ABOUT THE AUTHORS

Golf historian Roger McStravick is a double winner of the USGA's Herbert Warren Wind Book Award (2015, 2020) and the British Golf Collectors Society (BGCS) Murdoch Medal (2016) for *St Andrews – The Road War Papers, St Andrews in the Footsteps of Old Tom Morris.* This Allan Robertson biography also won for Roger and Bill, the BGCS 'Outstanding book of the year' (2025). His other titles include *The Fine Art of Golf, Little Tommy Morris, A History of Golf, 9 The Links, St Andrews – A Comfort Blanket for the Hapless Golfer* and *Little Lady Margaret Scott.* Editor of the BGCS magazine *Through The Green* for three years to 2022, Roger has written for many global golf magazines and is frequently on-screen, including for The Golf Channel, the films *Loopers* and *The Greatest Golf Story Ever Told.* An avid collector of rare book on St Andrews and Scotland, he lives locally with his wife and two children.

This would have been Bill Williams' fourth project, having previously written two books about Harry Vardon and one on Edward (Ted) Ray. As a sports fan, history fascinated him since his school days. He split his time between Florida, where he could play golf all year round, and the Kingdom of Fife, where he could also play golf 12 months a year. He was a proud member of the British Golf Collectors Society, the Golf Heritage Society in the USA and the Leith Rules Golf Society. He was also a member of The St Andrews Golf Club. Bill Williams died in July 2020 and is sorely missed by all but especially his family, including Bill's son Liam Williams, daughter Emma Mihlenstedt and his grandchildren Billy Mihlenstedt, Marcus and Freddy Williams. This book fulfills Bill's wish that Allan Robertson finally receives the plaudits he so rightly deserves.

The King of Clubs

Allan Robertson of St Andrews

ROGER McSTRAVICK
AND BILL WILLIAMS

ARENA SPORT

First published as *Allan Robertson of St Andrews: King of Clubs* by St Andrews Golf Press in 2025

This edition published in 2026
by Arena Sport, an imprint of
Birlinn Limited
West Newington House
10 Newington Road
Edinburgh
EH9 1QS

www.birlinn.co.uk

ISBN: 978 1 913759 27 8

British Library Cataloguing-in-Publication Data
A catalogue record for this book is available from the British Library

Typeset by Lexis Books

FSC www.fsc.org MIX Paper | Supporting responsible forestry FSC® C117931

Printed and bound by MBM Print, Glasgow

This edition is dedicated
to Roger's wife, Farah

The real 'King of Scotland', in regard
to golfing, reigns in St Andrews, and
is well known as Allan Robertson;
all others taking that dignity are
usurpers, and guilty of high treason.
Allan is the legitimate and
indisputable King of Clubs.

Fifeshire Journal,
Thursday 9 June 1853

CONTENTS

ACKNOWLEDGEMENTS

THE AUTHORS would like to thank Wally Uihlein, The Royal and Ancient Golf Club of St Andrews, United States Golf Association of America, Chic Harper, Mrs Sheila Walker, Peter Crabtree, David Hamilton, Ian Pattinson, Rand Jerris, Peter Lewis, Dr Eve Soulsby, Iain Crawford, David Joy, Angela Howe, Hannah Fleming, Kieran George and team at The R&A World Golf Museum, St Andrews Preservation Trust, Fine Golf Books, Peter & Anke Grunwell, Edward Playfair, Stephen Proctor, Connor Lewis, Joe McDonnell, Melvyn Morrow, Colin McAllister, Prestwick Golf Club, Andrew Lochead, Geoffrey & Harry Sprot, John Giannuzzi, the late John Still, Brian Matheson, Gary Cole, Virginia Rundle, Tony Corsini, British Library, Kathy & Mike Whitehead, Rob Freel, Stonehouse Heritage Group, Karl Jensen, Harry Ward, University of St Andrews Special Collections team, Olivera Cejovic, Pam Wood, Neil Laird, the late Seonaid McAinsh, the late Francis Melville, Terry McCullough, Jim Fitzpatrick, Pat Campbell, Elmer Nahum, Hugh Jolly, Jurek Alexander Putter, Richard Sowerby, Jim Davis, Adrian Milledge, John Pearson, John & Jordan Morton, Matthew Smith, Pehr Thermaenius, Dougy Watson, Christie's, National Portrait Gallery of Scotland, Bob Gowland, Adrian Milledge, James Eric Verden-Anderson and Joshua Verden-Anderson for their kind support, advice and assistance.

Thanks are also due to Bill's family, especially Emma Mihlenstedt and her husband Jack, for not giving up on Bill's remarkable work.

Roger would like to offer his thanks to his family Farah, Saam and Ana for their good humour and kindness.

FOREWORD

It is often said that Arnold Palmer – the most charismatic of golfers – was also the father of modern professional golf as we now know it. If that is so – and few dispute this – it is equally true to say that the father of all professional golf was Allan Robertson.

How many Open championships, then, did Allan win? Sadly none, for he died at the age of 43, a year after becoming the first golfer ever to hole the Old Course in 79 strokes (a prodigious feat given the equipment of the day) and two years before the first championship was played at Prestwick in 1860.

Without any doubt, Allan Robertson was the best golfer of his era by some distance and held the title of 'Champion Golfer' for 19 years. His premature death was not only tragic, but also created a massive golfing void, to the extent that one member of The Royal and Ancient Golf Club of St Andrews is said to have commented: 'They may shut up their shops and toll their bells, for the greatest among them is gone.'

The search for a successor to Allan Robertson, as the undisputed champion of his generation, acted as a catalyst in the search for who might be worthy of his crown. The only proper way to ascertain this was held to be by the establishment of a championship, the winner of which would be the Champion Golfer of the Year. The Open was born.

The story of Allan Robertson and his massive impact on golf in the 19th century has hitherto largely been confined to footnotes and anecdotes which are parenthetical to the accounts of other major figures – Tom Morris Snr and his son Tommy and Willie Park Snr, the first champion golfer.

In this book, the authors trace Allan's introduction to golf by his father, Davie, an expert featherie ballmaker. He too was a champion golfer who died at a young age, leaving Allan to take over his father's business at the age of only 21.

Allan would go on to play Willie Dunn Snr in challenge matches, attracting a large following of golf enthusiasts, young and old, from all social classes. Allan was both an exceptional golfer and an equipment innovator and would pioneer the use of iron clubs for pitch shots to greens. The R&A named its state-of-the-art equipment testing centre 'Allan Robertson House' for good reason.

He was undoubtedly the golfing hero of his time and both Roger McStravick and Bill Williams do a fine job of explaining how and why Allan Robertson became known as 'The King of Clubs'.

Ian R.H. Pattinson
Captain, The Royal and Ancient Golf Club of St Andrews
September 2024

*

The claim in the history of golf that Allan Robertson is the greatest golfer ever is often made, but proving it is difficult, since good historical sources for Allan's time in the earlier part of the 19th century are lacking. But serious historians have a mantra that 'there is always more', namely that there are always new sources to find. Roger has already shown, in his two important books on St Andrews golf, his talent for uncovering new material and here he and Bill Williams again show that there was indeed more to find on Allan's life and times.

We don't have a satisfactory name for the featherie ball era. A 'Golden Age' doesn't quite fit, but 'Heroic' is a bit better. The game was dominated by a small group of skilled players who could afford the expensive game, needing short-lived feather balls and long-nosed brittle clubs, and they had a high profile through their play, in their red coats, on the St Andrews Links.

Allan was a respected member of this golfing community, as was his father before him, living beside the links and serving their needs in many ways, notably with equipment (and even bottles of ginger beer, then an alcoholic drink). He even helped arrange the gentlemen's matches and handicaps. Allan might act as a caddie, but more often played as a partner in foursomes with the gentlemen, and, when nursing a weak player, Allan could turn on his power to 'snod them at the Burn' and win the match at the Road Hole.

Allan was entrusted with modernising the links, creating the double greens and he even brought in strengthening of the bunker faces with turf. Added to that, the St Andrews golfers made sure, through judicious challenge matches, that their man could be formally called the 'Champion Golfer' and they even referred to him as 'The King'.

The affection shown and his part in the St Andrews golfing world, a role taken up by Old Tom, whose relations with Allan are carefully looked at here, suggests that the snobbery and strict separation of amateur and professionals was not to come until later in Victorian times. Allan's scrapbook shows he was a literate man, reading widely and with interests beyond golf.

This book, with its new findings and many new images, gives us, at last, a much better understanding of Robertson and his times, and certainly puts his eminence in the golfing pantheon beyond doubt.

David Hamilton
Golf Historian

PREFACE

It was never a thought of mine to write a book on Allan Robertson. I am a devout Tom Morris fan and have relished researching his life over the years. Allan, or what little I knew of him, was a dubious character, who in a match would ask his caddie, Da' Anderson, loudly for two clubs more than the shot required, knowing the caddie would hand him two clubs less, hoping to confuse opponents. Some call it harmless gamesmanship, but I never warmed to this. I saw Allan as a peacock who did not like his champion golfer title to be challenged, like a boxer choosing his battles. Willie Park has always had my sympathies as an amazing golfer whom Allan would not face. Allan was simply not an attractive subject to study.

How wrong I was.

Bill Williams came to St Andrews to discuss his idea of writing a book on Allan. The R&A World Golf Museum's archives are incredible and include Allan's scrapbook, filled with press clippings of matches from that era. It is a wonderful time capsule of exciting moments on the links. It always seemed strange to me that so much of the book was not about a vainglorious Allan, but rather Tom Morris' achievements or matches that had nothing to do with Allan. Bill met various historians in town and listened to a variety of opinions about Allan. Over coffee at the museum cafe, with historians David Hamilton, Peter Lewis and yours truly, he told us about the idea and was given some constructive advice, including useful resources.

After the meeting, Bill and I chatted for a while, overlooking the St Andrews links. Little did I know that this would be the last time that we would meet. I encouraged him to write the book, that it would be good to have an equivalent of Rev. W.W. Tulloch's 1907 book *The Life of Old Tom Morris*, or the 2008 HWW USGA Book Award-winning *Tom Morris of St Andrews, The Colossus of Golf*, and said that if there was anything he needed me to do in St Andrews, just to let me know. We agreed to keep in touch and that he would send me a note about his next visit.

I liked Bill, an East London boy who had made his fortune in the UK before moving to the States. He was not your run-of-the-mill historian. Bill was feisty and if he had an opinion he certainly would let you know it. Confrontational in various online forums, Bill was always searching for the truth to be told. He was a straight shooter and, at heart, as kind and generous a man as you could meet.

Plans were afoot for his return, and I was looking forward to seeing him again in town. He emailed me to say that he was a little under the weather but would be back in touch soon.

One morning on Facebook in July 2020, my heart sank when a notification said that Bill had died. I got in touch with his daughter Emma through my friend and author Stephen Proctor and offered my sympathies.

When Emma and her family came to St Andrews to release some of Bill's ashes, we met at the Fairmont St Andrews Hotel. She asked me if I would consider taking on the book. I was blown away and felt honoured that she asked me. Of course, I said yes, whilst feeling a little daunted about doing a good job for Bill, his family and Allan. He had written an early draft of a few chapters and, in his research papers, had found out new things about Allan.

I soon found that I had been so wrong about all things Robertson. Instead of this braggart and shady character, what comes out is a very different, kindly, jovial Allan Robertson. Kind, funny, popular and well loved from all classes, with just a few colourful foibles thrown into the mix. I wrote on Jamie Anderson's headstone, 'We are all in life but human', and that would apply equally to Allan.

Allan was without doubt the champion golfer in the 1840s and 1850s and was hailed then as the king. There is a reason Sir Thomas Moncrieffe wanted him as a partner. There is a reason why he was put in charge of the links. There is a reason for the seemingly eccentric behaviour around the guttie ball. There is a reason why his own scrapbook is not just filled with clippings about himself but more about friends such as Tom Morris.

With Bill's passing, it was a little tricky at times to decipher what was Bill's own writing or simply his typically excellent research. I truly apologise for any credit or reference that has been omitted. It has however been a joy, and I have felt Bill close to me every step of the way.

I dearly hope that this finished book captures what Bill wanted to say and brings to life his hero, and now mine, Allan Robertson, the 'King of Golf'.

Roger McStravick

INTRODUCTION

ALLAN ROBERTSON, like Old Tom Morris, is synonymous with early golf history and the auld grey toun of St Andrews. Many will have read books and articles that have some reference to both these early pioneers of the Royal & Ancient game. Unlike Old Tom, who has had many books written about him, the same cannot be said of Allan Robertson. In fact, we know of only one book that devotes all its pages to the man, that being *Allan Robertson, Golfer – His Life and Times* written by Alistair Beaton Adamson in 1985.

In the last 30 years, there have been enormous advances in the digital world. These advances include British newspaper and magazine archives from the 1700s to modern day. Social media has enabled private collections to be open to the world. Writers of yesteryear could only dream of having more than 20,000 people with a love of golf history – as has The Society of Golf Historians Facebook group, founded by Connor Lewis – to share stories and request support from. Notwithstanding, the records pertaining to a golfer who died in 1859 are relatively sparse and difficult to find, especially understandable when one considers that golf as a pastime for wellbeing was only just gaining popularity in the mid-19th century.

With some justification Old Tom Morris was known in later life as the Grand Old Man of Golf. His acute knowledge of every element of the game, gained from the days when he started out as a young boy caddie to when he became the world's greatest golfer and then in later life laid out and re-designed over 100 courses, was second to none. Many of his natural skills were sharpened by Allan. Tom, at 18, joined him in his shop, known locally as the golf parlour, where the gentlemen golfers stored their clubs.

Tom and Allan made featherie golf balls together and, when the occasion arose, went out to the links when a challenge match came their way. Please remember they were only five years apart in age. Allan was born in September 1815 and Tom in June 1821. Rather than the well-worn storyline of Master and Apprentice that has been repeated ad infinitum, they were, in all likelihood, more akin to brothers. Tom would have already been an incredible golfer, having played golf from as soon as he could walk. Indeed, many golfers peak around 18, when university or work life takes over. He would also have been skilled in making a ball, as necessity would have dictated so. Tom came from a working-class family. They were weavers for many generations. It is not beyond the imagination to think that if Tom damaged his expensive featherie out on the links, he would try to repair it himself at home.

It would, however, be simply wrong to write off Allan's influence. Tom would undoubtedly learn a lifetime worth of skills with Allan and in interviews always talked of Allan as his friend. They were close. Even when Tom went to Prestwick, Allan would visit and play a game on the links with Tom. Much is made of their fall-out in 1848 but, as we shall show, there are some bonds in life that cannot be broken.

It was never our intention to include a lengthy preamble before discussing the subject matter; however, the more we delved into Allan's life, his family and their times, the more relevant it became to set the scene. The heritage of St Andrews, golf, the links, the rules, and indeed the Robertson family name itself, are all factors that shaped Allan and his peers.

Dispelling myths such as the somewhat fanciful claim that Allan was never beaten, the portrait we are painting is not the age-old one. We hope that these new insights into the life of one of the most iconic men in golf, who encountered so many highs and lows in his life, the champion golfer of Scotland, will give a true picture of this exceptional man.

This is Allan's story.

Major players

Throughout Allan's life there was a cast of influential people who played major roles in his story. For simplicity, they are listed below showing how their names appear in this book.

Allan – Allan Robertson, Champion Golfer

Davie – David Robertson, Allan's father, Champion Golfer

Alexander – Tom Alexander, Champion Golfer, Musselburgh

David – David Robertson, Allan's brother

Peter – Patrick Robertson, Allan's grandfather, Professional

Lang Willie – Willie Robertson, Allan's cousin and employee of Allan

Tom – Tom Morris, close friend, golfing partner and employee of Allan, Champion Golfer

Thomas – Thomas Morris, Tom's first son,

Tommy – Thomas Morris Jnr, Tom's second son, Champion Golfer

John – John Morris, Tom's father

Sandy – Sandy Pirie, playing partner of Allan

David Pirie – David Pirie, brother of Sandy

Andrew – Andrew Strath, playing partner of Allan, Champion Golfer

Moncrieffe – Sir Thomas Moncrieffe, playing partner of Allan

Dunnie – Willie Dunn, Musselburgh golfer, Professional

Jamie – Jamie Dunn, Musselburgh golfer, Professional

Park Snr – Willie Park Snr, Musselburgh golfer, Champion Golfer

Auld Da' – David Anderson, caddie and employee of Allan

Playfair – Sir Hugh Lyon Playfair LL.D., Provost of St Andrews

One

THE ROBERTSONS OF STROWAN

St Andrews is an ancient town on the east coast of Fife. The designation of the links as common land dates back to at least the 8th century but quite possibly much earlier. It is truly ancient.

There are two principal stories about the origins of St Andrews. The first is that around 732, Bishop Acca from Hexham, Northumberland, is said to have brought to Fife some authenticated bones of Saint Andrew, which had been obtained by his mentor, Bishop Wilfrid, who had created a church dedicated to the apostle in Hexham. Acca brought them north to create a church for King Óengus, who wanted to replicate the Roman church that Wilfrid[1] and Acca had established with choirs, libraries, paintings and statues. There was nothing quite like it in Scotland. It simply stirred the senses. In doing so, Acca created a place of pilgrimage that would last centuries and eventually give the town its name. This in turn would create prosperity for the area, with pilgrims needing accommodation, clothing, food and drink.

Around the 12th century, monks creatively devised a new story about the origins of St Andrews. According to them, Saint Rule (also called Saint Regulus), from Patras, had received a vision from God, sailed with Saint Andrew's relics and duly landed here, albeit by crashing his boat on the rocks. They would go on to build St Rule's Tower, which can be seen today in his honour. It was all quite fantastical.

The tall tale of Saint Rule does not hold much sway with historians today and the tower dates from the time the tale was created, if not later.

The reason why the version about Bishop Acca from Hexham holds credence as the true origins of St Andrews is because it involves real people whose movements were recorded at the time by historians such as Venerable Bede, who visited Acca's library in Hexham.

We do, of course, have to add the caveat that we may not be correct, but the balance of probability points to the Hexham lineage. Furthermore, the 8th-century sarcophagus of Óengus was discovered in the grounds of St Andrews Cathedral in 1833, near the tower. In fact, some believe that the very first church Acca created was the small church beside the Cathedral, which is still standing, hiding in plain sight.

The Robertsons of Strowan

The auld grey town of St Andrews has had a mysterious aura from the earliest of times. It is a mythical place where ghosts and witches, saints and martyrs all have tales to tell. Books in the 1700s and 1800s sold well when they touched upon Scottish heroes and eminent men of business. Stories were shared around the fire or at boisterous golf gatherings. Poems by the Scottish bard, Robert Burns, were recanted proudly and with much humour on Burns night from 1801. It was an age of romanticism and imagination.

On 9 January 1861 the *Inventory of the Personal Estate of Allan Robertson, ballmaker* was presented in Cupar by Stuart Grace. In his will, Allan left his house Sandyhill to his brother David, who was a merchant in Sydney, Australia. He included a right for his wife Jane Kyles to live the rest of her days in the house and also borrow against it, if needs be, to the maximum of £50. All the furniture, money, gold and silver coins went to Jane, but there were a few items that were given to his brother, including a history of the bible book dated 1712, his grandfather Peter's old penknife in the shape of a hare, dated 1800, and his late father Davie's old Pinchbeck watch. Pinchbeck had been creating watches for 100 years, since Christopher Pinchbeck in the 18th century, so Davie's watch had become a valuable family heirloom.

There was also a solitary book *The History and Martial Achievements of the Robertsons of Strowan and the Poems On Various Subjects and Occasions By The Honourable Alexander Robertson of Strowan, Esq.*[2]

It is this book[3] almost more than any other Allan artefact that explains why Allan was who he was. The perception of Allan as a working-class man who had quite pompous ideas above his station is clearly quite wrong, and this book that he kept for his brother evidently meant something to him.

It was intended for David, and it is not beyond the imagination to think that it was also meant equally as much for future generations of Robertsons, so that they too could know of the Robertson lineage.

Inside the book, he wrote his name four times plus his home address, *Sandy Hill, Links, St Andrews, 1844*, on the title page. This was clearly important to Allan. It was not some far-fetched populist re-writing of history. It was the story of the Robertson clan.

King Robert the Bruce (1274–1329)

William Forbes Skene (1809–92), Historiographer Royal of Scotland, described the Robertsons of Struan, as Strowan, which was by then widely known, and said that they were unquestionably the oldest family in Scotland, being the sole remaining branch of that royal house of Atholl which occupied the throne of Scotland in the 11th and 12th centuries. Modern historians may vary on this point, but the thinking when Allan was growing up was that it was true. This Strowan (Struan) is situated in Perthshire.

According to 19th-century historians, the Robertsons' origins are to be found in Gaelic Clan Donnachaidh. Their history goes as far back as King Malcolm II, who ruled from 1005 to 1034 and was a direct descendant of Kenneth MacAlpine who is seen by some as the founder of Scotland, as he united the Irish Scots and the Picts around 843. Malcolm's grandson, King Duncan I, ruled from 1034 for six years, before being murdered by Macbeth of Shakespearean fame.

The first noted Chief of that Clan Donnachaidh was 'Stout Duncan' (or Duncan the fat or corpulent as he was also known), who was so named for his stiff resolve to protect and serve King Robert the Bruce and not actually for his portly figure. He was awarded the lands of Atholl due to his clearing the area of wolves, and given various parcels of land, including Strowan in Perthshire for his loyal service to Robert the Bruce, as noted in King David's book of charters, no. 42, *Roberto filio Duncani de Atholia, omnium terrarum nojtraarum de Fordill in feode et hereditate*, dated 24 May 1362.[4] In honour of the king, there follows a long line of lairds of Strowan, including Duncan's own son, Robert.

Author Robertson said of the early clan,

> They were warlike men who had the courage and spirit, to fight for the freedom of their country, and when Balliol and his party arose in opposition against King Robert Bruce, they valiantly weakened that power of that party, and contributed greatly to the establishing of King Robert's authority over all that part of the country. In short, they were loyal subjects to King Robert, and no less to his son King David.[5]

This would be King Robert's eldest son, King David II (1324–71) who was the last of the Bruce line. Sons of Stout Duncan became Duncansons.

After James I (1394–1437) was murdered, Robert Riabhach 'Grizzled' Duncanson, the fourth Laird of Strowan, crushed the hopes of the regicides who hoped for civil war. He apprehended Walter Earl of Atholl and Robert Graham and handed them over to the crown, where they were tortured and executed in the Grassmarket area in Edinburgh.

Their deaths were grisly even for a brutal era. Over three days,

> Walter was put in a cart with a crane, hoisted up, dropped, and jerked violently to a stop to stretch his joints. He was then placed in a pillory and 'crowned with a diadem of burning iron' bearing the inscription 'King of all Traitors'.[6]
>
> On the second day, he was bound to a hurdle and dragged along the High Street of Edinburgh (some claim he was also blinded and tortured with red-hot iron pincers on this day, but Buchanan speaks only of the hurdle). On the third, he was disembowelled while alive, his entrails burnt before his face, and his heart was torn out and burnt. Finally, his corpse was beheaded and quartered, and the quarters displayed around the realm.[7]

It is from this 15th-century Robert that the Robertson name comes. Prior to this, the name Robert was merely used as a Christian name along with the surname 'de Strowan' depicting land ownership. Modern day chiefs of the Robertson clan still have the right to be buried in the family burial ground in Struan.

The Robertson crest

King James II, on coming of age and power, offered to reward Robert's service to his brother. On 15 August 1451, among many gifts, the lands of Strowan, Perthshire, were elevated to the Barony of Strowan. The family coat of arms was augmented and a motto added, which has not changed to this day. Allan included it on the inside cover of his own scrapbook. The arms consist of

> Gulles, three wolves heads, reflecting the early achievements of Stout Duncan, Heads raised *argent*, armed and langued *azure*; crest, a dexter hand holding up an imperial crown proper; motto, *'Virtutis gloria merces'*, with a wild man, namely Robert Graham, in chains. The motto *Virtutis gloria merces*, means 'Glory is the reward of valour'.

The proud ancestry of the Robertson clan is indeed noble. However, there is more. Rev. James Robertson states in his *Barons Reid-Robertsons of Straloch*, that they had a descendant Robert, as noted above, who did service to King James I that his whole lands became a free barony. He also mentions that Robert arrested the murderers of James I and how Robert refused any reward other than the lands, which included Straloch (and Strowan), and insisted that they should be made into a free barony in 1457.[8]

This is our hero Robert and the reason we have the Robertson crest.

The Robertsons of Strowan and Straloch feature regularly in history, with frequent mentions of bravery in battle. Importantly, they are noted for serving with honour and approbation.

With unwavering pride, Alexander Robertson notes of the Robertsons that 'They have been connected in marriages in Royal families both in Scotland and England, and among many noble families in Scotland and England, which is well documented by the Scots and English historians.'[9]

This may have struck a chord with Allan. The Robertsons were the oldest Scottish family, saviours of the king; they even fought heroically in the Jacobite Rising of 1745.

Modern historians might have a less colourful or less romantic take on the Robertson family history, but, in the 1800s, this was the world in which Allan saw himself.

Did he believe that he was a genuine heir to those great Scottish heroes? Was this reflected in his undoubted self-belief? Did their blood flow through his veins? Among the archery medals in St Andrews of the 1600s, there was a Robertson of Struan listed as one of the winners. Is this the connection between Allan and the gentry Robertsons? Alas, probably not. The Robertsons were landowners, and tradition shows that the workers on their estates took the laird's name. That is likely where Allan's surname Robertson came from.

The book by Alexander Robertson in Allan's will was written a mere 40 years before Allan was born. It is a book he kept and passed on.

His family may not have been royal, but they were Robertsons.

Two

MEDIEVAL BALLMAKERS OF ST ANDREWS

THE STORY of the Robertson shoe and ballmakers in St Andrews begins in the 16th century. The actual Robertson family line in St Andrews dates back to well before records began.

In 1585 the ballmaker Thomas Buddo was born. He married Agnes Gourlay around 1610 and had a daughter named Christian Buddo (b.1612), who married John Robertson (1620–1704) on 16 June 1642. They had five children, including David Robertson I (b.1655), who married Margaret Disher (b.1664) on 2 December 1680. This Robertson marriage produced six children, including Patrick (1684–1762) and David II (b.1686).

The Morris family, including Open champion Tom Morris' father John, would come from Patrick, while the Robertson line, including Allan's father Davie, would come through David II.

Thomas Buddo's other daughter, Agnes, is said to have married another David Robertson, but no records of such can be found.

The dawn of golf

What an incredible and tumultuous time it was for the early line of the Robertsons. The *Mona Lisa* was painted by Leonardo da Vinci in 1503. During a violent storm in 1505, Martin Luther entered the St Augustine Monastery seeking refuge and started his spiritual journey that would ultimately lead to the Protestant Reformation. In an age of adventure and exploration, when new marvellous worlds were being discovered, Christopher Columbus died in 1506.

Fear of plagues and hunger haunted St Andreans. A significant outbreak of plague struck London in 1509 and St Andrews itself suffered regularly, with outbreaks in the 1560s, 1605 and particularly the late 1640s; fortunately the last big outbreak that struck London in the 1660s did not make it a far as Scotland.

As featherie balls were being made for the golfers, religious fervour and belief in the existence of witches were common-place and normal: over 6,000 people in Scotland were tried for witchcraft. This context was real in the St Andrews of ballmaker Thomas Buddo. Anyone accused of witchcraft in St Andrews would be taken to what we know as the Scores' clifftops and would suffer trial by water. They would be bound and dropped into Witches Lake at the foot of the cliffs to see if they floated or sank. If they floated, they were deemed a witch, as God's water had rejected them. They were then executed near to where the Martyrs' Monument is today, which was called Witches' Hill by locals right up to the late 19th century. Many people in the 1879 Road War case in St Andrews still referred to the area as Witches' Hill and the area below as Witches' Lake.

Although we have seen dramatic re-enactments of witches being burned at the stake, damp wood was used so it was the smoke that killed them, rather than the burning. Bessie Robertsoune was accused of being a witch due to her non-attendance at church. Fortunately, she got off with a warning. Alison Pierson and Agnes Melville, who helped the Archbishop of St Andrews back to health with a concoction of herbs and flowers, were accused of witchcraft after they requested payment for their services. The working-class Pierson was tortured and burned to death. Melville, who came from a well-connected family, was flogged, but the stain of the witch accusation hung about her and after she was accused of witchcraft again, suffered the same grim fate as Pierson.

While plague receded from the mid-seventeenth century onward, other diseases were common. Under the 18th green of the Old Course today is a cholera pit, found when Tom Morris was building the new green around 1869, that was filled with the bodies of those who died. As we shall see, the original course itself was away from this area and, with no houses in sight, was deemed out of the way.

A golfing evolution

These early Robertsons witnessed golf's evolution into a popular sport. As historian and retired surgeon David Hamilton plainly makes it clear in *Golf, Scotland's Game*, golf was undoubtedly a Scottish game. There was no smoking gun or eureka moment, but it is the current consensus that it was a uniquely Scottish sport and not a Dutch creation. Of course, there were similar stick and ball games all over the world, including Chui Wan in China, but the long form of golf played to a hole in the ground was Scotland's creation. Hamilton has also found connections to the Scottish game of shinty, which is a much older game. Sandy Herd certainly talked of making shinty sticks in the 1800s, from the trees at Strathtyrum woods and hitting balls with it.[1]

King James I banned football in 1424, so that the people could focus on their archery as that was a skill needed in war: clan disputes and more importantly battling the English were relatively commonplace. This Act did not mention golf, but a generation later the very first written mention of the game came in 1457 when the Scottish Parliament of King James II prohibited both football and golf. Modern historians believe that golf was first played in critical numbers – and therefore had become a distraction to the populace – sometime between these two Acts, of 1424 and 1457. Golf could have been played earlier than this, in either the short street form of the game or our royal long game over common land, away from prying eyes. At some point in the 15th century, golf had apparently become a distraction to the populace, showing that golf was a game for all, and certainly not an elite sport.

The wording of the March 1457 Act, courtesy of the National Archives of Scotland, states:

> *Item it is ordanyt and decretyt that Wapinschawing be haldin be ye lordis and baronys spirituale and temporale four tymes in ye yeir. And [th]at ye futebawe and ye golf be uterly cryt done and not usyt. And [th]at ye bowe markes be maid at all parochkirks a pair of butts And schuting be usyt ilk Sunday ... And touchand ye futebaw and ye golf We ordane it to be punyst be ye baronys unlaw. And if he tak it not to be tain be ye kings officars.*

> Item it is ordained and decreed that the lords and barons both spiritual and temporal should organise archery displays four times in the year. And that football and golf should be utterly condemned and stopped. And that a pair of targets should be made up at all parish churches and shooting should be practised each Sunday ... And concerning football and golf, we ordain that [those found playing these games] be punished by the local barons and, failing them, by the King's officers.

The outright ban of playing golf and football effectively came to an end in 1502 at the signing of the *Treaty of Perpetual Peace*, when James IV of Scotland and Henry VII of England agreed to put an end to centuries of sporadic warfare between the two nations. As part of the agreement, the marriage of James IV and Margaret Tudor, daughter of Henry VII (sister of Henry VIII) was arranged. This union would eventually have far-reaching consequences for the monarchy of England. The peace would only last until 1513, but golf was once again – legally – an unrestricted pastime for all.

Records and charters

After 1502 there are numerous references to golf in Scotland. In the 1502 accounts of the Lord High Treasurer of Scotland, an entry shows the purchase of clubs from a bowmaker in Sanct Johnestoun, *aka* in the Robertson's homeland of Perth, which were possibly for King James IV when he visited the area. In 1504 further entries in the accounts indicate the purchase of clubs and balls for the king, which confirms that James IV was a golfer, in contrast to Mary, Queen of Scots, who was not, as brought to light by Professor Neil Millar's seminal studies on the young queen.

Despite many seasoned claims, there is currently no documentation or accounts like those of James IV showing payment for clubs or balls, which adds to Neil's conclusion that Queen Mary, in fact, was perhaps not the golfer she has been made out to be. It was merely another reason, written by her enemies in the book of evidence against her, for her execution. They said that she was seen golfing days after the death of her husband Lord Darnley and therefore complicit in his murder.[2]

Just over 30 years before the birth of St Andrews ballmaker Thomas Buddo, the first mention we have of golf in the ancient city is in Archbishop John Hamilton's agreement in 1552, just prior to the destruction of St Andrews' Catholic faith-based economy. Golf could be played on the open links land, which was perfect for the game all year round, especially in the winter when the harvest was done.

Hamilton's agreement permitted golf to be played on the common links land. The larger aim of this agreement was to establish for himself the revenue from the rabbits on the links and is not a charter, still less a golf charter. While Archbishop Hamilton appears to be confirming the ancient right of the people to use the common land, which was their right to begin with and had been so for hundreds of years, he was more concerned with establishing a revenue stream for himself on the people's land. Hamilton was a devoted advocate of Mary, Queen of Scots. He baptised her son, the future King James VI, and was the authority who pronounced the queen's divorce from Bothwell. Hamilton would die a grisly death at Dumbarton Castle where he too became implicated in the death of Lord Darnley and was hanged.

We have studied the common land of St Andrews and have gone back as far as the 8th century. Alexander I's gift of large areas of land in 1124, called the Cursus Apri, merely re-affirmed the gift made centuries before by the aforementioned Óengus. This gift of 'using and possessing the common pasturages' for the benefit of the people was ratified by various charters, including the final one by George Gladstanes (*c.*1562–1615), the Archbishop of St Andrews, on 18 August 1614 with approval of the king. It included

> all and hail, the lands of Pilmure, and that piece of land called the Salt Grass, and all and hail the links of St Andrews, as they lie, in length and breadth towards the water of Eden, as far as the sea ebbs and flows, together with the mussel scalps … [including] North Haugh … South Haugh and their common lands …

Even today, when people talk of the ancient links land of St Andrews, this is a very fitting description, dating back to the 8th century.

By means of these centuries-old charters, agreements and contracts, the people retained indisputable rights to the links. It has been common open links land for over a thousand years and used for cattle grazing and public leisure, including football. No green fees were charged until 1946, when locals faced a princely sum of 30 shillings a year. This also explains why the people in St Andrews are to this day so headstrong about the links.

It was, and remains evermore, the people's land.

The lady golfers in St Andrews are a slightly different affair. Largely thanks to the work of Mrs Boothby, the wife of Colonel Robert Tod Boothby and Mr D.L. Burn, the ladies were allocated an area of the links where they could putt freely. From 1868 the St Andrews Ladies Putting Club paid a rent to Mr Cheape of Strathtyrum and to the town council when they bought back the links in 1894. According to archivist Dr Eve Soulsby, 'Members paid to play in matches, while visitors were charged to play from 1919. The club was abbreviated in its Minutes to the LGC, not LPC, until 1941, so that the sport was thought of as golf, albeit a shorter form of golf.'

The fall of St Andrews

It is not beyond the imagination that Thomas Buddo's parents and grandparents were witnesses to the most dramatic moments in St Andrews history. Were they there when Mary, Queen of Scots lived in the mid-1500s in a house on South Street, close to the cathedral? Did they see her play archery? Mary said herself that she was glad Elizabeth I's Private Secretary could come to St Andrews and see her/Mary living like a 'bourgeoisie': she meant in a lowly middle-class house. They could well have been there when Reverend John Knox gave his infamous speech in the Holy Trinity Church in the summer of 1559, which followed a pattern of Knox's previous speeches elsewhere, including Crail. In St Andrews the riled-up locals tore down not only the emblems of Romanism inside the majestic St Andrews Cathedral and Greyfriars and Blackfriars monasteries but, in essence, they also crushed their own futures.

Did they not foresee what would happen if the administrative structures of the cathedral fell? Up until that time, St Andrews had been the thriving ecclesiastical capital of Scotland, with much employment and wealth, through the administration of the large cathedral and monasteries in town. Almost 30 per cent of job opportunities came from church and related activities. Pilgrims had been coming to the town for centuries to pay worship beside the bones of Saint Andrew the apostle. They needed accommodation and food, much akin to our golf pilgrims today.

It should be said that the locals did not destroy the cathedral but, as time moved on, the building became abandoned. When they left the cathedral on that night in June 1559, it was not the wreck of a building we see today, merely ransacked.

Higher education institutes in St Andrews had been in existence before the university was founded in 1413. In the Buddo era, the university was almost two centuries old. While Buddo's grandparents would have seen St Andrews in all its glory, with the greatest cathedral in Scotland, beautiful castle, vast shipping fleets and a wealthy vibrant city, Buddo would have witnessed the beginning of the slow, desperate decline of St Andrews.

The city limped on after the 1559 riots, as the new faith tried to emulate the Roman Catholic administrative structures that had worked successfully for hundreds of years. Slowly, year by year, however, St Andrews with its decaying empty buildings became a ruinous, decrepit shadow of its former self. The once majestic cathedral became nothing more than a crumbling edifice and an open quarry, with the stones being used to re-build the East Sands pier, which a storm destroyed in 1655.

As Bess Rhodes states in her book, *Riches and Reform, Ecclesiastical Wealth in St Andrews, 1520–1580* (2020), 'For the residents of St Andrews (and perhaps other Scottish urban centres) the Reformation was not merely a religious turning-point, it was an economic revolution.'[3] The beautiful classical city, with a population of less than a few thousand, which had attracted royalty for hundreds of years[4] prior to Knox's drive for reformation, was economically bereft. The pre-Reformation benefits of St Andrews being the religious centre of Scotland were not only the wealth of all the churches being established in St Andrews but everything that surrounded it. Scotland's east-coast burghs were economically vibrant, and St Andrews port was one of the busiest, exporting pelts, wool and salmon.[5]

Faith also got in the way of the golfers in the 1500s. The minutes of the Kirk Session of the Town Church in 1598 noted that it was regretted that steps had to be taken against members of the church for golfing on the sabbath. This is the same reason why the Old is closed on a Sunday, the sabbath.

In 1582 there was a shooting on the links when Patrick Learmonth (Lermonth), son of the town Provost, shot at Archbishop Adamson, who was on the links and not preaching at the time. This murder attempt was more about the new Adamson being an early Protestant archbishop after the Reformation than about golfing.[6]

In these tumultuous times for St Andrews that the early Robertsons lived through, Archbishop Sharp suffered a cruel death, seven years before the birth of David Robertson II, on 3 May 1679, when his coach was intercepted by Covenanters who were waiting for and intending to kill Carmichael, the Sheriff of Fife, who oppressed Covenanters. It was a stroke of misfortune for Archbishop Sharp that he happened to be passing by in a coach with his daughter. At a gathering on 11 April the gang, led by James Russell, had plotted to hang Sharp and Carmichael 'over the port' in St Andrews. Having failed to find Carmichael on 3 May, they were thinking of going home, but were informed that Sharp's coach had been seen near Blebo.

The thirteen men raced to intercept Sharp and shot at him with pistols. Halting the carriage at Magus Muir, just outside Strathkinness, they told Sharp that he should prepare for death for his treatment of Covenanters. His daughter left the carriage to remonstrate with them, but it was no use. In the words of one of the murderers, after 'waiting some time, and then calling again upon him, to commend his soul to God's mercy, for that he should immediately die; we fired upon him with our pistols: when finding he was not yet dead, and remembering that it had been reported, that he had used sorcery in order to defend his body, and that he was invulnerable; and withal to rid him of life, with as little torture as we might, we slew him with our swords, and departed.'[7]

For Thomas Buddo and his grandchildren ballmakers Patrick and David II, this was a violent time to be in St Andrews, with life having seemingly little value and religious intolerance at its zenith. Fortunately for them, their sewing skills were needed, as there was still demand for items such as shoes and featheries.

How strange that among all this brutality and religious fervour there was a living to be made in ballmaking? There is evidence from earlier than 1585 that it was a lucrative business.

It was not only the fall of the Roman faith or the decline of St Andrews that the family line witnessed. They also saw the original 22-hole layout of the St Andrews links. The next generations of Robertson ballmakers knew where it was, how it was played, and why it was logically cut down to eighteen holes. Little did they know that this little change in St Andrews would set in motion the future for the entire game of golf around the world.

Three

THE DARK CENTURY

St Andrews in the 1700s was heading towards its lowest ebb. A far cry from the flourishing, majestic and spiritually inspiring city of the 1500s, it had fallen into a woeful state. Lang called it a 'filthy starveling village', with polluted waters.[1] Churches that shone the light of God were now abandoned ruins and housing sheep. The crumbling harbour was patched and patched again, which reflected the overall downfall of the shipping trade.

With streets filled with manure and the stench of herring guts, the university was said to have considered, in 1697, moving to the wealthier and more central Perth. The reasons given for moving were quite strange, as they included:

- 'This place [St Andrews] is a most thin and piercing air … and this is the reason why old men coming to this place are instantly cut off [die].'
- 'This place being now only a village, where for the most part farmers dwell. The whole streets are filled with dunghills, which are exceedingly noisome and ready to infect the air, especially at this season when the herring guts are exposed in them, in all corners of the town.'
- Poor relations between the town and the university … 'may prove impossible … to keep Gentlemen and Noblemen's children from incurring great hazards, being exposed to the "rabble of this place". Their future threat could involve burning the town.' Citing an example of one Mr Henderson, who luckily escaped the burning of his house, thanks to a Master getting advance notice of the threat.

- Further evidence to the threat to the students included the story that, in 1690, students were chased into their colleges and cannons were brought to blow down the colleges. One of the local tradesmen went into the college and threatened to murder Dr Skeen and another local threatened to drag the same poor Dr Skeen into prison.
- Uncharitably, it noted the locals' hatred and aversion to Learning and Learned Men and stated that the only person from the town worthy of being a student was the then 'Bibliothecar' (librarian). Everyone else was apparently of sub-standard intelligence.

As observed in Lyon's book on the history of St Andrews, 'infectious diseases have been observed to begin and rage here, as in the visitation in 1640, when Dr Bruce died; and last year a most malignant flu, whereof dyed upwards of two hundredth persons in a few weeks, which much prejudiced the universitie'.[2] The Scores, which was called Swallow Street, was said to be utterly ruinous, with not a house in sight. With only 945 houses in St Andrews and 159 of these said to be uninhabitable, the town had a population of around 4,000 people. Two bakers were all that was needed to supply the entire town. According to William Douglas, 'many of them [the townspeople] are idle and half starved, there being neither Trade or Manufacturers in the Place'.[3]

That last statement needs qualifying, as around the year 1525 shoemakers in St Andrews formed themselves into a guild. *The Guild Book of the Cordiner [cordwainer, or shoemaker] Craft of St Andrews* includes names from 1525 to 1796 of locals and elections.[4] With the Robertsons being leather ballmakers, there may well have been distant family relations involved in the guild. Seven trades formed their own groups, namely the hammermen, wrights, baxters (bakers), tailors, cordiners, weavers and fleshers. They joined together as the Seven Trades, with no religious character attached. It was a way to protect their prices, standardise apprenticeships, levy fines and regulate trade. Anyone working in town had to be a member of one of the craft associations. Their joint Trade Court dealt only with offences against fellow members, but not civil morality issues. Pre-Reformation, the fines were a donation of wax, which went to the trade altar in Holy Trinity. After the Reformation, monetary fines were used for general purposes of that trade, including wine for the officers at the craft organisation.

Locals simply had to do what they could to make ends meet and improve their fortunes.

We know that some houses were becoming derelict and dangerous, for in 1744, the town council ordered that they should be demolished.

In this fallen city, there was another generation of Robertson ballmakers. The wealth of the young academic students was a sharp contrast to that of the working-class and bereft locals.

David Robertson II (1686–1758) married Elizabeth Corsar on 21 October 1707 and had four children – David III (1707), Margaret (1709), Patrick (1711) and James (1716). David II later married Ann Robertson, a daughter of George Robertson, in 1721 and had two further children, Robert (1722) and David (1726).

Clubs and balls

The golf equipment of the early Buddo and Robertson eras would not have been very different to the set that Tom Morris played when he won his Open titles. These were beautiful, long-nosed clubs that demanded an upright swing to get the ball elevated. Fine craftsmanship would be needed to create sets that were carried under the arm. To the modern golfer they would look like wooden hybrids, with the addition of the small-headed rut iron, which was used to play out of narrow cart tracks and a lofter, an example of which can be seen in Tommy Morris' picture with his father.

The Robertsons, however, were not and never would be clubmakers. They created featherie balls alone until the arrival of the guttie.

According to the papers of the late Jim Fagan, on 28 February 1728 both Patrick and David Robertson II 'were admitted to the Cordiners Incorporation of St Andrews as Freemen Ballmakers'. The skills of a shoemaker would have made them naturally adept when it came to stitching together the leather pieces to create a featherie ball. These were in popular use until 1848, and a comfortable living could be made from their manufacture and trade. According to www.scottishgolfhistory.org, 'There is a reference in the Edinburgh Testaments (vol. xlvii, 123b) to 'fyve scoir twell flok goiff ballis [112 flok golf balls]' in a will in 1612. Flok, from the Latin word *floccus* meaning a tuft of wool or hair, is also used to refer to 'the down of unfledged birds' as well as 'a tuft of feathers on the head of young birds', and is thus probably an early reference to featherie balls and may explain their origin.

The manufacturing process began as three pieces of leather stitched together and turned inside out leaving a quarter inch slit through which the feathers were pushed with the 'brogue' using the chest. The feathers and leather were wet and, as they dried, the feathers expanded and the leather shrank, creating a two-way pressure and a tight ball with characteristics only recently matched by modern balls. Opinion is divided as to whether the feathers or leather were boiled, and there was more than a 'hat' full of feathers in each ball. Afterwards, the balls were painted white for protection and so that they could be found more easily. Early reports say a ball maker would make 2 to 3 balls per day. The New Statistical Account of Scotland 1838 estimated an expert ball maker could make 50 to 60 balls in a week.[5]

Rumours of medieval wooden or hairy golf balls are received with scepticism by today's historians. Although the hairy, so called due to being filled with cow hair, was used for golf in Holland, it is not believed to have been used in Scotland.

David II made his livelihood making balls. The students, university staff and the professors would have been among his largest clients. According to William Croft Dickinson (WCD) in *Two Students at St Andrews, 1711–1716*, portraying two students discussing golf at that time, 'their diversion, which figures prominently throughout, was golf'.[6] A letter in the book from an Alexander Munro to John Mackenzie, dated 27 April 1691, said,

> Receive from the bearer, our post, ane sett of Golfe-clubs consisting of three, viz. an play club, ane scraper, and ane tin fac'd club … if you stand in need of more, I think you should call for them from me. I have also sent you ane dozen of Golfe balls. I am told they are good, but that will prove according to your play and the fields.[7]

The scraper was used, as we shall see later, for playing your ball from a rabbit scrape.

These young students were allowed to play golf twice a week. There were notably different standards to their featherie golf balls. One student, Alexander, would pay four shillings, while his companions, Kenneth or Thomas, would pay two. Clubs cost 12 shillings and a single club-head four.

WCD says that the mention of an iron club for £1 4*s.* on 11 November 1714 is probably the earliest mention of an iron club. 'There are several references to "a horn to Thomas's club", or a "horn to Kenneth's club", always at a cost of two shillings, and this was probably the strip of horn fastened to the driving-face of the wooden club as, until recently, was still the fashion with modern drivers and brassies.'[8] Even in the 1700s, just like today, many St Andrews University students got distracted in their studies by the pull of the links.

The Goff

The year 1743 was important for golf. In May the ship *Magdalen*, captained by William Carse, left the port of Leith at Edinburgh and arrived in Charleston, South Carolina, in August carrying items for one David Deas, a successful Scottish merchant who lived there. It contained two boxes totalling eight dozen golf clubs and three gross (3 × 144) golf balls.

An Edinburgh business record discovered by Professor David Purdie in the National Archives of Scotland suggests a possible earlier shipment of clubs to Charleston on 29 June 1739, to businessman William Wallace. As an aside, at least nine of the 56 signers of the American Declaration were of Scottish origin.

Also in the year 1743 we have our first published mention of a golfing Robertson. It is in Thomas Mathison's poem *The Goff.* Although it does not say which ball-making Robertson or the name Robertson itself, modern historians believe that the Bobson mentioned is indeed a relation of Allan's.

Written by Edinburgh-based Mathison in praise of golf, it tells the story of Leith golfers in a match and offers glimpses of the sport in the mid-1700s. As a kirk minister, Mathison was one of a long line of churchmen who passed their free hours writing about the game and places to play. Rev. A.K.H. Boyd's books capture the spirit of St

Andrews in the 1800s. Rev. Tulloch wrote the first biography of Tom Morris in 1907 and Rev. Dr John Kerr's *The Golf Book of East Lothian*, published in 1896, is one of the most collectable books in golf.

In the second Canto of three, *The Goff* reads,

> Lo, tatter'd Irus who their armour bears,
> Upon the green two little pyr'mids rears;
> On these they place two balls with careful eye,
> That with Clarinda's breasts for colour vie,
> The work of Bobson; who with matchless art
> Shapes the firm hide, connecting ev'ry part,
> Then in a socket sets the well-stitch'd void,
> And thro' the eylet drives the downy tide;
> Crowds urging crowds the forceful brogue impels,
> The feathers harden and the leather swells;
> He crams and sweats, yet crams and urges more;
> Till scarce the turgid globe contains its store:
> The dreadful falcon's pride here blended lies
> With pigeons glossy down of various dyes;
> The lark's small pinions join the common flock,
> And yellow glory of the martial cock.
> Soon as Hyperion gilds o'er Andrea's spires,
> From bed the artist to his cell retires;
> With bended back, there plies his steely awls,
> And shapes, and fluffs, and finishes the balls.
> But when the glorious God of day has driv'n.
> His flaming chariot down the steep of heav'n,
> He ends his labour, and with rural strains
> Enchants the lovely maids and weary swains:
> As thro' the streets the blythfome piper plays,
> In antick dance they answer to his lays;
> At ev'ry pause the ravish'd crowd acclaim,
> And rend the skies with tuneful Bobson's name.
> Not more rewarded was old Amphion's song;
> That rear'd a town, and this drags one along.
> Such is fam'd Bobson, who in Andrea thrives,
> And such the balls each vig'rous hero drives.

The phrase 'with matchless art' suggests that Mathison regarded Bobson as the finest ballmaker in St Andrews, which would certainly be a moniker of which the Robertsons, including Allan, were all too aware. This was Allan's heritage. Mathison's final charge was as Minister in Brechin, where he died in 1754.

The Society of St Andrews Golfers, 1754

It was not until the 18th century, when the game began to grow in popularity, that groups of gentleman golfers began to form golfing societies. The Company of Edinburgh Golfers set the standard with the formation of their society in 1744 and a competition to play annually on Leith Links for a silver club.

This type of prize was emulating the sport of archery, in which a silver arrow was typically awarded to the victor and a badge with his name attached to it. The Society of Edinburgh Golfers also set out 13 rules of play, which would form the bedrock of the game at that time. It is the minuting of the setting out of the competition and the rules, signed by Duncan Forbes of Culloden, President of the Court of Sessions and first captain of the club, earlier that year that makes the Honourable Company the oldest golf club in the world. All clubs are dated by their minute books. The Silver Club has been played for each year since 1744, apart from 1746–47 and 1832–35. On 26 March 1800, the society became The Honourable Company of Edinburgh Golfers.

In St Andrews, golf was possibly played since the 1400s, coinciding with the formation of the university in 1413, but the gentlemen golfers did not create a formal society here until 1754. The Society of St Andrews Golfers created a competition for a silver club that was held on 14 May that year. On page one of the minute book, the names of 22 noblemen and gentlemen are listed. The Silver Club is dated 1753, which suggests that plans for the society had been made earlier. The winner would become 'Captain of the Golf' for the following year. Although this was a competition for members only, there would be opportunities for the ball-making Robertsons and also for local caddies who would carry clubs for the aristocracy and gentlemen taking part.

After the slow 200-year financial strangulation of the town by the

Reformation, such new opportunities and prospects would have been very welcome.

St Andrews links

David II died on 12 October 1758, aged 72, and was listed in the parish death records as 'David Robertson Senior, Ballmaker in the North Gate'. This is North Street today. There used to be an archway akin to the West Port archway, just beside where Tom Morris lived as a boy, at 121 North Street today, but, like the other gateway arches into St Andrews, it was removed. David II had a long life for those times and would have witnessed the all too vivid decline of the town.

The only course David II knew would have been the 22-hole original layout of the links but there is unfortunately no routing of that course. We do know a few things though, and from that can make an educated guess.

The original St Andrews links layout

It was 1764 when the course was cut down to 18 holes. The Society of St Andrews Golfers' minutes on 4 October are clear that the layout of the holes did not change drastically, other than to cut out the short opening holes. It stated that 'The Captain and Gentlemen Golfers present are of the opinion that it would be for the improvement of the Links that the four first holes should be converted into two. They therefore have agreed that for the future they shall be played as two holes, in the same way as presently marked out. Wm St Clair.'

The key phrase is 'in the same way as presently marked out', which meant that there were no holes elsewhere, such as stretching up to the Martyrs Monument. The holes stayed where they were; they just turned the opening short four holes into two longer ones.

Over time, *Hole o' the Hill* title may have confused those who did not know that the original 18th green would have been to the south of where it is now.

As can be seen in the A.A. Martin map of March 1821, the original final green was approximately 50 yards south of where it is now, in the approximate location of the gardens behind Golf Place and The

Links road. There were no houses back then, not even Allan's father Davie Robertson's, which would be built the following year, so it was all open links common land.

We also know from the 1879 Road War precognition statements, that the land there was also used for dumping rubbish. This must have been after the closing green was moved to approximately its present location. Being sandy soil, there were few things that the land could have been used for, so it was ideal for golf.

The entire back nine that we play today was, for the 18th-century ball-making Robertsons, the entire width of the course: it was very narrow. Allan never played the anti-clockwise course direction that we now play, nor the front nine. All his grand matches against Dunn or in foursomes with Tom against the Dunn twins or Park and Willie Dunn were played over the land of the back nine today. The new front nine was part of Old Tom's revolution of the links after Allan's death, bringing in the new 18th and first greens, and new bunkers. It was a simplification of the links and it certainly made an easier course than the one Allan knew.

In the 1700s the Robertsons played the 22-hole layout and the front nine in reverse. From near their 22nd green, they would drive off, back down the fairway. There was a large bunker called Halket's bunker about 180 yards away. In the June 2011 edition of *Through the Green* Peter Lewis set out the case that the original first hole green must have been somewhere in that general location. Given that the shoreline on the right was close to Halket's, the bunker may have been towards the front of the green.

The second hole would have played from there to today's 17th green. Remarkably, from the left of the fairway, where the road is today, the Road Hole green is a welcoming and gently rising target. For the first time, from that angle, the green makes perfect sense and is an attractive approach shot. This was simply how it was meant to be played.

Given the dogleg of the land where we play the 17th, the original third hole would probably have been a straight hole with the green somewhere around Cheape's bunker. Players would have to play over Progressing and Scholars. These bunkers and those beyond Cheape's bunker pretty much line up to give us an idea of the direction of play.

A hand-drawn map of the bunker, surveyed and drawn by W. & J. Chalmers, Perth, in 1836, shows the original Cheape bunker and a possible green site, with Cheape's bunker being possibly front right of the green.

The fourth hole would have been a simple short hole to today's 16th green, with possibly three bunkers to be carried and one guarding the green. All in all, this would have been an attractive golf hole.

One can see that these four opening holes are quite short; by losing two of the opening and closing holes, the course goes from 22 holes to 18. This is the reason why we play 18 holes. It has nothing to do with whisky shots in a bottle; more prosaically, that is all the land would allow to create a good course in St Andrews. When the golfing world looked to St Andrews for rules and guidance for regulations, they wanted to emulate what St Andrews had. If St Andrews had only been 12 holes, we might today be looking at a very different golfing landscape.

David III (1707–67) married Margaret Smith on 30 July 1741. They had a son on 17 June the following year, also named David, but Margaret died eleven days later, possibly due to childbirth issues. In 1743, ballmaker David III married his first cousin Marion, who bore six children, namely William (1745), John (1747), Patrick (1748), Marion (1749), Andrew (1752) and Helen (1756).

Patrick (1748–1803), who was known as Peter, followed in the family line and became a ballmaker and was known as a 'professional golfer'. This was Allan's grandfather.

What was a professional at this date? Was it a person who made money from the game? Perhaps the best description is an artisan who could be called upon to play with a gentleman in a betting golf match. It seems to be a loose, yet all encompassing role, that also included caddying, tending to a links, and perhaps teaching the game. The professional role would evolve to include having a golf parlour. The modern era, where caddies can earn fortunes by carrying a bag for a tour player, is a world away from those with clubs under the arm or joining a gentleman for a match. Nonetheless, it was certainly a life wedded to golf, and that could be said of many generations of Robertsons.

Few families hold the premier positions in St Andrews as much as the Robertsons, with many generations looking after the golfers' needs, be it for golf balls or refreshments. They were also present as the links evolved. From the time of the 22-hole layout to the 18-hole routing, there was a Robertson providing a range of featherie balls or tending to the green. In good times and bad, there was a Robertson there. This explains why, when guttie balls come in to play, Allan could see the fading of his heritage; he reacts accordingly.

In 1780, according to the St Andrews Society's minutes of 4 August, new red coats were needed for golfing as their old ones were in bad condition. The new ones would be 'red with yellow buttons. The undermentioned gentlemen have likewise agreed to have an [sic] Uniform Frock-viz. a Buff colour with a Red Cap. The Coat to be half lapelled, the Button white. Signed Balcarres and Ten others.'

As the 18th century came to a close, there was a storm brewing. The town council was in trouble financially and, as a result of poor and somewhat illegal decisions, the very St Andrews links itself would be put at risk. The Robertson clan would be key expert witnesses in court as the future of the links hung in the balance.

Four

UNPARDONABLE BLUNDER

On 15 June 1774, it was registered in St Andrews that Patrick 'Peter' Robertson had married Elspeth Gibson on 19 May. Their son, Davie Robertson (David IV), was born the next year, on 6 July 1775. He was Allan's father.

In Peter and Davie's time St Andrews was still not a pretty sight. This was the era of Dr Samuel Johnson and Mr Boswell's famed visit to the town. Now akin to a mere village with around 1,000 'inactive … and gloomy' inhabitants, St Andrews was a shambles, the detritus left after the Reformation. The only manufacturing was that connected to golf or sailcloth. Flocks of sheep meandered on grass-filled dirt paths, which were the town's roads. Buildings were crumbling, and the stench of foul manure and herring guts filled the air. For a population that lived without, as Lyon says, the Christian glory of yesteryear could be captured in this poem by Virgil:[1]

> Ardea, a place renowned in days of yore,
> But now her perished glory is no more.

Locals drank polluted, discoloured water that was said to have included lead. The open water source was also used to wash all sorts of items, including dirty clothing and bed linen. Fish were washed and gutted in it. It was a recipe for disaster and, not surprisingly, disease associated with poor water and sanitation were prevalent in St Andrews, including outbreaks of typhoid, dysentery and cholera.

Street lighting using oil lamps was suggested in 1796 but not installed. Clean water pipes were also suggested in 1781 to take the water from the reservoir behind Holy Trinity Church, but they too were not built. The town could simply not afford such luxuries. Despite all this, visitors still came to St Andrews. Sir Walter Scott wrote of his time here, as did many other authors. Even back then, the ancient, wonderful, brutal history of St Andrews lured writers and stimulated imaginations.

Among the deprivation, there was a living to be made in the family ball-making business of Peter and his son Davie Robertson. The golfers and students gave our historic families such as the Robertsons a way to feed the family. If you could stitch featheries, you could also turn your skills to making shoes or sailcloth if needed, and many did. Among the makers of sailcloth were the Dempster family, about whom we shall learn more of shortly. History has been somewhat unkind to the Dempsters, due to the rabbit issue discussed below, but they were one of the town's biggest employers, offering a lifeline to many during a very harsh period of St Andrews history.

Build-up to the Rabbit Wars

One of the truly remarkable episodes in the history of the links came in 1797 when Davie was in his 22nd year: the town council chose to sell the links.[2] This controversial and, what some might claim, illegal decision by the council to sell the people's land eventually led to what is known as the Rabbit Wars. The court case that ensued was acrimonious, but for us the testimony in court given by many golfers, including Allan's grandfather Peter and Tom's grandfather John Morris, gives an insight to life on the links in the 1700s.

With only around 1,000 people paying taxes, the council could ill afford to maintain roads or fund much-needed public health improvements. There was a diminishing population and certainly nowhere near enough revenue to pay off the town's debts. The main list of debts listed in the minutes of the town council on 21 January 1797 were £410 *7s.* 11*d.* to the Bank of Scotland, £300 to the heirs of Dean of Guild Landale for repairing and building the flour mill, and £120 to John Brown (merchant) for building houses for the millers.

In total, this was £830 *7s.* 11*d.* Furthermore, another debt was for their proportion of the £1,500 cost of repairing Holy Trinity, the town church, plus the long-term outstanding bills for 'the Laying of the

Public Streets. Bringing water into the town. Reparation of the new miln and Grammar School'. £90 loss was incurred giving the poor a meal at a reduced price. The Council were in a dire situation.

By the 18th century, the sale of common land was allowed by law only if it benefited the inhabitants. Many argued this could well have been the case in St Andrews at the time.

From David Hay Fleming's notebook in the University of St Andrews archives, we learn of the woeful state of affairs.[3] All the town's assets were plundered to try to sort out its debts. With all avenues exhausted, on 21 January 1797, a council meeting decided

> to endeavour to borrow a sum of money upon their Lands of Pilmour Links and Commonty, the Gray [sic] Friars Yard, and the Town's proportion of the area of the Town Church, or even to feu or sell the same, for the above purpose; and in the meantime, the Town Council request the magistrates [local legal authority] to grant their own personal security for any purposes before mentioned.

This allowed the council to relieve the local lawmaking magistrates of their obligations to the public, and 'to grant them a Bond and Disposition in security over the said subjects. The magistrates, however, were not to sell without intimation to the council assembled.'[4]

This is legal double-speak, where the council gave the magistrates (who were often the very same people, thus the council gave to themselves) a Bond and Disposition, over the linksland. This at first appeared to enable them to sell the links. However, this was ultimately deemed legally flawed and could probably not hold up against the people's longstanding inherent interest.

The letting or leasing of the linksland was not in itself unusual. In 1659, it was ordained by the council that 'Pilmure Links and Commonty' should be 'rouped' (parcelled off) and let for three years for grazing cattle. Some of the council minute books and records have been lost and it would not be surprising that the links common land were let by the council well before 1659. Clearly the activity did not hamper the golfers. In fact, the sheep and cattle would have kept the grass short. It was a perfect partnership.

On 24 September 1726 William Gib, Deacon of the Baxters (head of local bakers), was permitted to farm his black and white rabbits on the links and the privilege of disposing of them. Importantly, however, this permission set out that the links was 'not to be spoiled where the golfing is used'. The Council could withdraw this permission with a month's notice. This did not interfere with golfing so must have been on a manageable scale.

In 1751 James Lumsdaine leased the linksland, but was told not to interfere with the golfing ground, or he would be fined £20. The lease reserved to the locals the specific liberty to tack (trap) and destroy rabbits. The 3 February 1786 lease of the links and commonty for £42 to James Ritchie was very specific in that he could not use the links as a rabbit warren.

All in all, it was a very active piece of land, with a community of golfers, linen bleachers, cattle, sheep, occasional footballers and rabbits. However, in difficult circumstances, painful decisions had to be made.

A difficult path

Two local merchants, Robert Gourlay and John Gunn, knowing the bind that the council were in, offered in a little legal jamboree, to act as Trustees for the Town and to advance £2,080 7*s.* 11*d.* and grant their own security, on condition that the Town grant them a bond for the advance and a disposition in security over the lands. The Council agreed, and on 27 February 1797, duly gave Gourlay and Gunn the power to do what they could not, that is sell the links. Anything over £2,080 7*s.* 11*d.* was to go to the council and anything less, made up by the council. On 12 June 1797, the 'Lands of Pilmor [sic] and Pilmor Links' were put up for sale, but no buyer came forward. On 30 October 1797 they were put up for sale again for a reduced price of £700. Cathcart Dempster offered £800, but Thomas Erskine, later Earl of Kellie (*c.*1745–1828) and owner of the Cambo estate by Kingsbarns, offered £805. Ownership of the links duly passed over to Erskine.

It is worth mentioning in passing that the Dempsters and Erskines held high office in St Andrews, be it Deans of Guild or the Provostships. Those curious may question insider dealings, but it should also be noted that this move by the council gave them a financial lifeline and it was as a last resort that the action was taken. It could also be argued that it was their determination that the links should remain a golfing links evermore, that saved the golf course for future generations. Without that zeal, the council, in their desperation, could have made alternative decisions which, in turn, could have led to much worse scenarios for the ancient common land.

When the St Andrews links land was transferred to Erskine in liferent and his daughter Miss Anna Engelhert in fee, it was to be a brief ownership. Anna was his daughter from a previous relationship in Sweden. He adopted all of Anna's children and her eldest son, David, became the first Baronet of Cambo in 1821.

The feu (permission to purchase land in return for an annual rent) granted to Erskine had conditions which protected the rights of the golfers and, over the next two years, no action was taken that would be to the detriment of the links. However, he made it known that the previous leaseholder, Ritchie, had given up his lease and a new tenant could make a good business from a rabbit warren on the links. He even offered some of his own rabbit stock from the grounds of the Cambo estate in Kingsbarns. Stuart Grace, Secretary of the Society of St Andrews Golfers and Town Clerk, drew up the missives that included the ability of the land to be pastured for rabbits and they were let to George Forgan for 19 years.

A high point in the Dempster and Erskine family relationships came in 1799. Following the death of Provost Duncan in January, Charles Dempster nominated Sir Thomas Erskine of Cambo as Provost – a post he would retain for a decade. Sir Thomas Erskine at this point decided to sell the links and made it known that the purchaser could breed rabbits on the links. Forgan never got around to creating the rabbit farm.

So, in lieu of the time-old storyline that the Dempsters bought the links and filled it with rabbits, they actually bought a piece of land with that aspect clearly advertised and, in truth, its only capital-generating source apart from cattle grazing. Erskine alerted potential buyers to the rent currently achieved and the potential income and rent that could be achieved from the rabbit warren. It caught the interest of their colleagues on the town council, the Dempsters.

There were always rabbits on the links but, as shown in the various leases, they were kept away from the golfing links and never in any number to do real damage. Locals also were free to help themselves to the wild and natural food source.

On 29 August 1799, three months before he became the 9th Earl of Kellie after the death on 28 October 1799 of his nephew and Crail Golfing Society founder Charles, Thomas Erskine petitioned the council saying that he wished to sell the links to Charles and Cathcart Dempster, without the consent of Anna, as she was a minor, 'under the same restrictions and reservations as granted to the petitioner and Miss Anna Engelhert'.

They agreed on 11 October 1799 (the disposition is dated 4 December 1799) to sell all of the 280 acres of 'Pilmor' links lands belonging to the city, but with the following conditions:

- '... reserving to the Town of St Andrews, the whole ground to the eastward of the Swilkin [sic] Burn'. In other words, the land where we play for the 1st and 18th today. This land has never left public ownership and has always belonged to the people of St Andrews.
- '... reserving the Bleaching Ground to the west thereof as marked out by march stones, on which the inhabitants of St Andrews are to have the liberty and privilege in bleaching in all time coming'. This included the land on and near today's St Andrews Ladies Putting Club.
- '... reserving to the Burgesses of the City, power and liberty to cast and whin divots upon the links and commonty, for flanking and rigging, for repairing the Town's mills and dams.
- '... that no hurt or damage shall be done thereby to the Golf Links; nor shall it lie in the power of any proprietor of the said Pilmor Links to plough up any part of said Golf Links in all time coming, but the same shall be reserved entirely, as it has been in times past, for the comfort and amusement of the inhabitants and others who shall resort thither for that amusement; as also Reserving free access by a foot-path of road from the Town, through the said Links, to Eden water, to the

> Town's mussel scalps and cockles, according to use and wont; or as said subjects may be otherwise more fully described in the ancient rights … thereof, together with all right, title and interest, claim of right, etc., etc.'

Notice that there was no specific mention of not using the links as a rabbit warren. It was also agreed that he would pay a feu of £42 twice a year, which would double each time it was transferred to an heir, and the term of entry was given as Whitsunday 1799.[5]

In the agreement Charles Dempster reserved with right to sell, dispose and burden with debt the links land without permission of his son, Cathcart. They bought out Forgan's 19-year-old lease, even more than they paid Erskine for the land purchase, and let to James Begbie for nearly double the amount that Forgan had paid. This would have been an eye-watering amount and certainly questions would have been asked about their reasoning at the time. Was it that Charles was drawn to the 'Laird of the Links' title, or did they actually think that they could make a good financial return on the links?

What is clear is that the Dempsters would not have thought that their rabbit ambitions were in the least contentious.

Honourable citizens such as Erskine, as the Captain of the Society of St Andrews Golfers, and Grace, as Secretary and Town Clerk, would have led them to this train of thought. Their first attempt at raising revenue from the links with sheep was unsuccessful in 1799. Of the 120 sheep placed on the land, half of them died and the other half were deemed unwholesome and barely suitable to sell.

Their second attempt the following year was with rabbits.

The original sale by the council was naturally abhorrent to later generations. How could they sell the links which, for hundreds and hundreds of years, were owned by the people? Historian David Hay Fleming explains in part,

> It was an unpardonable blunder … [but] it is very easy for us to condemn their short-sighted policy; but it is only fair to remember that, in those days, the powers and limitations of the town-councils were not so clearly defined as now … the City … had reached its lowest ebb and that soon there would be indications of a change for the better. And no doubt they

> thought that they had conserved all the liberties and privileges over the Links.[6]

The town was in trouble, and this financial deal offered a bridge out of it. When the golf boom started in earnest, the fortunes of St Andrews would transform from those dark unlit days, but for now they had stabilised the town's finances.

Thus, far from being history's rogues, the Dempsters simply bought a piece of land in good faith. It was they who would suffer the consequences of that very questionable, and quickly forgotten, rabbit advice.

What did the Robertsons make of all this? Fortunately, it is they as links experts who were called to give their opinion in the court case on the damage the rabbits were doing to the links, and in doing so would give us an insight into their lives.

Five

RABBIT WARS

LITTLE did the council know that this financial reprieve would lead to over 20 years of strife in St Andrews and a protracted, ten-year court case. With no other viable alternative way to make money from their land purchase, the Dempsters turned to the very source that the earl had advised – rabbits. They brought in rabbits from England and nearby Tentsmuir. The one thing different from Ritchie, the previous tenant who also bred rabbits on site, was that their new tenant, James Begbie, did not manage where the rabbits were living or how many there were.

Locals were also under no doubt that they could no longer tack (trap) and destroy the rabbits, as they were all now under the ownership of the Dempsters. Loud proclamations of this change in access to the links' rabbits were announced in the town by drum. Dogs were prohibited on the links. Poison was laid down and some locals' dogs perished. Mr Cheape lost his own pointer dog.

So, with unmanaged numbers and unlimited warrens, the breeding started to damage the links as the number of holes and rabbit scrapings increased.

After a year of rabbit breeding and importing rabbits onto the links, enough was enough. On 8 October 1801 a letter was given to the council from George Cheape, Captain of the Golfing Society of St Andrews, complaining about the deterioration of the links and referencing the town's rights:

> Gentlemen,
>
> The Golfing Society are extremely concerned to find the Golfing ground so much cut up and destroyed by the Rabbits

> in the Links and which if not speedily prevented must land in the total destruction of the Golf ground … The Society are informed that the Good city were extremely guarded in the Sale of the Links by providing that nothing should be done to the prejudice of the Golf ground but that the same should be preserved entire as in times past for the Comfort and amusement of the Inhabitants and others …

New golf rules were formulated to address the new hazard. This is the origin of the rule on rabbit scrapings that exists to this day. Back then, it felt nothing less than an invasion.

On 15 January 1803, the Golfing Society of St Andrews, with Hugh Cleghorn as Captain, decided to bring the issue to court and raised funds for the case through subscribers, which were to be paid to their appointed agent, Adam Bruce. It was said that some of the subscribers came from Calcutta to maintain the case.

It was not the only dispute Cleghorn would have with the Dempsters. In 1804, there was difficulty between Hugh Cleghorn and Cathcart Dempster regarding the Fife Militia, with Cleghorn declining 'all commerce of confidence and friendship with you'. In this case Erskine tried to broker the peace.

Observing the reaction that the rabbit farm was having, the Dempsters suggested two weeks later that they would pay a person to tend to the links and all the rabbit scrapings, at the same wage the golfing society was paying. This offer was not taken up, possibly due to other squabbles they were having at the time.

On 23 April 1803 a summons was created by many well-known and recognisable names under the title of Golfers of St Andrews, and on 30 April it was executed. The pursuers' names included Hugh Cleghorn, Dr James Playfair (Principal of United College of St Salvator and St Leonards of St Andrews, Sir Hugh Lyon Playfair's father), James Cheape of Strathtyrum, George Cheape, plus an all-encompassing phrase 'all the inhabitants residing in St Andrews', albeit not the town council. They were perhaps cautious that they could also be sued for mismanagement of the common good. It was traditional at the time that the inhabitants would sue the magistrates if such an infringement was felt, and in fact this case was the first where the locals went after the taker of the feu, that is the Dempsters and not the magistrates. Remarkably one name on the list stands out – Thomas Erskine, Earl of Kellie. Such was the detriment to the links that even the seller, who had encouraged a rabbit farm, had issue with what the Dempsters were doing.

The summons complained about the damage to the links, how the rabbits had also come onto Cheape's land at the Balgove, and destroyed crops, and about the poison that had killed dogs including that of Mr Cheape's Balgove tenant, John Hood.

They wished that the Dempsters and Begbie desist and furthermore remove the rabbit stocks, which they had imported to the links, said to be about 100 pairs. They wished that the golfing ground be returned to its previous good order. Cheape and Hood wished to be compensated £50 sterling for the damage to their grounds and crops. The Dempsters and Begbie should also pay the pursuers £100 for damages.

The Dempsters

History has been very unkind to father Charles (1742–1809) and son Cathcart Dempster (1764–1839), aided by prose from writers such as George Bruce, who in *Reminiscences of St Andrews Bay* (1884) described Charles as 'a pompous, self-interested, opinionative' official. However, the full picture is less dramatic and far more human. Also, Bruce calling anyone opinionated is ironic in the least, as he seldom had a kind word for anyone.

Charles was born in 1742, three years before the rebellion of Bonnie Prince Charlie. He married Jean Methven on 30 October 1763. They had three children, Cathcart (1764–1839), Mary (b.1766) and Peggy (1769–1842). Cathcart married Mary Glass (1768–1802) on 16 January 1790 in St Andrews. They had eight children, Janet (b.1790), Jean (b.1792), Mary Anne (b.1793), Charles (b.1795), Margaret (b.1796), Harriet (b.1798), another Charles, so named after the first died (b.1799) and finally Thomas (b.1799). It was a large family. Being a family of considerable importance, the dowry costs of the girls' marriages must have been considerable in the second decade of the 19th century.

The Dempsters were no town pariahs. Creating a formal business partnership on 2 August 1790, as Charles Dempster & Son, they were one of the biggest employers locally, with a philanthropic outlook. Cathcart was the *de facto* chief magistrate, stepping in for Sir Thomas Erskine when the latter was away, which was often.

In 1792 they brought the first bank to St Andrews. They bought the land for the town hall. They founded the Butter Market, which brought revenue to many. They were the ones who proposed lighting in St Andrews in 1779. Cathcart aided the fisherfolk by bringing in experienced fishermen from Caithness to help them improve their livelihoods (though George Bruce had a different take on that), created the sale of the Eden mussels for bait, and organised the licensing of seaware for cutting on the rocks. This in turn led to improvements in the harbour. He also bought the steelyard for the harbour in 1798. It was said of Cathcart that 'His mind was most thoroughly practical, scientific, charitable, and void of selfishness'. They funded a type of sailcloth that became one of the town's biggest sources of revenue. In fact, far from being the town outcasts, Cathcart's years were known as the 'Dear Years', as he also established a poor folk fund that gave subsistence to those in dire need.. It raised 1,000 guineas from subscribers.

Cathcart himself enjoyed practical jokes. On one occasion he invited famed golfer Samuel Messieux and friends to dinner. Cathcart appeared to have difficulty in swallowing and was struggling to eat. Messieux enquired over the issue. Cathcart said,

'Oh, I am bothered by a tuft of hair growing under my tongue.'

'How very extraordinary! I have never heard of such a thing!'

'Why, sir, you can feel it by putting your finger in my mouth.'

When Messieux naturally obliged, Dempster bit down on his finger. He had been seeking revenge over a trick Messieux had played on him.

'I have been owing you for a pair of "Swiss gloves" for a good while and that is payment!'

In this Rabbit War controversy, Cathcart tried to settle all matters before it even went to court, by offering in a letter dated 25 January 1803 to pay for someone to 'keep the Links in as good order as ever they had been kept, and to hold himself responsible for the same, and would even pay, from his own pocket, the difference betwixt the sum presently paid to the Links Keeper, and what should be required to do the business completely'.

If this reasonable offer had been taken up – and it is still not clear why it was not – all of the Rabbit War legal controversy could have been avoided. Throughout the court case, Cathcart employed men to repair the links, albeit with admittedly mixed results.

This is not a family determined to destroy the links. Far from it. Yes, the rabbit controversy is a painful period in the history of the links but, like all human stories, neither party was totally good nor bad. In fact, it is not an exaggeration to say that the Dempsters finally deserve to be recognised for their service to the town. For too long the established narratives have remained unquestioned.

For further information on the Dempsters, see this extract from *St Andrews in the Footsteps of Old Tom Morris.*[1]

A Question of Title

This is a time in the early 1800s when there were almost no other golf courses in England, Wales or Ireland, bar Royal Blackheath in London. It truly was a Scottish game that would later spread throughout Britain, America, and then to India and the rest of the world. Wherever there was an Officers' Mess, there would be a form of golf, for example the Dum Dum Club in India *c.*1829 (Royal Calcutta Golf Club today), which was founded by Major Hugh Lyon Playfair, its first Captain and son of Principal James Playfair, who is mentioned frequently during this case.

The case would require expert testimony and that would come from the various Keepers of the Green or ballmakers, and many of them, as we shall see, were Robertsons.

In the Rabbit War court case, the defenders were Charles and Cathcart Dempster, and their tenant James Begbie. On 1 June 1803 judge Lord Polkemmet in the Outer Court in Edinburgh, allowed John Macfarlan, who was acting on the defenders' behalf, to give written defences the day following the summons, and directed both parties to be ready for debate the following Friday.

Having heard both parties as noted, Lord Polkemmet asked on 11 June 1803 for the pursuers to give in a condescendence, which is a legal note, explaining their basic title or right even to bring the case, within eight days. Could the pursuers, who were not the town council but mere locals, have the right even to bring the case? If not, the case would be over.

The Pursuers pleaded:

1. The right by which this property is held contains a reservation in favour of the pursuers.

2. The privilege has been reserved to the whole inhabitants, so each individual may apply to the court of law whenever their right is deemed violated.

3. The proprietor cannot object to the condition under which he received the land when purchased.

The Dempsters' counter responded:

1. A personal servitude must cease with the life of the person it was created for. This servient tenement right cannot be bestowed upon a whole class of individuals, such as every person who golfs. In other words, they were questioning the legal validity of the commonty.

2. The reservation made by the Magistrates was for the Magistrates alone and not the indefinite multitude who golf. Therefore, as the Magistrates were not part of the case, none of this was answerable.

On 11 February 1804, and signed on the 14th, Lord Ordinary Polkemmet's interlocutor said 'having considered the said condescendence, with the answers thereto, and haill [whole] process … made avisandum with cause to the Lords; and Appoints the parties to prepare, print and box informations thereon, and therein state what may occur to them on the point of title, as well to the merits …'

So, the case was still in limbo but inching forward. The issue of title was as yet undecided, but certainly not refused out of hand, which is what the Dempsters desired.

The Inner Court

On 9 January 1805, the Dempsters filed 32½ pages of information that were boxed and signed by Adam Gillies, with the Dempsters insisting again that the pursuers had no title and therefore no right to bring such a case.

On 8 February 1805 Hugh Cleghorn and other pursuers boxed 25 pages of information signed by John Clerk (later Lord Eldon), claiming an incorrect application of law by the defenders, as the case law referred to by the defenders had been disregarded in later court decisions.

Three months later, on 17 May 1805, the Lords sustained (affirmed) the title of the pursuers in the first instance. That firmly settled the first issue of Cleghorn and fellow pursuers' basic right to bring the case. The case was then remitted to Lord Ordinary with instructions to receive condescendence from the pursuers, and to proceed with the case.

Now it was time to look at the case evidence itself. After receiving written evidence from the three parties including Cheape, it was decided on 9 July 1805 that proof was to be provided. David Douglas Esq. (later Lord Reston), advocate, was duly appointed to take this proof – that is expert witness statements in St Andrews.

The Robertsons' evidence

This is a truly engaging part of the Rabbit Wars saga. Within the statements, we have legendary golfing names such as Robertson and Morris, looking after the links, illuminating the 1700s and early 1800s.

From 3 to 7 September 1805 Douglas took statements in St Andrews from the Pursuers' and Defenders' witnesses. Of the 39 witnesses examined for Pursuers, 16 were for Cheape. The Defenders had 16 witnesses. Some 53 pages of evidence were gathered over the five days and what is very apparent is that there are a lot of Robertsons giving witness statements as seasoned ballmakers, golfers and caddies: that is to say, the St Andrews golfing experts, alongside John Morris, Tom's grandfather for the pursuers, while his great uncle, a lone Robert Morris, then current Keeper of the Green, was called on behalf of the defenders.

Charles Robertson (*c.*1752–1810) was the first witness on 3 September 1805. He was 52 and knew more about the St Andrews links than anyone, having worked them for 25 years, from around 1776 to 1801, 12 years after the 22 holes became 18. He eventually left when the rabbit damage made it impossible to continue.

Who was Charles? He may have been a relation of Allan's, but with people being called not the names with which they were christened, it makes it impossible to trace. There was a Thomas Robertson born on 25 March 1753, which would make him 52, and he is also the only St Andrews-based Robertson born that year. There was an Andrew, Allan's great uncle, born in 1752, but we simply cannot be certain who Charles is. There is one lone entry for the death of a Charles Robertson, ballmaker, on 10 March 1810. What we do know is that the expert of the links was a Robertson, as so deemed by many of those who gave testimony.

At the very outset, the Dempsters objected to Charles giving a statement. How could the evidence of a ballmaker, whose very business rested on being on good terms with the golfers, be anything but one-sided? They claimed that he had a vested interest in the case and would benefit from the very cause of the case itself. The Commissioner rejected this and allowed testimony to continue. For the sake of repetition, the Dempsters' legal team did this for every single golfer and each time were refused.

Charles confirmed that he had worked the links for 25 years and was paid to do so by the golfers. This was the Society of St Andrews Golfers, which would become, in time, The Royal and Ancient Golf Club of St Andrews. It is their vital support over the years that kept the links in play.

The primary job of Charles was to make new holes on the green for every monthly meeting, and he was down on the links on a daily basis throughout that time. He confirmed that there were few rabbits on the golf course in that time before the Dempsters, and that he, like all the locals, freely shot rabbits as desired. This informal but effective management kept their numbers down.

His shooting time was between 6 a.m. and 9 a.m. After the Dempsters came and sent the drum through the town prohibiting everyone in town from destroying the rabbits, the population of the rabbits exploded, and the number of scrapes increased vastly. These new holes and scrapes did severe damage to the links.

The local rule was that if your ball went into a hole or scrape, lift the ball, drop it over your head and play the next shot without penalty with a ponderous heavy rut iron club. At that time players' clubs were mostly woods, akin to modern hybrids. The rut iron, which was used as a means to escape, would not have moved the ball very far at all. The lofter, with which Allan was said to have introduced the high approach shot, came later. For now they were using the rut iron, the face of which was barely larger than the ball.

Alarmingly, Charles said he thought if the rabbits were to continue unabated, the links would be unfit to play golf. In other words, the very game of golf in St Andrews was at stake; such was the threat by the rabbits. On a links that has since had such luminaries as Allan Robertson, Tom Morris, Tommy Morris, Bobby Jones, Arnold Palmer, Jack Nicklaus, Seve Ballesteros, Tiger Woods and Rory McIlroy, how much would have been lost if Hugh Cleghorn, the Society of St Andrews Golfers or the locals of St Andrews had not fought vigorously to protect their links? It was that serious.

Charles maintained that scrapes were repaired, but just as fast they opened up again. Matches were suffering with players getting caught in holes or badly repaired scrapes. Note that matchplay, just like Muirfield today, where foursomes and matchplay are pre-dominantly played, was also the principal forms of the sport at this time.

Charles confirmed that the Dempsters asked him to help with the repair, but he refused as there were just too many holes, especially in the bunkers. For the first 20 years, he was paid 20 shillings (£1) for tending the links, but such was the state of the links they doubled his allowance for the remaining years. Charles confirmed that there were always sheep on the links.

When it came to the defenders questioning him, he confirmed that when the Dempsters sent the drum through the town, they warned people not to bring their dogs there. However, the Dempsters' questioning was largely poor and ineffectual. Charles confirmed that the golfers often lost their balls in the bents (whin bushes) but not so often in the holes and scrapes of the rabbits, unless the hole was deep. He also confirmed that the Dempsters did have sheep on the links, but many of them had died.

Towards closing, he confirmed that Thomas Robertson took over the links after him but the latter did not last a year, due to his employers being unsatisfied.

As the next Robertson lined up to give testimony, I do wonder what Charles' life on the links was truly like and whether it would have ever occurred to them what the town would be like some 200 years later. Halket's bunker, on the opening and closing hole, would have been waiting to trap their errant balls. Situated about 50 yards from where The New Golf Club is today, at the time it may have only been a natural hazard where the winds had worn away the grass and sheep sought shelter. Remember this is well before Sir Hugh Lyon Playfair's land reclamation, which gave us the land for today's first hole.

For some at the time hazards added to the fun of the game. As they played out and back to the same holes, effectively on the narrow land of our back nine today, with not a house in sight, they could not have dreamt of the global scale of the sport and of St Andrews. Those houses' existence, as we shall see later, were a direct consequence of the financial burden of the rabbit war.

George Robertson (1768–1831) was next. A North Street ballmaker and caddie, George married Janet Aikman on 21 July 1792 in Edinburgh. Working as a caddie for 25 years meant that he, as many of his contemporaries, started working on the links from the age of about 10 or 12, which raises questions about the schooling, or lack thereof, for working classes in those days.

George said that when the Dempsters came there were 50 times more scrapes than before the Dempsters. He confirmed that Charles Robertson told George that he would not do the job of keeper of the green for three guineas (£3 3*s.*), given that the course was nearly completely ruined. He testified that John Morris (Tom Morris' grandfather) and he counted the number of scrapes that had been repaired, which was 895 and that he also observed 1,137 new scrapes. It was clearly getting out of hand.

One player, Mr Black, said George, snapped his iron club in sheer frustration after his ball went into scrape after scrape. Tourists had also complained about the state of the links. It was not a happy situation.

George was asked by Begbie to shoot a dog which had been caught in a trap. Although he does not state whether he did shoot the dog, numerous locals, including Mr Cheape, lost their dogs due to the Dempsters and Begbie laying down poison balls or traps.

Cheape's pointer dog was called Pompey. Remarkably, when George died around 1836, he had £1,052 5*s.* 10*d.* in his will, but, according to Fife Family History Society in *Golfing Skeletons in Family History* (page 47), there was no cash in the house and the value of clothes and contents came to just £2 12*s.* 6*d.* In 1818 he was given a personal bond for £1,000 from William Dalgleish of Scotscraig and Andrew Murray Guthrie of Craigie. No reason for the money is offered, but it would have made him a very wealthy Robertson.

Next to give evidence was ballmaker William Robertson, who was the son of David III and Marion Robertson, born 25 February 1745, the year of the Jacobite rising. He was the eldest brother of Peter, Allan's grandfather. In 1766 he married Margaret Thomson; his aforementioned son, George, was born two years later.

Now aged 60, he had worked as a caddie for 50 years. This means William probably saw the original 22-hole layout when the links was arguably at its wildest. At that time there were no houses, bar the shepherd's cottage, and no main roads on the links. Paths criss-crossed the links as routes for carts to the shoreline for collecting mussels or seaweed. Bunkers were unraked and unmanaged; they were mere hazards that nature had created. Greens were kept short by the sheep and the naturally salt-rich soil. It would have been a challenge to the golfers of the day.

Most noteworthy among William's testimony is that the course was much busier in 1805 than in the 1750s, due to the success of the university, which was well attended. This is not an inconsiderable point. As much as we have the gentlemen golfers to thank, we should also note the university's part in keeping the links alive, with resulting work for caddies and ballmakers alike.

Peter Robertson (d.1826 aged 50 or so), spoke next. This was not Allan's grandfather; it was another Robertson who, confusingly, was also a ballmaker. This Peter was the son of William above and nephew to Davie, Allan's father. This made him Allan's cousin. He notably owned a half share of a sloop ship called the *Southwick* of St Andrews, which was valued at £122 in his will in 1826. His house contents were £15, making a noteworthy £137 estate for another Robertson.

He married Margaret Ramsay (d.1820) on 4 November 1791. Peter was a caddie as a young teenager to around age 38 and worked on the links every day. He also noted that his father William used to tend to the links and got paid five shillings a year for doing so. His duties were confined to making new holes and filling up the old ones as necessary.

The final Robertson, also a ballmaker and a caddie, to give testimony was Thomas, aged around 40, who merely confirmed what most had said already about the links deterioration since the Dempsters had taken over.

No other family name is as prevalent as the Robertsons in the witness statements. They were simply the experts, with generation after generation of ballmakers and Keepers of the Green. This history would not have been lost on Allan.

Non-golfing Robertsons

There were other Robertsons who also gave testimony, who, unfortunately for us, have the same names as the golfers and thus add to the confusion. William Robertson, labourer and gardener, aged 47, in discussing the damage to Cheape's property, observed ditches and drains filled up and choked by rabbits. Charles Robertson, tenant in Kirkcaldy, aged 31, confirmed that he sold rabbits to a John Leitch who confirmed he would be putting them on the links. Peter Robertson, 60, butcher, said that he had tried to cure the Dempsters' sheep by rubbing six or seven score of them with butter and brimstone and also put the combination down their throats. It was thought this got rid of ticks. Small wonder many did not survive.

Pursuers' witnesses of note

John Morris, Tom's grandfather, was aged 53 at the time and was said to be a weaver and a caddie. Like all the caddies, his testimony was objected to by the Dempsters, but again, their objection was repelled. John reported that he had been a caddie for 30 years. He said, as a boy around the age of 10, he would kill rabbits for food and pelts, by digging them out of holes, but he became a weaver not long after.

Domestic handloom weaving was then the most common employment among working-class families, but the trade eventually declined, and such work had become scarce by the end of the 19th century. In addition to cotton cloth, weavers also produced beautiful items, including silk scarves and handkerchiefs for the home market, as well as exports to India. At its peak, it is said that cottage weaving was so lucrative that in the early 1800s weavers could afford their own houses. The era around 1815 and the Napoleonic Wars is known today as the 'golden age' for handloom weavers.

It is said they had valuable skills and could negotiate lucrative terms. The rise of the socially minded building societies in the 1830s also saw a rise in new, affordable houses being built. It should be noted as an aside that there is a question mark over the actual ownership of the houses on North Street at the time, as records tended to say whose abode it was, not who the owner was. What we do know is that Allan's father owned Sandyhill and Tom Morris owned his own golf shop and 6 Pilmour Links. For the other caddies and ballmakers, we simply do not know, but there is a clear history of weavers owning their own homes, so it would not have been remarkable for the weavers on North Street to be the actual owners of the houses.

By the 1820s the golden age was over. The buoyant trade of being a handloom weaver began to decline as larger, more efficient and faster power looms in factories took over. It also coincided with the 1825–27 depression and the crash of the Bank of England, which was helped out of the situation, remarkably, by the Bank of France, a country with whom they had been at war.

It would be wrong to categorise weavers as poor, and certainly there was no social stigma attached to being a weaver until much later as the trade dwindled. Weavers' income could go from around 26 shillings a week to around 6 shillings, and food prices also shot up, leaving many weavers bereft, with some facing starvation. This explains why many took to caddying whenever they could to supplement their income. At the time of the Rabbit War it was the golden era for the handloom weavers.

The constant source of rabbits on the linksland would have fed the Morris generations in the 1700s. Like Charles Robertson, John Morris warned of the ultimate loss of the links for golfing if nothing changed.

He highlighted that the links had been repaired two years earlier, but, in the interim much damage had been done.

He also confirmed there had been a recent repair, but that fresh scrapes had been opened up. John stated that he thought the links would be best for golf if pastured by sheep.

The Dempsters' legal team asked him to confirm that the ground was often first broken by iron clubs, especially those swung by unskilled players, and that the rabbits usually then scraped there. In other words, the bad golfers themselves had no one to blame but themselves as they were making openings for the rabbits to dig into. John reiterated that no amount of repair could keep the links in good order while the rabbits continued in their present numbers.

Various witnesses lamented over the loss of the links' playability. George Mitchell said he lost a match as his ball got into a scrape for three successive holes and had never seen the links in a worse state. He ventured that it used to be so rare to even see a rabbit that he remembered hearing a caddie say, 'Bless me, I saw a rabbit!'

Rev. William Thomson, a young preacher in St Andrews, aged 28, said that it got so bad that a new rule was brought in that, if you get into a scrape, your caddie must retrieve your ball and drop it over his head, and that the next shot must be played with an iron club. Even the patience of a man of the cloth was being sorely tested.

In evidence regarding the damage to Cheape's property, David Balsillie said that for two years he herded cattle for Mr Hood on the low ground near the links. He said in that time Mr Hood's crops of corn and turnips were much destroyed by the rabbits and that his dog died in great pain due to the poison administered by Begbie on the links. His dog bit at stones in the wall, foamed in the mouth, and had his belly 'much drawn up' after coming back from the links. It sadly died 30 minutes later. Begbie threatened anyone seen pilfering rabbits that they would be sent to Botany Bay.

John Balsillie said that he knew of David Fowlis' dog which had also perished, and also how crops were destroyed on the land of Cheape's tenant, Mr Hood. He also confirmed Begbie's well-used Botany Bay threat, having been so threatened himself; he added that initially there was very little damage to the crops but that in the second year, it got much worse. He confirmed to the defenders that he did not see any noticeable rabbit scrapes on Mr Hood's low ground in the first two years.

John Butcher said that a full year of wheat was destroyed, possessed by Mr Hood, on what was known as the Clayfaulds, adjoining Dempsters' ground, due to rabbits. The Clayfaulds were separated from Strathtyrum by a public road.

David Peatie said he was employed by Cheape to kill the rabbits that strayed onto his land because they were destroying the corn. He estimated that he and Alexander Fernie killed 60 pairs of rabbits. It was an unwritten rule of employment that Mrs Cheape would get two pair of skinned rabbits a week. They killed as many as they could but he said it would be nigh on impossible to kill all the rabbits. He also said that he prevented others from killing rabbits on Cheape's property and low ground.

Mrs Betty McGuffog, housekeeper to Mr Cheape, talked about another of Cheape's dog disappearing on the links.

Cheape, who was a member of the Society of St Andrews Golfers, had witnesses lined up to talk about destroyed crops, hedges, trees, ditches, drains, and dogs. David Fowlis, the links shepherd who lived in the solitary house on the links, confirmed that his dog was poisoned there. He provided a little more detail about the sheep on the links that perished, calling them rotten and full of water, which was discovered during dissection. Remarkably, he stated they were the wrong type of sheep for the links. They needed more fertile grass than the salty links could provide. Some 80 sheep died in the first year. David reiterated the point that, before the Dempsters, rabbit numbers were managed as folk were regularly killing them for food. His wife, Christian Reid, also made the point that sheep were kept by various tenants of the links land, but Dempster simply brought the wrong sheep to the site and that is why they perished.

James Pringle said that his father was a tenant of the links, along with Provost Lumsden, and they kept sheep very well before Nicol and then Ritchie.

James Mason complained that Begbie killed a dog of his on the links and they often fought due to this. There is a line of witnesses whose dogs suffered due to the poison on the links, or they knew someone whose dog had died. It was a truly woeful situation.

Donald Fraser wrote an advertisement for the Dempsters telling folks to keep their dogs off the links as poison was going to be down to kill vermin. David Tod was a member of the town council when the links were sold to Erskine. He said that the town had no right to sell the land as a warren, and would have been prevented in doing so by the people if they tried. The town council would certainly have expected more financially from the sale.

Defenders' proof

Where there was a chorus of people lining up to say how bad things had become, how they knew of someone who had lost a dog, or that the very sport of golfing on the links was at peril, the defenders did not enjoy such. Their testimonies relied on people who clearly had eyesight or memory issues.

The first defender was Robert Morris, brother of John Morris, Tom's grandfather. He was noted as 49 years old, working as a weaver and also as a caddie for the last 20 years. His links knowledge was extensive, as not only had he been around and on them for 40 years, but he was also currently employed by the golfers to keep the links and would have been doing so for two and a half years come that October. It does not appear to have been a full-time job as we would know it now. The fact that his profession is noted as weaver speaks volumes. Robert confirmed that Principal Playfair, Sir Hugh Lyon's father, forbade him from repairing the scrapes and Dr Melville told him to let them be. Until that point, he had been repairing them. This explains why for two years the course had fallen into a ruinous state.

It also sheds a slightly different light on the Dempsters, who historically had been deemed to have been at fault. It turns out that it was the senior golfing authorities who forbade any repair work for around two years. One can understand the Dempsters' bewilderment of the situation.

Robert said that if the links were in good order, he would manage them for £4 or £5, this being the running cost, rather than his wages. He did not know what it would cost to put the links right, but he did confirm he was paid £2 by the golfers.

All in all, his testimony was not exactly helpful to the defenders. Though it was a minor point, it did show that far from the Dempsters being the sole cause of the problem, golfers themselves initially prevented the repair of the links.

Town clerk Stuart Grace, aged 50 and upwards at the time, had the most remarkable amnesia. Grace did not remember mentioning that the links would make a good rabbit warren or that tenant George Forgan had liberty from Erskine to turn the links into a warren, with the help of Cambo rabbits, and that he himself, Stuart Grace, had written a missive detailing such. He also claimed that the council would never have allowed a warren.

However, George Forgan aged 36 years, who was the above Erskine's tenant, said in stark contrast to Grace's testimony that Erskine did indeed promise him some Cambo rabbits to put onto the links. The missive was written by a clerk at Grace's firm; it also stated that he would not have agreed to the £70 rent if it were not to be used as a rabbit warren. He confirmed that the missive in question was put into Grace's hand but that he had not seen it since. Grace had said that such a missive could not be found.

This is the Dempsters' strongest point in the case, as it clearly shows that they bought the property in good faith as a potential rabbit warren, regardless of the lost evidence.

Adding to Grace's woes, Alexander Kirk, council member and an innkeeper in St Andrews, said he heard Grace and Bailie Richard in the town council saying that it would make a good rabbit warren, but Alexander Walker, also on the town council, said that he heard the conversation too, but it was only a joke!

It was a very curious testimony indeed from Grace, who was by all accounts the town's most respected clerk. Clearly trying to distance himself from the events that had demonstrably occurred, he seemed to have lost the one piece of written evidence regarding Erskine letting the links to Forgan as a potential warren.

Of the other witnesses called, Archibald Brodie said that he played the night before and he got into no scrapes, and that all scrapes had been repaired. He talked a little about the clubs he used: an iron putter on the green, but otherwise rarely using an iron club. His set was mostly woods, like Tommy Morris some 70 years later. Only when he got into a bunker or a scrape would it necessitate the iron club. On cross examination by the pursuers, he changed his tune slightly and agreed that since Dempster's purchase, the number of scrapes increased vastly and that the course was in terrible condition, although he immediately contradicted himself by adding that he seldom saw any scrapes. The defenders' legal team must have had their heads in their hands.

One of the oldest witnesses was John Pringle, aged 75, who said that the club used to get out of a scrape was called a scraping club. On cross examination, he said he had not played golf for 30 years, but that he had walked the links looking for mushrooms. He paid no attention to the number of scrapes and could not advise on their numbers. The pursuers in later evidence on 7 September claimed that Pringle suffered from palsy and loss of memory. With an aging witness with memory issues, it is curious that the pursuers would want his testimony ruled improper. It is a struggle to find any comfort for the Dempsters in his testimony.

In fact, it is very hard to see any overly supportive statements in their chosen witnesses. Peter Robertson, the butcher, talked of balls lost in the scrapes. He noted that, along with George Law and Thomas Buddo, they counted the scrapes the day before, which was considerably fewer than the number John Morris, Tom's grandfather, had claimed. Being questioned by the pursuers, Peter said that the scrapes mentioned are over and above the ones mended and he did not include the mended ones. Law had covered one side of the links and he, the other; when they met on the green, they tallied numbers. Buddo marked down the numbers: hardly scientific, and easily proved wrong.

George Law said that until recently he had been a ballmaker at Leith and Bruntsfield Links. He said there were 20 times more golfers many years ago, due to the success of the university back then, and the fact that golf balls (featheries) were so much cheaper than now. When they used to cost 3*d.*, tradesmen could afford them, but now at 10*d.* there was less golf. However, it must be said that this is patently not true as others testified that the links were busier than ever, due to the success of the university. He also added unhelpfully that there were ten times more rabbits on the links.

What was useful to us is that he named previous Keepers of the Green, including George Mill, Peter Robertson, Charles Robertson, Thomas Robertson and the current Robert Morris.

In addition to working in Edinburgh, Law said that he always returned to St Andrews in winter. This was possibly because the course was at its busiest during winter months, when the harvest was complete.

Andrew Cochran said that he fixed scrapes on the links for 18*d.* a day, and he thought it was some unknown men who had undone his repair work. He also attested that it was crows or pigeons who damaged Cheape's crops.

Alexander Fernie talked at length about the rabbits and confirmed that the killing season for rabbits was between 16 or 18 November and 1 March. He also mentioned the price of a pair of rabbits, including carcass and skin, was two shillings.

With that, the evidence was complete. There was considerable evidence against the Dempsters and, as much as they tried to offer an alternative account, there was very little that could have made them feel secure in the case. Where most families might have accepted the flow of decisions against them and withdrawn, the Dempsters fought on. If they truly believed this was a cause they could win, they were mistaken.

Six

HOUSE OF LORDS

ON 17 February 1806 the town council joined the case. On the 19th the interlocutor (ruling decision) came through in favour of the pursuers once more, declaring that the town's inhabitants did have a right to take or destroy the rabbits as they wished as they had done so in years gone by. Far from being a decision that would bring peace, it created a powder keg with locals, while the Dempsters believed themselves to be in the right.

The Dempsters appealed this interlocutor, as it included an element that was not part of the original summons. No one asked whether the public could destroy the rabbits at will. In May a reclaiming petition was given against the 19 February 1806 ruling. The court recalled it with a new ruling on 18 May which went, yet again, in favour of the pursuers. The Dempsters appealed both.

Thinking that the case was all but won, many locals started to avail themselves of the overly plentiful supply of rabbits on the links. The Dempsters still had an appeal to be decided upon and rightly believed that the case was not yet over. It caused much tension between the Dempsters' staff and locals. In July the Dempsters produced a newspaper advert, notifying rabbit hunters that they were acting unlawfully. They also said that they had bought the property with the burden of a tenant who was going to use it as a rabbit warren.

The Council responded with their own advert, detailing why locals did have the right to kill rabbits and that if anyone tried to stop them, they would prosecute.

On Monday 7 July the Dempsters presented a bill of suspension, asking for a ruling that prevented the killing of their rabbits before a court decision was made. Lord Armadale initially refused, but requested that the Dempsters' petition be answered with a reply from the pursuers. For some reason, they chose not to reply and, with little alternative, the suspension and interdict were duly granted by Lord Armadale on 29 December 1806. It was to be a very fleeting victory for the Dempsters.

In granting their petition Lord Armadale ordered that informations about the case be prepared, so that the full court could assess it. That court ruled that 'the chargers must confine themselves to what has been the immemorial Practice of Killing rabbits on what is denominated the Links or Common of St. Andrew's [sic], exclusive of such parts thereon as shall happen to be under crops at the time and to this extent recall interdict'.

The end of the Rabbit War

The judgement came through on 10 June 1807 by Lord Armadale, which confirmed that locals should confine themselves to killing rabbits on the golfing links.

In a highly intricate legal case, the Dempsters then appealed to the House of Lords.

The pursuers themselves also appealed, as the 19 February 1806 decision did not require the defenders to destroy their rabbits and preserve the links entire. They also appealed the interdict decision stopping people from killing the rabbits.

The case took seven years to reach the House of Lords, due to the backlog of cases from Scotland in the 19th century.

In the meantime, the pursuers took legal advice from advocate John Clerk, who confirmed that both the interlocutor finding the right to shoot rabbits on the links and that the recalling, or cancelling of the interdict that stopped them, remained, in effect, subject to appeal. Therefore, the rabbits could legally be shot with guns or killed with snare traps.

Whether there was a decline in the number of rabbits in the area, or whether the Dempsters could see the way the wind was blowing, the fire seemed to have gone from the fight. Some say that there was a myxomatosis epidemic that wiped out the majority of the rabbits and therefore, with the rabbits gone, there was no longer a need for the case to continue.

Certainly, the death of Charles Dempster on 11 July 1809, aged 67, was a significant event. Perhaps it was a financial decision and, with his father gone, Cathcart may not have wished to pursue it so vigorously any longer. It certainly took a few years to sort out Charles' estate.

Following in his father's footsteps, Cathcart was the Dean of Guild on the town council and a civil dispute against his own council may not have been in his best interests. Perhaps it was the expense that concerned Cathcart, with so many daughters and having to pay dowries when they married. Whatever the reason, the hostility of the golfers may have been buried with Charles and certainly the subscriptions asked from the members of the golfing society to cover legal costs had stopped by 1817.

Either way, in St Andrews, life carried on regardless. No longer were there angry notes about the state of the course. In fact, things were going so well that, on 18 April 1812, the Society of St Andrews Golfers advertised for a clubmaker. Applicants should apply to Mr Grace, secretary of the club. It was a role that caught the eye of a young furniture maker, Hugh Philp (1786–1856), who had taken to repairing clubs as a side line. Philp worked on country estates such as James Cheape's Strathyrum House. This house is still there today and still with the Cheape family. That is the joy of St Andrews, where history is tangible.

Hugh Philp would become the greatest clubmaker of his day, with his clubs even being compared to the violins of Stradivarius. Peter Baxter, in his 1899 book, *Golf in Perth and Perthshire* said, 'Hugh Philp greatly improved the style of wooden clubs, and his models held the field until the bulger type took root'.[1] H. Thomas Peter in *Reminiscences of Golf and Golfers*,[2] said, 'Hugh was a dry-haired man; rather gruff to strangers, but quite the reverse to those who knew him; with a fund of dry, caustic humour, but withal a kind heart. If a man after a match went to him complaining of a club, Hugh would merely say, "You'll hae lost yer match …".'

In *Golf and Golfers, Past and Present* (1891) Dr McPherson said, 'Philp was … the most painstaking of all club-makers. No maker of the violin in Cremona devoted more passionate attention to his work than did this framer of "ball-compelling clubs". Yet, strange to say, Hugh was a very indifferent player.'[3] Philp later goes on to say, 'Hugh in a match lost all the nine holes out; but gathering himself together he made a splendid three at the first return hole; and taking hole after hole from that turning point, halved the match.'[4]

In 1819 Hugh Philp was formally offered the post as clubmaker to the Society of St Andrews Golfers. He took over the cart shed that had been Willie Fairfoul's, which would evolve to become Tom Morris' shop on the links at number 7 The Links. Philp's daughter Mary, who married Thomas Fleming, said in the 1879 Road War case testimony that she remembered her family living there in the premises on the links, which Tom Morris owned.[5] These premises went from Willie Fairful's old cart shed to Hugh Philp, to G.D. Brown and then to Tom Morris. It is the oldest continuous golf shop in the world and today sells merchandise for The Open. Many locals do lament the loss of the Tom Morris signage above the door, yet, if the premises had to alter, then a continuing association with The Open is some compensation. For the fellow devotees of golf heritage, Philp's walls are still there today.

In the same Road War case, Thomas Fairful, 62, the son of Willie, said, 'I am a labourer in Argyle Street. My father lived 50 years ago where Tom Morris is now. He built Tom Morris' workshop. Philp got it afterwards. My father built it for a cart shed. It had an entrance from the Links, and all the stones to build the shed were driven on to the Links. There was an entrance down at Clark's Wynd.'[6]

The wood Philp used was taken from the orchard at Edenside and carted to him by David Ritchie, who was a farmer and public carrier from Dundee to St Andrews. Philp's assistant would eventually be his son-in-law, Robert Forgan, who turned the little business from 1856 into a thriving club-making one, fit for an industrial age, in the premises next door, today called Forgan House. Forgan made clubs for many golfers, including Prince Edward, the Prince of Wales, who would become king, and whose coat of arms was displayed proudly above Forgan's door.

Philp was said to be quick to lose his temper and Lang Willie Robertson, with his off-colour remarks, would often test it. The great clubmaker Philp died in 1856 and was buried in the cathedral grounds. His skill with wood was one of pure artistry and that is why today they are still one of the most valuable items in golf.

The House of Lords appeal

In late 1813 the Dempster appeal came to the House of Lords. Lord Eldon (John Scott, 1751–1838) noted the inconsistent interlocutors of the Court of Session. One had said that the Dempsters had no right to keep rabbits, but another said that they were not duty bound to kill them. The locals had a right to destroy them, but only on the golfing ground. However, the authority for locals to kill them was not even part of the pursuers' case, so should not have been part of any interlocutor.

It was confusing.

To summarise, the defenders were not to keep rabbits but not bound to destroy them. If they were not bound to destroy or remove them, yet bound not to keep them, what was the answer?

Lord Eldon also thought, incorrectly, that the issue of title was deemed not to have been addressed by the Court of Session. In October 1814 the House of Lords, with regret, felt duty bound to send the case back to the Court of Session with instructions to review those confusing interlocutors, saying that it was a strong thing to say that the golfers, playing on a man's land, may destroy the produce of that land which offered the biggest yield. He certainly had sympathy with the Dempsters. Lord Eldon added comically, 'If it were profitable to feed Black bulls there … if these Balls got into what they [the bulls] occasionally left behind them, they would be in a worse scrape than if they got into a Rabbit scrape.'

On 2 September 1814 funds were raised for the debts and costs of the ongoing case, with an annual charge of one guinea to the members of the Society of St Andrews Golfers. Resignations were not accepted until 'the debts incurred by the Club in conducting the appeal against Mr Dempster [Cathcart] shall be paid and discharged as these debts were incurred while those gentlemen were members of the Club'.

This is where the story of the Rabbit War peters out.

Cathcart Dempster does not take up the option to continue the case. In 1816, he was elected to the town council as Dean of Guild, so presumably the case had been dropped. It would be awkward in the least to try to get elected to the council on the one hand, while taking them to court with the other. He certainly would have seen first-hand the dire financial condition that the council was in with a never-ending cascade of debt after debt.

In 1817 Cathcart was in fear of his life and petitioned the provost, baillies and town council for protection from Thomas Wemyss, for worry of murder. Wemyss was cautioned. Nonetheless, Cathcart continued with his work in the same year, of improving and deepening the harbour. Life for Cathcart and the Robertsons simply carried on.

By 1818 there was still no Rabbit War activity, and the Court of Session never ever reviewed the case. Years of acrimony, with poisoned dogs, lapsed memories and questionable ethics, had truly come to an end. Locals freely hunted rabbits on the links once more, without reprisal. Cathcart's name also appeared at golfing society meetings, so perhaps, as John Behrend and Peter Lewis mention in *Challenges & Champions*, the matter was settled privately.[7] It certainly ended discreetly.

Although it has been written that a disease like myxomatosis eliminated most of the rabbits, evidence shows that when Cheape became the owner of the links he employed someone every year to kill rabbits. So perhaps the end came more due to Cathcart's political hopes than anything related directly to the poorly rabbits.

No one exits this case cleanly, but perhaps now we can see a fuller picture. The Dempsters were not pariahs and we in St Andrews owe much to their benevolence. The good humour of Cathcart and the fact that he was an active golfer show us that his relationship with the town was, in fact, more cordial than previously believed.

For Davie Robertson, the passing of Charles Dempster in 1809 would not have gone unnoticed as the Lairds of the Links for over 20 years were Charles and then Cathcart Dempster. The Dempsters were not the ogres of St Andrews. Far from it. Maybe now their time, known as the 'dear years', can get the respect it so richly deserves.

Hugh Lyon Playfair arguably took over where the Dempsters left off. St Andrews was built on the shoulders of giants such as Sir Hugh Lyon Playfair, John Milne, Tom Morris, George Rae, Allan Robertson and George Bruce. Alongside those names should sit Charles and Cathcart Dempster, who did so much for the town of St Andrews.

Seven

THE ST ANDREWS OF DAVIE ROBERTSON

ONE YEAR after their marriage, Peter Robertson and Elspeth's first son, David 'Davie', who would become Allan's father, was born. The very next day, 6 August 1775, David was christened by Dr Gillespie. The witnesses were Philip Gibson and Peter's brother William.

The links that Davie would have known when growing up was quite different in that most of our front nine did not exist. Whin bushes covered many of our fairways. Sheep and, on occasion, cattle walked freely across the land. The seashore lapped on the shore beside a very narrow first fairway. The land for today's first hole did not exist and was simply the West Sands beach and shore. Tides threatened to erode the 18th fairway away. It would be reclaimed some 30-plus years later during Playfair's revolution, when rubble and earth, dug up for making foundations for new houses, plus the rubbish from the town, were dumped on the beach, levelled off and seeded. It is our first hole today. Where the houses are situated on The Links road was mere undulating, open land, akin to the Himalayas putting course today. Rough, wild, barren and unkempt, the links was a 'play it where it lies' dream.

Like most boys of that time, Davie was a weaver's apprentice, working for Robert Gourlay Snr for four years from Whitsunday 1787. The life of the weaver was not an easy one. It was a slow and laborious job with frequent health side effects, be it from the dust or back problems from being positioned in one place for long periods.

Although this poem below speaks of the Irish industrial age, the realities of working in the weaving trade, at home in the cottage or in a factory with larger machines, resonate through the ages.[1]

Speaking For My Father

I am tired of hearing middle class poets
mouthing words about linen and weavers.
They did not hear or know words
like heddlehook, slubs or shears,
or shuttles which flew like bullets
across the space behind the red brick wall.
They did not know a word like hemstitcher,
where my mother sewed the edges of handkerchiefs
woven by my father behind that grim wall.
They did not hear the clackety clack
of loom upon loom or put their child ear
to the wall and hope to hear their father's voice over the din.
They were never wakened by the wail
and warning of a factory hooter hissing steam.
They did not hear the slap of shoe or clog
on hard flagged pavement,
or the new macadam road hissing with bicycles
down to the factory gate.
Instead they romanticise a hard
legalised slavery of exploited men and women.
One was my father – no rhyming weaver –
He was too busy surviving with his shears
tucked into the chestpocket of his dungarees,
white faced, bloodless with toil which never tanned,
his light sinewy frame dancing
between the looms he fed and watched.
When let out at week-ends, far from beams
of cloth and ruthless linen lord and master,
he showed me honeysuckle and berried holly
and he sang like a caged lark in the chapel choir.
So do not tell me vicariously poet
of linen and flax.
My father's blood was the oil
for that product.

And I am proudly the rhyming son of a weaver
of looms and dreams.

Poem by the late Brendan McStravick (1999)

It must have come as a shock when Davie's father Peter died on 1 December 1803 at the age of 55. It was noted in the press that Peter was bending down on the Burn Hole (the 17th) to tee up a ball and died doing so.

Twenty-eight-year-old Davie would have to fend for himself and his family. Allan never met his grandfather but no doubt would have heard tales from his father about the great golfer Peter Robertson. We will address the relatively early deaths of the Robertsons later, when we discuss Allan's own demise.

Amid the noise of the Rabbit War court case five years later, on 14 February 1808, 32-year-old Davie Robertson married Ann Bell from the parish of Cameron. Ann was born on 21 November 1787, almost twelve years after Davie, in Largo, Fife. They had two children, Allan (1815–59) and David (1824–64). Allan was named after his maternal grandfather, Allan Bell, as noted in Allan's mother Ann Bell's birth record.

Coincidentally, the River Allan runs through the Robertsons' ancestral homeland of Perth. Allan has an ancient meaning of 'to flow, to stream'. If Allan had been gifted with children, tradition follows that they too would have shared the name Allan, David or Peter, after the names of his father and grandfather. That was not the destiny for our king.

The *De'il's* bargain

Davie's St Andrews was moving on from the 1700s but was still in dire straits. The population in 1821 was only around a few thousand inhabitants.

As we have seen, with increasing debts plus the Rabbit War court case, and having even sold the links, the town council was still struggling to find revenue. Seeing no other alternative, they decided controversially to portion off a part of the links that was still under their ownership and to feu (sell) it for house building. In Scotland feuing was the selling of land for perpetuity, in return for an annual fee to the landowner. The land in question was the land where the original opening and closing holes had been played.

> **Town Council Meeting – 3 March 1820**
> The Council agree to feu by public roup, for building stances, and yards behind the same, that piece of ground leading from the south west corner of Mr Robert Richard's park down to the Swilcan Bridge, agreeably to a plan drawn by Deacon Edie, now produced to the Council, and marked by the Provost as relative hereto; and they appoint the said roup to take place on the first Monday of April next, and the Council nominate as a Committee to fix the upset feu duty of the different lots, and sign the Articles of Feu, the Provost, Dean of Guild, Mr Dempster, Mr Mitchell, the Convener and Deacon Edie – the Provost to be Convener, any three a quorum, and to report to a future Council.

The feu plan was drawn by John Edie, Deacon of Wright in St Andrews, but sadly it could not be found by historian David Hay Fleming and is deemed lost.

The feuing of part of the golf links was undoubtedly a direct violation of the rights of the inhabitants. Lord Curriehill, the Outer House judge who heard the evidence in the 1879 Road War case brought by town councillor John Paterson, observed it as 'a very great encroachment upon the rights of the community'.

The golfing society was against the proposal. This common land had been in play for centuries.

In the minutes of The Society of St Andrews Golfers on 5 May 1820, it stated that the captain had called an extraordinary meeting of the club for the purpose of authorising such measures as might appear necessary for the prevention of a proposed encroachment on the golfing course between the first and second holes. The minute read,

> The meeting having this day inspected the part of the golfing course above aluded to, and the line staked off for feuing by authority of the Magistrates of St Andrews, are unanimously of

opinion that the same is an encroachment on the ground which has from time immemorial been appropriated to the game of golfing as appears from the evidence of the oldest caddies and ballmakers, and they therefore resolve to resist the same; at the same time they are desirous of settling the business amicably, and with this view have to-day caused a line to be staked out as the south boundary of that part of the golf course, but in case the Magistrates shall not agree to the line proposed, the meeting resolve to take all legal measures to maintain their rights to the ground in question, and to prevent any encroachments thereon, and at the same time declare that they shall not be held responsible collectively or individually for any accidents occasioned to individuals, or injury to property, arising from the measures adopted by the Magistrates; and they appoint as a Committee on the part of the Club the Captain, the Medal Holder, Lord Kellie, Mr Guthrie, Mr Murray, Mr Bruce, Mr Cheape, Mr D'Oyly, Mr Thomson, Mr Dalgleish, Mr Cheape, Strathtyrum, Captain Ramsay, Major Cameron, Captain Mason, Dr Mudie, Mr Moncrieff and the Secretary, any three a quorum, and in absence of the Captain, Mr Murray to be convener, and the Secretary to call a meeting at the request of any two of the Committee. With power to attend to the interests of this Club, and to take care that a road of ten feet is preserved from the south west corner of Mr Richard's park to the first hole, as fixed to-day at the ground. Signed in name, presence, and by appointment of the meeting, by Thomas Bruce, Captain, *pro. tem.* [i.e. '*pro tempore*', 'for the time being'. In other words, a temporary position that could be applied in absence of the actual captain.]

On 14 July the society minutes noted that no progress had been made in stopping the magistrates and, in fact, buildings had been put up already. They agreed to try to find an amicable solution with the council but, 'to take all legal measures for the recovery of the ground so unwarrantably taken possession of; and with this view the Club resolve that a subscription shall be instantly set on foot among the members for defraying the expenses which may be incurred, and that the inhabitants of St Andrews, not members, and who may conceive their rights in that course to be infringed on, be invited to join in such subscription.'

The council was in an unenviable position. They were struggling with debts and now the powerful golfing society was against them. With the threat of litigation and further expense, what was to be done?

At the council meeting on 14 October 1820, the note of a meeting between the society and council was handed in and read,

> At St Andrews, the 5th day of August 1820 – In a meeting of the Magistrates of St Andrews respecting the golfing course. Present – Robert Meldrum Esquire, Provost; William Haig Esquire, Dean of Guild; Robert Bruce Esquire M.P., Captain; Colonel Murray of Lintrose; Edward D'Oyly Esquire; Major Holcroft. The committee of the Golf Club having in terms of the remit from the Club of date the (omitted in Minutes) July last, this day met with the Magistrates of St Andrews respecting the ground lately feued by the town betwixt the first and second holes of the golf course, and the Magistrates present having pledged themselves and the Town Council of said city to enter upon their record at the first meeting of Council a minute and resolution declaring the golfing course as now fixed by the plan of feuing betwixt the first hole and the Swilcan Burn to be the unalterable golfing course in time coming, and that it should not be in their power or in the power of their successors in office to feu, build or encroach further upon the said course on the north or west sides, and also to allow the Golf Club a piece of groundon the east of the present first hole sufficient for the site of a new golf house, when they shall think proper to erect the same; and the Committee, having deliberated on these proposals, unanimously agree (upon these being implemented) to stop from all further proceedings, and to accept of the course as now fixed on; and they instruct the Secretary to procure for the Club an extract of the minute of Council when passed, to be entered upon the record of the Club.

To summarise, all legal problems for the council would stop if they gave the society, for free, a vacant piece of land for a clubhouse. This would become, in time, the site of the R&A clubhouse.

The council duly considered and approved. They also bound and obliged themselves and their successors in office to preserve that part of the golfing course for the game of golf, and not to encroach in any manner thereon in all time coming.

This was a double win for the Society of St Andrews Golfers. They had protected the course evermore and also got a portion of land for a clubhouse. The town council had narrowly avoided another expensive court case.

This was all happening in front of Davie's eyes. Houses were built on the golfing land upon which he perhaps played as a boy, but even at this time, around 1820, it was referred to as a quarry and public tip. Either way, it would be links no more.

The 18th green is believed to have moved long before this feuing. What a fun opening and closing holes the 1st and 18th/22nd must have been.

A new laird of the links

The Dempster links rabbit farm era drew to a close about 1818, when the property was sold to Major Angus Cameron, who was on the committee of the Society of St Andrews Golfers. There are no papers in the St Andrews archives that detail the sale, but it is believed to be around this time.

On 21 March 1821 Alex Martin created a map that showed the feus. This map was paid in part by the town council and Cheape, and clearly showed Major Cameron as the owner of the links.

Cameron's ownership was to be brief due to bankruptcy, which caused a few complications with the sale of the property. The St Andrews links was eventually sold by Major Angus Cameron's creditors to James Cheape for £3,150 around July 1821.

Following advice from his lawyer, as shown below, Cheape announced at the autumn meeting that 'the Society have been in the habit of destroying the rabbits to prevent that injury to the golfing ground, which these animals occasion. I have lately made a purchase of the Feu of the Links, and although the former Proprietors have not availed themselves of the judgement of the House of peers in their favour, which entitled them to carry on their Suit before the Court of Session, yet there seems … to be nothing to prevent me or my successors from doing it; but strongly desiring to put a stop to all future litigation, I shall relinquish every right that I may have on this score, and confirm to the Society, so far as depends on me, the entire privilege of the golfing ground, as they at present possess it, and in doing this I am confident that … I am rendering a service to my successors as well as to the Society.'

For this, he was roundly applauded with three cheers. The Rabbit War was over.

The March Stones

On 5 December 1821 Cheape commissioned Alex Martin to make a survey of the links. This is the oldest full map of the course. Martin was told to lay out 'march stones' to separate the golfing ground, so on one side of the stone today you see the letters G for golfing ground and C for Cheape. Today, they offer an insight to just how narrow the links was then.

At first glance Cheape's offer to set out the links boundary line and avoid any future litigation might appear altruistic – as he was offering to pay for this surveying and map work, on his own land, by Alex Martin and for the stones – but we also know that if the golfing society did not agree to them being placed, he might well re-open the rabbit case, which the House of Lords' decision had left open to him.

It may be a little surprising just how litigious they seemed to be in the 1800s. Even the autumn meeting statement, saying that all litigation was over, did not last a year. Cheape was threatening anyone who hunted rabbits on the links without his permission. Against those very poachers whom he was backing during the Dempster years, he was now threatening litigation. Claims of common rights that he had fought so vigorously for before, Cheape, as laird of the links, now strongly refuted that any such right existed.

One poacher, William Carmichael, was fined one pound by the magistrates of St Andrews for laying traps and catching rabbits on the links. Who was chair that December day in 1822? Sir Thomas Erskine.

Cheape said in a letter that he had allowed his friends and gamekeepers to hunt, but no one else. Furthermore, in 1822 he claimed, though unsuccessfully, that the beach and salmon fishing rights on the West Sands were granted in the sale. It was ruled that the title deeds would have said so if this was the case, and his claim was refused.

What is beyond doubt is that the turmoil Davie Robertson grew up with in St Andrews due to the rabbits, changing owners of the links, and the controversial feuing of the links was coming to an end. Peace and stability would reign for half a century or so until 1879, when the 1820 decision by the council to feu the links was widely criticised and deemed somewhat illegal.

For now, Cheape had indeed brought about peace and for St Andrews folk, including Davie, the opportunities to earn a good living from golf were about to begin. Where most caddies remained as such or as weavers, Davie had other more ambitious ideas. He and Allan would be beneficiaries of the feuing controversy and thereby created the first 'golf parlour' on the links.

It was a decision that would shape their very lives and the life of Tom Morris.

Eight

LIFE AT THE PARLOUR

On 5 November 1821 it was reported that on the previous Saturday, there had been drama on the West Sands. At 6 a.m. two men, with their friends accompanying them, gathered to settle a dispute with pistols. It was carried out very professionally, as all duels required to be in line with the royal code of honour. The site was measured appropriately, and the guns checked. The two men walked 10 to 15 paces, turned, and fired upon each other. Fortunately, neither of the two was a very good gunman. In their first round they both missed, possibly due to shaky hands, either because of nerves or the temperature on the beach that time on a November morning. In the second round, a Mr P's ball (bullet) went through Mr A's coat without causing injury. After a few seconds, possibly realising that they could have died, an honourable reconciliation took place.

This was the world in which Davie was bringing up his young family. A fallen city, once called the darkest town in Scotland, was beginning to find its feet again and enter one of the most important periods of growth and development in its history. Old superstitions and traditions, like shivering dawn duels, were fading.

Journeys by horse-drawn carriage between Scotland's major cities of Edinburgh and Glasgow would have taken Davie's grandfather around 12 hours, but, as roads were improving and a road network slowly evolving, this would come down to around five hours. The journey from St Andrews to Musselburgh would have taken most of a day to get anywhere near the links.

New iron pipes were used in 1819, with cleaner water being taken from the reservoir at the rear of Holy Trinity Church. Unfortunately, they used narrow pipework and the supply was not nearly enough for the town. Market Street was paved in 1820 and no longer a horrid dirt track.

Oil lamps on the streets were installed in 1821 and in 1835 the streets were lit by gas. With the first stagecoach to and from St Andrews, the town was opening itself up to tourists and workers alike. The limited service went once a week to Cupar and twice a week to Dundee. As woeful as this sounds, it does show that St Andrews was slowly developing for the better and that there was a glimmer of light on the horizon.

Times were indeed changing.

Sandyhill

When many professionals, caddies and ballmakers followed the golf work and moved to Musselburgh, St Andrews or Perth, Davie's family remained in St Andrews and built the first golf parlour on the links, called Sandyhill. It was situated on the corner of what would become The Links road and Golf Place. It was a condition of the town council that houses should not face the links, so Davie's front door opened on to today's Golf Place.

Davie bought his feu on 20 March 1822. It was described as being '736 square yards … which is marked as No.12 on the plan drawn by John Edie, ordained measurer … David Robertson and his foresaids shall be bound and obliged, within three years from the 3rd of April 1820, to build … a dwellinghouse … with liberty to quarry stones from rocks at the Witch Lake for the purpose of building said house.'

Witch Lake, named as such after the witch trials and executions three hundred years ago, is the area at the bottom of the Scores cliffs. Scaur, from which Scores gets its name, is an old Scottish word for steep cliffs. These stretched all the way from the golf course to the castle.

The original controversial feu charter dated back to 1820. Although Davie bought his land in 1822, he still had to have it built by April the following year. By April 1822 the property was listed as being under the ownership of The Old Friendly Society of St Andrews, but it was in Davie's possession by 1831. The Old Friendly Society operated like a mortgage company today, where a lump sum would be paid and the mortgage paid back over time.

The 1879 Road War evidence

Sandyhill is where the golfers would congregate before and after their round of golf and store their golf clubs; it was also where Davie continued the centuries-old family trade of making featherie golf balls. The golf parlour was a hive of activity for the golfing populace.

So, what did the feued land around the links look like? During the Road War case in 1879 many witnesses talked about the evolution of the landscape by Davie's house. These descriptions come two generations after Davie, and only 20 years after Allan's death, so they often refer to it affectionately as Allan's house or Allan Villa.

Witness John Carstairs was the very stone mason who built the Sandyhill house. He remembered building the house, plus other details of note including the first house on the east of the wynd being built by George Clark, butler to Patrick Playfair, cousin of Sir Hugh Lyon Playfair. This would become known as Clark's Wynd and then affectionately as Grannie Clark's Wynd.

Carstairs also recalled carters taking seaweed from Witch Lake and the uneven ground by Davie's house. There was a large sandhill in front of Sandyhill and this was eventually removed to create a promenade. This is very likely the reason the house was called Sandyhill. 'The grass at first was as high up as Allan's villa window,' said John. 'The feuars built their garden walls just as they built their houses. They had their garden wall just as the boundary that was staked off to them. It is the same run of wall as there is at present.' He mentioned how, when the land was feued, there was a 'nasty soft road from the parlour to Clark's. It was formed about 1821.'

It was St Andrews labourer David Black, who, in the 1840s, removed the sandy hill outside what was by then Allan's house, to create a flat terrace for Playfair. Due to the work and the impact on the foundations of removing the sandy mounding, the Sandyhill house had to be 'coalwalled or underfooted'.

Local legend Da' Anderson, who was father of the champion golfer Jamie Anderson (1877, 1878, 1879) and worked for Allan Robertson in the golf parlour said in his testimony,

> I know Allan Robertson's house. It is the east most of the feus.

> When I first remember, a dyke [wall] ran along from that house towards the site of the present Club-house [R&A clubhouse today], dividing the Links from what is now Golf Place. That dyke was about two feet high. The road was lower than the Links. The Links sloped up to the top of the wall, and the road was two feet below the wall on the other side. That wall came up to the sill of Robertson's window. It was not possible while that wall was there for any cart or wheeled carriage to get on to the Links from Golf Place, or into Golf Place from the Links. There was a garden wall running along the back of the feus. There were always doors in that wall since I remember. I think there were six doors in it when I first remember it. Some of the houses have not doors at present. When you stepped out of those doors you stepped upon grass.

That is a fundamental point. The gardens of the feu houses, including Davie's, opened straight onto the links. It would only be at the resolution of the Road War case that the road, which today passes down the side of the links, was created.

Talking about the ground outside Sandyhill, he said,

> Sir Hugh Playfair made the first change upon that part of the Links about 1849. He macadamised the road where it went down to the flagstaff [outside the R&A today], and took a piece of this bank off to make it level. After that he took it down and made a proper terrace of it, and put up posts and seats for the public pleasure. Those operations extended over some time. He levelled the ground which had formerly been in hollows and hillocks. The terrace was levelled, with a slope upon it to Clark's Wynd. The width of the terrace would be about 20 or 30 feet. It was sown with grass. It stopped at Clark's Wynd.
>
> The grass grew quite well. After the terrace was made, it was used just as a seat for the people sitting upon to admire the play. There were seats put up on it. There are no seats now. The seats remained there till 1873.

Walter 'Watty' Alexander, who took over the care of the links after Da' Anderson for nine years in 1855, said he

> knew Allan Robertson; he was my cousin. A bank ran along between the Links and Golf Place from his house to the present Club-house. That bank was about three feet high. It went up to the sill of Robertson's window. When it was taken away, the wall of Robertson's house had to be underfooted. There was a retaining wall on the Golf Place side of that bank. The road was on the east side of the wall, and lower down than the Links. I know the garden wall of the feus on the south side of the Links. When I first remember, the ground immediately to the north of that wall was all heichs (bumps) and hollows. It was covered with grass up to the wall. It was different from the rest of the Links in this respect that there were more hollows into it. We had a range of short holes there when I first remember. I cannot exactly say how long that range continued; after the Provost made up the place next to the wall the short holes were removed to where the Club-house now is.

Giving detail of the feued land on which Sandyhill and other houses were built, William Conacher said, 'My father [Robert] was town's tenant of the Haugh, a little to the west of St Andrews. He was one of the original feuars of the ground to the south of the Links. He got his feu in 1820. I was then about six years of age. Before the feus were given out, the ground was partly used as a depot for manure, and was a rendezvous for any persons who wished to go there.' In other words, it was open land with multiple uses, even for those who merely wanted to walk on the links. This reiterates the point that it was open common land. William's father was Davie's neighbour.

Also, it is worth mentioning that with the links-facing gardens still open and visible bar the fencing between them, the area of links land of the original 22-hole layout was still in view to Allan and others until as late as the 1870s, when the building work started in earnest.

Conacher added, 'There was a cart track along the whole way in the line I have mentioned fro[m] Clark's Wynd to the Scores. After the feus were given out, my father and the other feuars used that track for any purpose for which they wanted it. My father took in potatoes there, and other feuars put down seaware there occasionally; and I remember James Berwick, who had the feu next to my father's, putting down a load of earth to cover his garden. The feuars all used their garden doors … I remember a feuar named David Robertson. He had the top feu – what is now called Allan's Villa. I have seen a cart slanting up the side of the bank to his garden. There was a bank at that time between the road and Allan's villa but it has been all carted away.' Bringing to life the links at Davie's time, he added, 'I remember the bleaching green at the Swilcan Burn; in my younger days it was on both sides of the burn. All the people in the town bleached there, and the clothes were brought down and taken away in carts. A man named Sandy Melville, who lived in Fish Street, used to cart clothes down from the Scores to the Swilcan Burn, and take them away again.'

David Melville, a joiner in St Andrews, and son of Sandy Melville, said that his father 'was a carter in St Andrews from the year 1835 to 1854. He carted clothes to the Links all that time, more or less he had set paths that he carted to, consequently at each washing every fortnight or so and he had occasional employment in that way from other people. I often went with him – he always went by Clark's Wynd where the clothes were bleaching on the east side of the burn.' The sight of carts loaded with linen traversing the links to the east of the Swilcan Burn, near to the ladies putting course today, would have been a regular sight for Davie and the young Allan.

Bob Kirk Snr, aged 69, was a ballmaker. 'I am a ballmaker, and have carried on that trade for about 30 years. Before that I was a shoemaker. I have lived in St Andrews all my life. My father [James] had one of the original feus, the feu up at Golf Place. Allan Villa was built on a sub-feu from my father.'

That explains how Davie bought the land which had already been divided into parcels by March 1821 but Sandyhill was only built a year later – he simply bought a portion of James Kirk's. With a touch of humour and perhaps rose-tinted glasses, he added, 'I took the Operative Medal [St Andrews Golf Club] four times running. I do not think the smoothing and macadamising of this road would do any injury to the golfing. I think it would be a grand hazard; but they want a bowling green, apparently; they cannot nip a ball clean as they did in my day.'

In all likelihood Bob would have seen Davie Robertson play, being in his twenties when Davie passed. Given that Davie was noted as an exceptional golfer, his matches would have garnished interest, especially among the young golfers. Just as I, at Lurgan Golf Club in the 1980s, looked up to the Magees, Hannas, Horans and Douglasses, not forgetting the late Stephen Guisley, the young Kirks too may have looked up to the great Davie Robertson.

Capturing his caustic humour, Bob Kirk Snr said, 'I like plenty of hazards. That is the science of golf.' The courtroom galleries chuckled. To add insult to injury, he continued, 'Ordinary players like a bowling green, I think.' Mackintosh, who was acting on behalf of the pursuers and thinking he had an opening here, put it to Kirk, 'There are plenty of hazards on that hole?' Kirk replied dryly, 'The mair the better,' to which the galleries laughed again.[1]

With a clear memory of how the land looked before Sandyhill, Henry Peattie, Church Officer, said, 'I am 79 years of age. Born in St Andrews and never been far away from it all my life. I recollect before the Town feued the Links to Hugh Philp and others. I also recollect of the houses being built. After they were built there was a road on the Links at the back of the gardens attached to the houses. The road began at the end of Clark's feu and ran up by Hugh Philp's shop, then it took a turn round a sand hill and out to join a road that led to the Witch Lake. This sand hill was at the back of Allan Robertson's house and has now been removed. I was a ploughman at Strathtyrum about the year 1839 and remained a year. Hugh Philp did all the wright work at Strathtyrum and I often went with carts to be repaired and driving implements for the same purpose to his shop. I always went by this road. There was no other road to Hugh Philp's shop. It was just a rough track like many other country roads.'

Captain of The Royal and Ancient Golf Club of St Andrews, John Whyte-Melville, aged 82, who became a member on 2 October 1816, shared his memories too. In the 1840s, Allan was frequently his playing partner and caddie.

Whyte-Melville said, 'I recollect the building of the first house in the vicinity of the Links. It was built by David Robertson, in what is known as Golf Place and the Members kept their clubs in it until the time of the Union Parlour, which was 1835. That was the predecessor of the present Golf Club.'[2]

More details on Sandyhill and the Road War testimonies can be found in *St Andrews, The Road War Papers.*

A busy parlour

At the centre of the golf world in St Andrews, the parlour was akin to a members' club where you could store clubs and arrange matches while at the same time purchase clubs, refreshments and the featherie balls that Davie, Allan and possibly young David had made.

More than just a shop, it was their very home. This was their life and it also remains very much the model of professional shops today. When we come to discuss Allan, it is imperative to see how his upbringing and heritage, which were steeped in golf, ultimately defined his life.

Time and again, Davie would be called on to give out the odds, that is, how many shots would be given in a match. Golf was mostly matchplay and that was the golf he knew. An armful of swan-necked wooden clubs tucked under the arm, featherie balls in his pocket, and an unkempt links, with balls flying between the sheep. The rabbits scraped holes all over Davie's links for the best part of 20 years. The wild St Andrews links that he knew played out and back over what is the narrow width of our back nine today.

In 1831 the St Andrews golfing society introduced handicaps in strokeplay, which opened the possibility of winning medals. This had the effect of improving the numbers attending meetings.

Davie's father Peter may have known the 22-hole layout. His grandfather David III, ballmaker, would have very probably played it. Given that Davie was in his forties when the feus were given, he probably knew where the old final green was. Davie knew featheries and how they would be of varying quality and pricing, but he never knew the guttie ball – that would appear some 12 years or so after his demise.

Davie, the champion golfer

In Scotland even back in the 1700s golf was available to all. They had their champion golfers and their betting favourites. Even a ballmaker could afford to play golf on the free, open common linksland. The title champion (and champion golfer by extension) was not a new invention with the Open at Prestwick. It was merely a well-worn phrase by 1860 for the best golfer. It was a grand title that could not be thrown away in any old match. It had to be a proper organised match, with organised money backers and an awareness of the game advertised well in advance.

The champion could decide when and against whom he would do battle, akin to a boxer picking his fights. It should also be said that although the title was nice to have, as it would add to the prestige of the player and his home course, there were only a handful of courses in existence, so the champion would still have to make ends meet by some other means.

Was it an honour? Yes. Did it pave the way to riches? Certainly not.

The artisan champions still made featherie balls and did whatever they could, such as working as a handloom weaver to make ends meet.

In *The Royal and Ancient Game*,[3] Robert Clark said when speaking of Allan, 'He came of a golfing race. His grandfather, Peter Robertson, who died in 1803, was a ball-maker and professional golfer. His father too, David Robertson, who lived till 1836, followed the same trade, and was moreover a good player in his day – nay, few were better on the golfing green.'

It was said he was competitive, and his giving of the odds would be to his own advantage. 'For pure dodgery no one ever came near old Davie Robertson, the father of "pawky Allan". He would give his greenhorns "half-one" when he could have given them "a stroke a hole", and after winning three matches go on to lose a fourth, that his man might play him again for double stakes.'[4]

Davie undoubtedly became a famed golfer and was for a time the champion of his era. Whenever a challenge came in from Musselburgh, Davie was invariably called up to defend St Andrews. Musselburgh, Perth and St Andrews had the finest golfers in Scotland, and therefore the world, and the moniker of champion golfer would would go back and forth between the areas.

People in St Andrews at Davie's time would be all too aware of Scottish-wide scandals. It was the era of Burke and Hare, whose murders of 16 people in Edinburgh in 1828 were the talk of the time. Not receiving enough earnings from raiding the graves of the freshly dead to provide bodies for dissection at student surgeon lectures, the duo took matters into their own hands and turned to killing. They were eventually caught. In the trial Hare turned on Burke and was rewarded with immunity. Burke was hanged on 28 January 1829 in front of 25,000 people and his skeleton, to this day, is on display at the Edinburgh Medical School. This was one of the biggest news stories of that time and would likely have been the talk on the St Andrews links in Davie's day.

Davie was affirmed the champion golfer in 1830 by beating Tom Alexander, as noted in the *Fifeshire Journal* of 27 August 1863. It appears that he held on to that title for five years. The *Fife Herald* of 1830 merely mentions that 'several interesting matches at Golf have been played during the week and various sums, in the shape of bets, have changed owners'.

A clipping from the *Fifeshire Journal* of 15 January 1863, to celebrate the opening of The Star Hotel in St Andrews, tells of a supper that was attended, among others, by landlord Mr Duncan and George Rae, architect of the R&A building. The chairman, merchant Mr Turner, gave a toast to Allan, who had died four years earlier. It was 'drunk in silence – a feeling tribute to the memory of one of our warmest-hearted men, and most scientific golfer that St Andrews, or Scotland has ever produced.' Mr Gowk then proposed a toast to all golfers. In reply to this, Allan's brother David got up to speak. He said that at one time his father was the champion golfer for *eight* years. There may well have been matches with Tom Alexander prior to the ones recorded, but the additional dates David provides in his speech are also not quite accurate, so it may be a simple mistake on his part. He also added with humour that the title would soon be returning to the Robertsons when he, in the not-too-distant future, would beat the reigning champion golfer Tom Morris. As good as David was, everyone knew this was a joke and laughter ensued.

Nonetheless, Tom Alexander (1802–41) from Musselburgh was indeed Davie's great rival. Most of their matches were not recorded.

It is hard to believe that, in an era when betting was a vital element of the sport, the two best players did not meet again and again. What we do know is from obituaries, when their finest victories were heralded and sins omitted.

According to the birth register the Musselburgh golfer was born on 8 October 1802 to John Alexander and Euphemia Dove in the parish of St Cuthberts. This was the same parish where Allan's second wife Jane Kyles hailed from. Tom was an exemplary golfer, with history in Burntisland, Leith and Musselburgh. His featheries are in much demand today among collectors, often selling for thousands of pounds.

Catherine Smith (née Sharpe) was Tom's first wife. His family were very much involved in the golfing community, with his mother working as a steward in Golf House, Millhill, Musselburgh. Alexander tended the Leith links for the Honourable Company of Edinburgh Golfers and cut the holes for £5 per annum at Musselburgh thereafter.[5]

Davie had witnessed how the Robertsons tended to the links and made featheries all his working life. The Robertsons of St Andrews were among the finest golfers, and that rich heritage ran through all the Robertson golfing blood. Even though Davie was arguably the best golfer in the world, he still needed to work as a caddie and ballmaker, and run the parlour to make ends meet. His matches with Tom Alexander alone did not keep a roof over the Robertson heads.

The last match

It was an exciting time for St Andrews. Finally, the town had started to recover after hundreds of years of decline due to religious zealotry. Now was a time of renewal and expansion. The next 30 years would be among the most progressive in the town's history. Land reclamation from the West Sands beach would ultimately create the ground for today's first hole. New houses, much in line with the New Town of Edinburgh, would be built and deemed desirable for middle classes. Street lines were straightened, roads cleared and the foul piles of manure and rubbish removed. It was claimed in *The New Statistical Account of Scotland for Fife/Kinross*, Parish of St. Andrew (1845, vol. IX, p.452) that 'The great width of the streets and the extensive gardens interspersed, afford the fullest ventilation, and except in some of the narrow closes, there is no obstacle to the admission of pure air into the houses of the inhabitants.' The *Fifeshire Journal* of 28 July 1836 reported, 'St Andrews is at present very gay, the influx of beauty and fashion having been for some time past considerable. The advantages which are afforded to bathers at this season generally render it a favourable place of resort.'

These may have been a little optimistic, as it was reported in the *Fife Herald* in January 1837 that a couple had been found starved to death and also that a young girl was found in the same house, near to death and suffering from starvation.

Nonetheless, despite these awful discoveries, Davie saw a different St Andrews from that for his forefathers. That was something in itself. From cleaner water and night lighting, to trainlines and a bourgeoning tourism thanks to buses and trains, the changes that were coming no doubt led to the growth of golf and made St Andrews a thriving metropolis once more. It would be nothing short of a revolution, Playfair's revolution.

Alas Davie would not see the fulfillment of these remarkable changes.

In 1835 Davie had what was to be his last great match. Tom Alexander came to St Andrews and this was a battle too far for Davie. The Musselburgh challenger returned to his home town as the champion golfer once more. How difficult it must have been for Allan, who was around 19 at the time, to watch his 59-year-old father being defeated. Davie must have been relishing an opportunity to win the title back again, but unfortunately, his time ran out.

When Allan was merely 20 years old, Davie died, on 7 May 1836, aged 60. Allan's young brother David was only 11. It was a huge loss for the family and the town, as one of their most prominent golfing figures, champion for many years, was gone.

His was the world of Mr Dempster, Mr Cheape, John Whyte-Melville, Lord Erskine and the changing so-called Lairds of the Links. His was the Rabbit Wars and feuing of a portion of the links. It was a time when the Society of St Andrews Golfers became The Royal and Ancient Golf Club of St Andrews (1834). He saw the town's lowest ebb and the bleakest times, including a number of epidemics such as the 1832 cholera breakout. Davie survived them all.

It was the end of a generation, whose great grandfathers were wary of witches and thought it prudent to throw them off clifftops. The generational link between the darkest days and the dawning of a new St Andrews was gone.

It is a pity that the *Fifeshire Journal* local reporter's suggestion in July 1835 of a painting to capture the scene at an R&A meeting was not taken up. He suggested, 'In the middle distance we would have the Union Parlour with the Archer's butts and the Methven's Tower, where a marquee might be pitched. On the left, the sea with a frigate, etc. in the distance. On the right a number of equipage and spectators; and in the foreground the players, in the uniform of the club, and purses in hand, settling the stakes ... Sergeant Ness, keeper of the Union Parlour, with his Waterloo medal on, might be serving round the ginger beer, while the caddies with "Davie, chief of all the cads" at their head would give a certain character to the whole.'

How glorious it would have been, even just to see an image of champion Davie.

Davie's life did not pass unnoticed like most golfers of his class. Two years before he died, golf poet laureate George Fullerton Carnegie had written in 1833, the humorous and satirical *The First Hole At St. Andrews On A Crowded Day*, where Davie is mentioned,

> For instance – Davie, oldest of the cads,
> Who gives half-one to unsuspicious lads,
> When he might give them two, or even more,
> And win, perhaps, three matches out of four,
> Is just as politic in his affairs
> As Talleyrand or Metternich in theirs.
> He has the statesman's elements, 'tis plain,
> Cheat, flatter, humbug – anything for gain;
> And had he trod the world's wide field, methinks,
> As long as he has trod St.Andrews links,
> He might have been prime minister, or priest,
> My lord, or plain Sir David at the least!

To start with the positive, he calls him a statesman, showing that he was no mere working-class caddie. Carnegie describes Davie as worthy of being as bright as the greatest in society. In a different life he might have held high office. This industriousness and business-like thinking were also evident in his sons, especially young David, who expanded the home into a hotel.

However, this is not a glowing endorsement of old Davie. The impression here is of a crafty, wily soul and unfortunately not in a positive sense. Carnegie gives a strong hint of deviousness about Davie that he could have been as conniving as a prime minister or a priest. It leaves the impression of a trickster who would have done anything to win. Similar accusations would later be thrown at Allan.

Repeating the 'eldest cad' line, after Davie's death, Carnegie wrote the following in *Another Peep at the Links*, in the third edition of *Golfiana* in 1842:

> Great Davie Robertson, the eldest cad,
> In whom the good was stronger than the bad;
> He sleeps in death and with him sleeps a skill
> Which Davie, statesmanlike, could wield at will!
> Sound be his slumbers yet, if he should wake
> In worlds where golf is play'd, himself he'd shake,
> And look about, and tell each young beginner,
> "I'll gie half-ane nae mair, as I'm a sinner."
> He leaves a son, and Allan is his name,
> In golfing far beyond his father's fame;
> Tho' in diplomacy, I shrewdly guess,
> His skill's inferior, and his fame is less.

As much as he tries to water down his tone, by once again calling Davie a statesman and diplomat, this poem is somewhat derogatory to both our Robertson golf heroes. For Davie, the repeated use of the word 'cad' has a distinctive double meaning of caddie, but also someone who was dishonest: someone who could behave in a dishonourable or irresponsible way. There is nothing in any archives to suggest such for Davie, bar this. It is harsh indeed. Even the giving of a half – in other words, a shot every two holes – has an edge to it and is certainly not generous to a beginner, making Davie the ultimate sinner.

Allan does not escape either this time, with the cutting double speak of the poem. Yes, he is far beyond his father's skill on the links but then that compliment is diluted by his supposed lack of talents in diplomacy. So, in other words, Allan has less diplomacy than a cad. More than unkind, having read many reports of people who knew him, I think this may have been for the writer's own comic effect, rather than a truism.

That they were working class might have induced class snobbery from a writer such as Carnegie. Maybe, he believed they would not even read it. Knowing how prolific a reader Allan was, as we shall see shortly from what was left in Davie's will, this was not the case. The language certainly was a sign of the times.

Maybe, and most likely the case, it was all just in keeping with the overall tone of the poem. It should be reiterated that Carnegie's poems are meant to be humorous, so he does poke fun at many well-known figures in town at that time. One could imagine it being read out in a boisterous golf dinner with claret flowing, to roars of laughter, rather than objective descriptions of the men.

He even includes himself with the self-mocking lines,

> That little man that's seated on the ground
> In red, must be Carnegie, I'll be bound!
> A most conceited dog, not slow to go it At Golf,
> or anything – a sort of poet.

It was an honour that in a roll call of the gentlemen golfers of the day, Davie and Allan, out of all the professionals in St Andrews, were the ones mentioned. Hugh Philp is the only other non-gentlemen golfer mentioned. Carnegie points to Davie's golfing fame and he certainly was a senior figure in golf, beating the best of his day.[6]

Despite his foibles, Davie's passing was a loss to St Andrews, and his humour and golfing prowess would have been missed keenly. Allan would possibly have felt that the responsibility had now been transferred to him. Not just the golf parlour and the family, but also the title of champion golfer. Not only for the honour of St Andrews, but for his own father. Tom Alexander had defeated the great Davie Robertson and the champion golfer title lay in Musselburgh, but Allan was getting better and better and, in time, his chance would come.

Davie's will

On 3 April 1837 Davie's will was lodged at the Sherriff Court in Cupar. It was valued at £92 5*s*. 10*d*., which included £17 and 5 shillings in cash in Sandyhill and £42 in the Bank of Scotland. Davie's will was not unsubstantial, showing it was indeed a healthy business being a ballmaker and the owner of the golf parlour. It also offers us a great insight into the golf parlour's operations and the contents of Sandyhill.

The will included an inventory of furniture and other items: 23 club boxes (lockers), 49 clubs, £2 worth of golf balls, some leather and six dozen ginger beer bottles. This is the financial equivalent of approximately 20 years of salary.

The list also includes tools of the trade; be it wheelbarrow or leather. There are also personal items such as an old cradle, which no doubt was for Allan and his brother.

Of interest is his collection of books, which was deemed worthy enough to be included in the inventory and certainly addresses any query over whether he read or not.

Davie's wife Ann remained in the Sandyhill home, as noted in the 1841 census some five years later.

With Davie's death, the mantle was passed over to Allan. He was a 20-year-old man, and yet the weight of the family survival fell squarely on his shoulders. Allan would quickly follow in the footsteps of his father and far exceed his talents, so much so that the press would hail him as the King of Golfers and the King of Clubs.

As Allan's golfing fame began to rise, so too did that of St Andrews. Few could have known that the town, thanks largely to Major Hugh Lyon Playfair, was also about to undergo a revolution that would make it fit and attractive for golfers, tourists and middle classes alike. It would be an era where St Andrews was at the forefront of the invention of photography and the faces of golf legends could be seared on to paper for the first time, lest we rely on a caustic satirical poem. The links would also improve, and Allan would do some of that incredible work.

The town that Allan knew was about to change rapidly.

Nine

THE BOY WHO WOULD BE KING

IN the private weather diary of J. McFarlane, 11 September 1815 was announced to be 'a fine day, much sun, no rain, wind light, west' in Edinburgh and the east coast of Scotland. On that sunny day, Allan Robertson was born in St Andrews and christened on 17 September by Rev. Dr Buist. This was the same Reverend who would christen Tom Morris in St Salvator's church approximately six years later, on 24 June 1821.

It was the time of the Napoleonic Wars, which were coming to an end. Napoleon returned to France from his banishment on Elba in March 1815 but after Waterloo was quickly sent to St Helena for his second exile. In November peace resumed, ending a turbulent and bloody period of European history that had been going on since the start of the Revolution in 1789. In America the war with the British was ongoing. In the Battle of New Orleans the American forces, led by Andrew Jackson, defeated Sir Edward Pakenham's British forces.

In time, Allan would become the champion golfer, and his persona became so well known that golf balls made in his parlour would be simply stamped 'ALLAN'. Everyone knew who that meant.

He would be the champion golfer of his day.

Knowing that many of the weavers and caddies were house owners, it may have been an altogether more egalitarian, church-going society than once thought. The image of vagabond, godless caddies is possibly erroneous, with all classes of society attending church services at Holy Trinity and the other town churches. The wealthier families would have had their own pews, but the fact that Tom Morris became a church elder points us to think that it was a more even-handed, cohesive society in St Andrews. When the craft organisations were created in St Andrews, the working class rid themselves of the shackles of church and wealthy landowners. Together they were a powerful force. When the bells tolled in St Andrews, it was a call to the people of all classes.

Growing up

Twenty years or so before the photography pioneers in St Andrews captured the first images of the town, the streets were still dirt tracks and the water quality questionable. Young Allan, however, was born into a different St Andrews to that of his father, with the town on the cusp of transformation.

Epidemic diseases, which may have been rife throughout Scotland and England, did not have too much of an impact in St Andrews. The 1818 typhoid epidemic was said to have missed no town in Scotland apart from St Andrews.

Davie, Allan's father, was noted on his birth register as a weaver, denoting that it was the main source of money for the family in 1815. Davie's hours working on the weave, ballmaking and caddying were more than mere sidelines; they were necessities to feed and clothe his family. Destitution was only a few bad breaks away. Ill health could be the ruin of a family.

In 1819, five-year-old Allan was living and playing on North Street, which, over time, was filled with the Robertson, Morris, Forgan, Hutchison, Gourlay, Pirie, Herd, Auchterlonie and Anderson families. It could justifiably be named 'Champions Street' as many of their sons would indeed earn the title champion golfer or, after 1860, win the Open. The young golfers would create a golf club or shinty stick from any suitable stick. Champion Sandy Herd said that he created shinty sticks from wood they found on the Strathtyrum estate and used a cork as their ball, with nails added to give it weight. North Street had been his and other champions' early training ground.

Up until the Reformation, the education of the children of St Andrews was undertaken by the priors of the city. There were only two options when Allan was a schoolboy. Firstly, the grammar school, created around 1570, taught Latin in a building near to where they would later build Madras College in the 1830s. The English School (number 4 on the map), where today's public library is, came later, around 1755, and gave an all-round education in reading, writing and arithmetic. This school was created by the great George Dempster of Dunnichen (1732–1818), provost of St Andrews 1760–76.[1]

Receiving his inheritance at the age of 22, Dempster was very influential in Scotland with his liberal outlook. He was an MP for Perth Burghs, which included St Andrews, from 1761 and by 1769 a director of the East India Company. It is he who convinced Dr Andrew Bell (1753–1832) to go out and visit Madras in 1787 as a lecturer on natural philosophy. While there, Bell created an education method where the older boys taught the younger pupils, and thereby improved their own knowledge. Bell came back, due to health issues, and created Madras College, which opened in 1833, the year after his passing.

This would have been all too late for Allan, who was 18 when the college opened, and the English and grammar schools amalgamated into one large school.

It is likely that Allan went to the English School, but with no school attendance records extant we can only go by what evidence we have in Allan's scrapbooks, which illustrates that he was a studious reader and could clearly write.

The children of North Street families, including Allan and Tom, enjoyed the same games, such as street golf, aiming for lamp posts with whatever makeshift ball or cork they could find. There was not much money around. Church festivities or birthday celebrations would have been celebrated in their own particular way according to their beliefs. Despite staunch social stigma at the time, not everyone went to church. Figures show that just over a third of the population attended church regularly in thc 1800s.

Christmas for young Allan would have been a somewhat subdued affair, with the Scottish tending to make more of a celebration over the New Year. There was no Santa. There were no gifts. There wasn't even a Christmas tree. Yuletide vacations and 'all observations thereof' were made illegal by the 1640 Act of the Scottish Parliament, and that even included the making of Yule bread. A merry feasting day prior to this, Cromwell banned the singing of carols and festive gatherings. Even the merry monarch Charles II could not lift the Scots' appetite for Christmas. Although the ban was lifted, the churches continued to frown upon celebration at Christmastime. It was not until as recent as 1958, when it became a Scottish public holiday (and the creation of Boxing Day in 1974) that attitudes changed. Many Scots will still remember the sombre Christmases of yesteryear and perhaps worked on Christmas Day.

The English celebrated a muted Christmas after Charles II but by the time of the Georgian era from 1714 to 1830, it had become immensely popular once more. In Jane Austen's *Sense and Sensibility*, she writes about John Willoughby partying at Christmas from 8 p.m. to 4 a.m. It was in the late-Victorian era when the traditions of Christmas cards, Christmas trees and our modern-day festive activities took hold. The coming together with family and friends is wonderfully captured in Dickens' *A Christmas Carol*, with the Cratchits excited about having a goose feast. Goose was the lowly roast bird for the working class due to its sparse meat. The plum pudding was Christmas cake that we would know today, but with plum being the main ingredient then.

In Allan's scrapbook of clippings from *Chambers' Journals*, on page 206, is a section on Christmas, under the title of Popular English Festivals. It describes Christmas as the 'celebration of an event the happiest that ever took place on earth, it is particularly a festival of joy'. It was a day for the 'mingling in brotherhood of all classes, "gentle and semple"'. Christmas carols were sung, and the article includes the words to *God Rest Ye Merry Gentlemen* and *I Saw Three Ships*.

One early Scottish tradition was the 'first-footer', which at that time was the name given to the first person to arrive on Christmas morn. They would typically come with gifts of coal or peat, whisky, black buns (a sort of Christmas cake made with raisins, almonds, citrus peel, all spice, ginger and cinnamon) and bread. Nowadays, first-footing is on Hogmanay, with guests arriving with coal or whisky and being welcomed with food and drink. This was the night, in the 1820s, that the Scots would celebrate.

Heroes of the age

Every era has its exceptional sporting heroes for that time. Before the age of Allan Robertson and Willie Dunn, the most notable of the early golfers were his father Davie, the David and Sandy Pirie brothers from St Andrews, and, as mentioned, the formidable Tom Alexander and Robert Oliphant from Musselburgh.

As each generation looks up to the generation before, these were the golfers that Allan had to study. They were known as the crack golfers. Papers at the time talk of competitions between the cracks, such as Highlanders versus Lowlanders, but often do not give their names.

Cupar-born artist Charles Lees (1800–80) immortalised Sandy Pirie (*c.*1795–1861) in his painting *The Golfers*, which was commissioned by Alexander Hill, the Edinburgh publisher, in 1847. A student of Sir Henry Raeburn (1756–1823), Lees' painting captured the 1844 match of Sir David Baird and Sir Ralph Anstruther of Balcaskie against Major Hugh Lyon Playfair of St Andrews and John Campbell of Glensaddell. An engraving was made by Charles Edward Wagstaffe (1808–50) in 1847, from which prints were produced. His work also includes portraits of royals and aristocrats, including an 1844 engraving of Queen Victoria's 1840 wedding to H.R.H. Prince Albert of Saxe-Coburg and Gotha by artist Sir George Hayter (1792–1871).

Sandy Pirie was named after his mother Margaret's father, Alexander Mackie. Discussing Sandy, W. Dalrymple, writing for *Golf* on the death of Allan Robertson's father Davie in 1836, stated, 'As a leal [loyal and honest] son of St Andrews, he used to also tell with justifiable glee of a fly-away and unexpected visit to this cold, grey town of redoubtable Tom Alexander of Musselburgh. There were no regular professionals at that time and most players had some trade or other. The only man considered capable of tackling the formidable Alexander was Sandy Pirie, the wabster [specialists who warped and beamed yarns for the weavers]; and he was away working in the harvest field! However, they sent for him post haste; and he came into St Andrews on pony-back, beat his man and went back to work!'

Many of the gentry golfers had their preferred man to caddie for them. Sandy Pirie was always partnered with Captain Maitland Dougall. Sandy also prepared his clubs for Maitland Dougall, so that they were freshly cleaned and polished.

In *Golf and Golfers – Past and Present* by Dr McPherson, it was said that 'he knew every foot of the green, and every point of the Captain's "play". He had the grand merit of silence during a match. He knew his master's mind by a sort of trained clairvoyance, and put into the Captain's hand the right club without being asked. Close behind he would faithfully follow, earnestly bent upon the match, carrying the clubs in his left hand, instead of the time-honoured method of carrying them within the left arm. On a passing player asking about the game, Sandy would remark, "We're twa ahint; but we'll mak' it up; we're no' in oor play the day." The "we" showed the fidelity and interest of the old caddy.'

He added, when talking about Maitland Dougall, 'He was a fidgety player, but by no means nervous. His anxiety was plainly marked in his features … Mechanically he went to work … and pawkily did old Sandy Pirie pilot him through. When a slip was made, a word of encouragement from Sandy restored his equilibrium, and he forgot the past – a secret worth knowing.'[2]

As an aside, if the caddies developed a good working relationship with a golfer, they would repeatedly caddie for them. Watty Alexander was the caddie for a chap called Old Campbell. Bob Kirk Snr looked after John Campbell of Glensaddell, who lived at The Priory on the Cathedral grounds. Andrew Strath looked after Old Sutherland. They didn't just carry their clubs. They cleaned them and had them under the arm, ready for the game. There was often a gathering of caddies at the house of John Morris, Tom's father, 121 North Street today. It is said that Pat Alexander gave a dozen of them an 'annual treat' lunch in John's.

Although Sandy was a prince of the links, all references refer to him as a weaver or caddie and never as a ball maker. He died in 1861 due to mortification of the lungs at his home on North Street. It may well have been working the loom and its known risk of lung damage that ultimately took him. Sandy witnessed all Playfair's changes to St Andrews and his protégé and playing partner Allan become the King of Golf. Sandy's legendary stoicism may explain in part his pupil Allan's mute response to Willie Park's very public challenges.

Sandy's brother, David Pirie (1799–1854), who also lived in that same golfing hub on North Street, worked as Keeper of the Green in St Andrews from 1823, as detailed in the Society of St Andrews Golfers (R&A) minute book, taking over from George Robertson, who was let go for being 'incompetent and incorrigible'.

When he passed away in 1854, his obituary confirmed his status as one of the Senior Caddies of St Andrews. 'David Pirie was one of the old guards of St Andrews golfers and upheld the celebrity of the Links some twenty or twenty-five years ago. The family of Pirie has contributed a respectable quota to the ranks and renown of St Andrews professionals, and David was, we believe, the first who made the name famous in a generation now past or passing away. He and his brothers were the "crack" men of our Links before Allan Robertson and the modern race of notables were known, or at least had acquired repute. The Piries figured frequently in grand matches during their period, against the heroes of the golfing grounds, singly as well as in "foursomes" with amateurs. David was the keeper of the Union Club-House in those days, such as it was, but retired from that office and the "turf " some 20 years past, and followed the trade of weaver, at which he conducted himself as an industrious man and a quiet neighbour.'

At this time, you could not make a career out of one single element alone of the game. Invariably, a working-class man would be a caddie, a weaver, a ballmaker and a Keeper of the Green all in a day.

Grand matches were not an invention of the Tom Morris and Willie Park era, and probably even before the Piries there would have been another generation playing matches between Musselburgh and St Andrews, with heavy betting throughout.

It was Allan who was pronounced champion golfer and king of golf by the press, but in the 1830s, the Piries were 'undoubtedly the first players in Scotland'.

A report in the *Perthshire Courier* found in Allan's own scrapbook recorded the Pirie brothers in 1835 playing a match against Alexander and Oliphant, the same year that Alexander defeated Davie Robertson. It proclaimed that the Piries were the best players in Scotland and therefore, by extension, the world adding, 'The competitors exerted themselves as if for "dear life", and achieved wonders, but all with the greatest apparent coolness. The tide of fortune varied now and then in the course of the day, but the Peeries [sic] kept still ahead, and ultimately triumphed.'

In 1838 Sandy is noted as coming second in medal play (not foursomes) for the inputs with a 97. Geddes, from Musselburgh, won with a 93. Remember they are playing the course in reverse and it is worth noting that the amateur winners that week came in with scores of around 111. Thus, Sandy and Geddes were approximately 20 shots better than the best gentleman golfers.

By the late 1830s Sandy and Davie Pirie seem to have done the opposite to Davie Robertson. Where he set up his own shop and created from nothing a valuable business that included exporting clubs, the Piries concentrated on being weavers and other manual jobs. Although this may seem short-sighted, it must be remembered that when the weaving cottage industry was thriving, it paid very well.

The *Fife Herald* of 10 November 1859 reported that Sandy's two sons had died. John as the captain of the Dundee ship *Rectitude*, and Stewart was the carpenter on board. When the boat in which they were travelling to shore capsized off Frederickstade on 27 October, they both drowned, and it was said to have hit Sandy very hard. The papers reported that he was never the same after this loss.

Sandy died two years later on 25 April 1861 of mortification of the lung, which may well be a loom-related death. His passing was covered in the Scottish press, lamenting this loss to the town and calling him a professional golfer. People often refer to Allan as the first professional golfer, but this is rather romantic.

Sandy got to see his young golfing partner, Allan, become the champion golfer of Scotland. He was also around when Willie Park Senior won the first Open, when the title briefly went to Musselburgh. His passing was noted in all the major Scottish papers. It truly was the end of an era. To him, the links went out and back to the same greens. The shoreline was pushed back and the beach reclaimed to protect the links. The squalid parts of St Andrews were all upgraded, and golf even had a new golf ball, although the majority of his matches were with the featherie ball.

It was a time of great improvements in the town and a consistent increase in the numbers of people playing golf. He witnessed nothing short of a revolution for both the sport and the town.

History would not glorify his protégé Allan to the same extent as the next generation with Tom and even more so with Tommy Morris. It is not hard to see why we have concentrated so much on the Morris family – even Sandy was around to see Tommy Morris as a ten-year-old. However, we would be quite wrong to dismiss out of hand just how good at golf Sandy and David were. When Allan was growing up, it was the Piries who wowed the crowds of onlookers. Just as you or I would have looked up to the older crack golfers in our own clubs, Allan, as a ten-year-old himself, would have looked up to Sandy, and just the way that Tommy looked up to Allan, the greatest golfer in the world.

The Pirie brothers were the first (that is, best) players in Scotland and therefore the world. They are buried in St Andrews Cathedral. If you may wander into the grounds on your travels, please doff your cap (or bonnet) to some of the finest golfers ever to come from St Andrews, the Pirie brothers.

The Red Coats

As a boy, Allan would have enjoyed the pageant of the red-coated members of the Golfing Society, and the pipers leading them to the links, and watching them play.

This poem by Principal John Tulloch, father of Tom Morris' biographer William, captures the buoyant scene on the links:

> It is, indeed, a goodly sight to see,
> Those red coat champions marshalled for the fray,
> Driving the ball o'er bunker, rut, and lea;
> And clearing, with imperious 'fore,' the way,
> Enlivening still the game with laugh and say,
> Whilst trotting club-man follows fast behind,
> Prepared with ready hand the 'tees' to lay;
> With nicest eye the devious ball to find,
> And of the going game each player to remind.

It was said that the red coats added to the spectacle of a meeting and 'added greatly to the vivacity of the scene'.[3]

On 11 October 1817 the Thistle Golfing Society in St Andrews was formed. Their choice of uniform was a green jacket with a black collar and buttons engraved with a Scottish thistle, surrounded by the motto of the society, and an upright Scots thistle of silver lace.

Their regulations stipulated that no member could play with another member unless in uniform, risking a one shilling fine. All funds raised by such fines would be put into a general fund. Their coat of arms has 1817 on it. Their first competition, on 2 September 1818, which was played on the open links without houses lining their opening and closing holes, was won by a John Buddo with a score of 120.

Thanks to the late Francis Humphries, we know that the Thistle Club's early meetings were held in the Crown and Oyster Inn and also in the Black Bull Inn at the end of South Street. However, meetings at the Black Bull Inn may have curtailed slightly after William Christie, landlord of the said inn, who was on the list of potential new Thistle Club members, did not have sufficient votes for admission. His less-than-Christian language that followed probably made many members realise they had made the right decision. The society ran until 1839, when it was agreed that the trophies should be sold. It commenced once more on 13 June 1865, although it was reconstituted as the Thistle Golf Club.

On 23 December 1824 Allan's brother David was born. He would go on to be one of the most influential pioneers of golf in Australia and send gold nuggets home as prizes in competitions that Allan would be arranging. While a baby, the family lived in Sandyhill overlooking the links and beach.

Schooled in life

There is no record of Allan attending school and the only viable school, as mentioned, for the working class was in the building that houses today's library, behind Holy Trinity Church on South Street. Sometimes missing school creates a strong desire to learn. His father had ambition, though and was clearly determined to improve the family's fortunes and not spend a life forever working on the handloom.

Davie left a number of books in his will that were valued at £1 13*s*. Given that Dickens' *A Christmas Carol* cost five shillings and that 20 shillings equalled a pound, we can estimate that he had at least six books and probably more. It is speculative to say this, but the evidence of Allan's scrapbooks, filled with information such as the English Christmas traditions in *Chambers Journals* quoted above, would suggest that he had a thirst for knowledge. Nor was this only on the subject of Scottish affairs: battles, wars, poets, history through the ages, diamonds, Paris and more were all of interest to Allan. The political chatter of the gentlemen golfers or discussions about the fluctuating events across the world would not be lost on him. The name of Allan's Newfoundland dog, *Tell*, whose passing was included in the papers in October 1853, on how well behaved he was, also points to Allan being well read. How many caddies would name their dog after a Swiss folk hero?

The portrayal of the clueless caddie and professional golfer did not apply to Allan or his father. Far from gormless, Allan was self-taught and clearly worldly-wise.

Allan's real education during those formative years was on the links, be it carrying clubs or possibly walking the course with his late grandfather's brother, as he set out the greens for a medal. It was a family affair. Without a formal education Allan learned the best way possible – by experience.

The Robertsons were, if there was such a category, upper working class, like the Morris family. The self confidence that came with that filtered through Allan's life and is evident in his branding of his featheries simply as ALLAN.

Life on the links

What was fortunate for Allan was that he was there when the St Andrews revival started. As the game was growing and the town gradually underwent re-building after centuries of decline, he was right in the middle of it.

As a five-year-old, Allan saw a portion of the links being taken over in 1820 for housing. Thanks to this, from around the age of seven in his boyhood, Allan's family moved down to the links and was in the heart of the daily hub of golfing activity. It was a smart move by Davie.

Even back then, the first and closing holes over a thin strip of land were like a theatre stage, especially around the opening tee, where there was always a hub of activity during the Society of St Andrews Golfers meetings.

One could imagine Allan at night peering over new gardens of the 1820 feu houses to the location of the original first green. How strange the old links land must have looked divided up now by stone walls. One such wall certainly still exists, in Tom Morris' garden, but back then it was still mostly gardens and grass. Over the years, that triangular portion of links would be covered with houses, starting with Golf Place and Pilmour Links and then slowly around the circumference to The Links road.

Willie Fairful's cart shed would be the nearest building to Sandyhill. In time this would become Philp's workshop and then eventually the Tom Morris shop. If you consider that Philp produced his beautifully crafted clubs in the closest building to Allan's house, what a learning experience it must have been to young Allan. To see crude blocks of wood get turned into beautiful swan-necked clubs would have been a fascinating experience, like watching a Cezanne or Turner painting come to life.

Allan would never see Rusacks, the Grand Hotel, the Bruce Embankment and most of the houses on the links road, such as Jamie and Da' Anderson's house and shop at 9 The Links. He would know Jamie as Da's little boy. It was 18 years after his death that Jamie won his first Open. The new Union Clubhouse, opened in 1854, would be a tiny, box-shaped building while Allan lived. The amalgamation of the R&A and Union Clubs would coincide with Jamie's first win.

What Allan could see was the site of the old Halket's bunker on the links, opposite Rusacks today, and he could stare at the waves lapping nearby, as all the land of the first hole that we know was shoreline at this time. On stormy days, Allan must have wondered about the possible damage to the first hole, which was only around 65 yards at its thinnest.

The 1887 book *Reminiscences of Golf On St Andrews Links* (page 14) by James Balfour, describes changes to the 18th green that Allan and Davie would have known. 'The principal difference on the last hole is on the putting green. That has been quite changed by the formation of an artificial table-land, which forms a beautiful green. Formerly the hole was on broken ground in a hollow, with the ground sloping down on both sides. Shortly before my time, there was another hazard made by the sea, which came up to the stair of the present Club-House. That hazard was a very serious one, as the sand at that place was as deep as at the high hole.

The last hole often placed near the edge of the green was close to the sand. But the Links have now been made much wider by the rubbish from the town having reclaimed a large portion from the sea, and there are no hazards on that side.'

It is worth noting that bunkers on the links existed long before golf. They were the natural sandy holes where the wind had worn away the grass and where cattle took refuge or slept – that is, bunked. In fact, the very mound in which the bunker sits was probably blown up by the sea winds. In 1833, when interest in golf was growing, a description of the game in *Chambers Journal* talks about the 'sand holes'. Adverts in the St Andrews newspaper show rooms available for guests and the landlady was known as a 'bunk-wife'. 'Bunker' was simply a well-worn phrase for these natural hazards by the time golf expanded in the 1800s. They were never raked. You played the ball as it lay, and that was part of the fun.

To Allan the 18th green was always a small green, which sat towards the back middle of today's green. Tom Morris' creation of the wonderful plateau green we have today would only be built in 1869, in time for the autumn meeting, ten years after Allan died.

The still darkness of Allan's night would give way to the dawn sunshine. At around 11 a.m. the trundle of early golfers would start the show all over again. That was Allan's daily routine for the rest of his life. As a wise close relation of mine once said, 'Must-do is a great master', and so it was for Allan and all his family.

Out of season and between meetings, it could be very quiet down on the links. One visitor described the Union Club scene on 8 October 1842 in *Chambers Journal*, 'It is about two o-clock of a fine August day. When, after a forenoon of useful avocations, I pop into the clubhouse to glance at the papers, and be in the way of any agreeable temptation that may arise. All is emptiness and silence within and without, for there are no visiting members, and many of the residing ones are gone, some to grouse-shooting, some to watering-places, some here and some there. Most of the cadies [sic], as servants who carry clubs are called, have gone to work at the harvest, in pure despair of so much as one job per day, leaving only one or two to attend to the business of the green – who are seen to be leaning listlessly against the corners of distant houses, as if they thought employment a thing to be wished for than expected. John Ness, porter to the clubhouse, and who is also a cady [sic], is heard through the open window remarking to a passing acquaintance, that things are most uncommon[ly] dull just now.'

To give a clear idea of how the course was habitually quiet, if there were 15 or 20 pairs attending the autumn or spring meeting, that would not be unusual.

It is little wonder that caddies worked in the fields when it was harvesting time. They really had to seek income wherever they could. The writer goes on to talk about a match that he subsequently plays when he finds a foursomes partner, as that is the preferred game, but of note he says, 'There is a ball-maker, Allan Robertson by name, who, besides having the highest character … is reputed to be the best player at St Andrews, and consequently Scotland – I may as well add, in the world. This is an eminence which golfers must needs admire; and in the little world of the links, men of estate and title will be heard speaking of worthy Allan as if he were a kind of king amongst them.'

Allan indeed would be king. Back then, in the 1820s, he was but a boy in Sandyhill, with the links for a playground.

Spirit of St Andrews

By day, young Allan would have seen his dad sorting out matches when asked and acting as referee for the always-sensitive process of how many shots would be given to one side or the other. The R&A archives have the original betting book from the 1700s and it gives a real flavour of the matches that took place, featuring, among others, great names such as Playfair, Whyte-Melville and Dalgleish.

'A half one' usually meant a shot every second hole. 'A third' meant a shot every three holes. People would be happy. Some would be disappointed.

It would be quite wrong to give the impression that golf was only played by the gentlemen. How did Allan become so good at golf? It was because the links was open, common land and free to all. That is the spirit of the game in St Andrews and Scotland. Allan could play the links as much as he liked. There was no financial barrier. His father could help him with rudimentary clubs to play with. He would find balls if needed, in the whin bushes on the links, like other boys.

Most genius shot makers like Allan or Bobby Jones start out with whatever clubs they can get their hands on. The creation of shots with clubs ill-suited for the cause was part of the learning process, like a boy Seve Ballesteros lofting a ball from the beaches of Pedreña with an old 3-iron.

From dawn to dusk, Allan could play. He could imagine being in matches like his father and becoming the champion golfer, the best in the world. That was an attainable dream. Davie did it. So could Allan.

To understand the St Andrews back then is to understand golf, a game open and available freely to all. No claim or right to play of one local was any greater than that of another.

The working classes playing the links would have enjoyed betting too, albeit on a lesser scale than the gentlemen. Perhaps for a ball or two? Even in those hard days, the workers relished their leisure time.

So, golfers of all classes and occasional visitors would come and go to the Parlour. Stored clubs would be picked up or dropped off. Balls and ginger beer were sold and the news of the day would fill their hours. *Who won what? Who beat whom?* Ruinous moments in bunkers that were hideous at the time would be re-told with much hilarity. Broken hickory clubs, split featheries and wounded souls were all there to be mended.

For Allan as a boy it must have been an exciting time. Not only the new house on the links but the growth of the game from the late 1700s to early 1830s meant that his father no longer worked as a weaver. His father concentrated all his efforts on ball-making, caddying, selling McEwan's from Edinburgh clubs, his own golf matches and the general day-to-day operations of the golf parlour in St Andrews. No longer would the town records have the title 'weaver' beside Davie Robertson's name – surely a proud moment for the Robertsons.

Peter McEwan (1781–1836) was a clubmaker from Bruntsfield, who took over his father James' business when the latter died in 1800. The business would continue for six generations, until 1920. Peter appeared at autumn and spring meetings, and Davie acted as an agent for him in St Andrews, selling McEwan clubs, which were known for their fine symmetry and shape. Peter and his eldest son, James, died on the same day on 26 April 1836. Douglas carried on the business thereafter.

The golfing world of St Andrews revolved around Allan's father's new parlour in Sandyhill from 1822 to around 1835, when the Union Club opened. More than just golf's heritage or the evolution of the links, this was Allan's boyhood.

Allan's hometown of St Andrews was about to undergo a transformation, with more change than at any time in over 300 years. It was thanks to the drive, or some might say despotic zeal, of the Principal of the University's son, Hugh Lyon Playfair. He had high ambitions for a new St Andrews and Allan was very much a witness to it all.

Ten

PLAYFAIR REVOLUTION

It would be impossible to write the story of Allan and not mention Lieutenant-Colonel Sir Hugh Lyon Playfair LL.D. (1787–1861), or 'The Major', as he was affectionately known. In the 30-year span from 1830 to 1860, Allan and The Major would have arguably the biggest influence on St Andrews since the times of holy pilgrimage and worship. As one was becoming the champion golfer of the world and widely celebrated as the King of Golf, the other was leading the St Andrews building revolution, tearing down the tired crumbling old St Andrews and heralding in a new, vibrant town.

Allan would have known him as The Major for most of his life. An exceptional golfer for his era in his own right, winning multiple tournaments in 1818, Playfair would become Lieutenant-Colonel Sir Hugh Lyon Playfair LL.D., Provost of St Andrews and a recipient of the Freedom of St Andrews. He transformed the town like no other before or after. Davie Robertson sadly missed the complete reinvigoration of the town. St Andrews for him was a mere shadow of yesteryear.

Of course, there were others, like George Bruce and John Milne, who did so much for the town, but this perfect grouping of Allan, Playfair, Tom Morris and what would be The Royal and Ancient Golf Club of St Andrews is the primary reason why St Andrews is the success story we enjoy today.

The landscape that Playfair was transforming was Allan's world and therefore to fully understand Allan's life, we must see it in context. To begin with, who was The Major and how did the St Andrews that Allan lived in transform?

The life of Sir Hugh Lyon Playfair LL.D.

Hugh Lyon Playfair (HLP) was born at Meigle on 17 November 1786 according to his own memoirs and his monument in the cathedral, although the birth register places it on the 18th.[1] He was educated there at Newtyle and at the grammar school of Dundee, now called the High School of Dundee. The school originated in 1239, when it was founded by the Abbot of Lindores. Past pupils of this historic school are said to have included Sir William Wallace.

As a boy Hugh Lyon Playfair would in all likelihood have played on the links of St Andrews from around 1800. He would have grown up though in the starveling version of the town. The degradation and squalor of the fisherfolk quarters in the east end of North Street would have been all too real. You could hardly miss it. If it didn't offend your eyes, it assaulted your nose.

Coming from the celebrated Playfairs of Perthshire, it is said that for 200 years his family 'occupied a prominent place in the Annals of Scotland'.[2] Relations include mathematician Professor John Playfair (1748–1819), Professor of Mathematics and Natural Philosophy at Edinburgh University, who has a memorial monument on Calton Hill, Edinburgh. The statue was designed around 1825 by William Henry Playfair (1790–1857), nephew to John.

Hugh Lyon Playfair was neither work shy nor afraid to share his thoughts. He studied at the University in St Andrews. After concluding his education in 1805, he began a military career in Calcutta. The 1861 book, *Memoirs of Sir Hugh Lyon Playfair*, may have been written by Playfair with his 23-year-old son, Lieutenant (later Major General) Archibald Lewis Playfair (1838–1910). A book in the family archives clearly has pencilled in the lieutenant's name as the author but it would be hard not to conceive that Playfair would have supplied personal notes and dictated sections to his son.

The book discussed Hugh Lyon Playfair's early career highlights including leading a detachment of European artillery across 800 miles in India to Cawnpore without having to punish a single soldier or any loss of life. He was clearly a born leader, bringing personal and financial discipline to his corps. The memoir also talked about numerous uprisings by locals, including one by the robber chief, Tumon Singh.

In 1814 Playfair was wounded when a spent cannon ball struck him on the chest, and his cheek was grazed by the shrapnel of an exploding shell. Battles and violent skirmishes with locals were all very vivid and painful for Playfair.

Given his success, he was promoted time and again. In 1815 he became Captain of the Horse Artillery and in 1817 he sailed to St Helena when Napoleon Bonaparte was in exile there.

In 1818 Playfair won the Society of St Andrews Golfers' most illustrious medals, the Gold Medal, plus the Gold Medal at the six-hole Scotscraig course on Tuesday 29 September 1818. At the dinner in St Andrews two days later, he said that he would play any Gold Medal winner in Scotland. Walter Cook, the 1806, 1807 and 1817 winner, took up the challenge and won.

As an aside, Davie Robertson was made the official ballmaker to Scotscraig in 1818, which creates the very real possibility that he was the person engaged to set out the first holes at Scotscraig. He was the go-to man for anything golf related, and few knew more about golf locally than Davie. We cannot know if the origins of the Scotscraig links are connected to champion golfer Davie Robertson, but evidence does point us in that direction.

In 1819, Playfair repeated his Gold Medal victory in Scotscraig and was elected captain there. His other golfing victories were in North Berwick, where he won the Glensaddell Gold Medal in 1835 and 1841. In 1840, in St Andrews, he won the Royal Medal, presented to the Club by King William IV in 1837, and followed that in 1842 with the Gold Medal once more.

In 1855 he was made Convener of the Links Committee of The Royal and Ancient Golf Club of St Andrews and in 1856 he was elected captain.

There was intimation that his first wife, possibly from Bendochy in Perthshire but not possible to verify, died in 1819. In the obituary in the *Edinburgh Evening Courant* of 23 January 1861, it says he was twice married, but does not provide the detail of that first marriage.

On 7 March 1820 Hugh Lyon Playfair married Jane Dalgleish (1798–1872), daughter of William Dalgleish of Scotscraig, Fife. William Dalgleish was captain of the Society of St Andrews Golfers in 1806, a founder at Scotscraig in 1817, and their captain in 1818. Indeed, many of the society players in St Andrews also played at Scotscraig. It is noted in the first betting book of the Society of St Andrews Golfers that at dinner on 3 April 1818, alongside the society's secretary Mr Charles Grace, Playfair arranged to play a match against Dalgleish and Mr Graham. The result is not noted but the bets were. Most games of this era had modest bets of a crown, which is the equivalent of £5 today, but they could get substantially more. One David Moncrieffe lost an entire fortune gambling.[3]

Playfair and his wife Jane had seven daughters: Margaret Adelaide (1822–48), Jane Julia (1823–1920), Eliza Ogilvy (1826–27), Mary Bayne (1828–86), Helen Macdonald (1829–30), Francis 'Fanny' Makgill (1837–1906) and Emma Louisa (1843–71), and six sons: William Dalgleish (1821–46), Hugh Arthur (1825–48), Col. Frederick Lyon (1830–1907), Henry Macdonald (1833–73), Robert Edward (1838–55) and Archibald Lewis, twin of Robert (1838–1915).

Playfair bought his new home at St Leonards for £2,000. The house as it was in 1847 was described[4] as: 'In the lobby, we found some optical [photography] instruments, which are occasionally called into use in amusing company. The parlour we found half hung round with calotype [sic] portraits, a perfect gallery of the family's circle of acquaintance, many of whom not live at the distance of half the globe. Amongst these sun-pictures are many presenting groups of ladies, gentlemen and children, seated in arbours, or under garden trees, or in parlours. There are generally combinations of some portion of the family, with their relations and friends, taken at times when the latter were living at St Leonards, or casually called. The pictures, therefore, serve as memorials of those meetings and associations which often survive so long in memory's waste. In the same apartment is a series of Indian landscapes, done by various officers in the major's regiment in Bengal and presented to him in gratitude for the care he had taken of them. In his own room, the active character of the man is strongly traced in the numerous philosophical instruments, maps, plans, books, bundles of papers, knock-knackeries of all kinds, which are seen around. One can see the retreat of a man who is never one moment idle.'

Playfair's exotic gardens reflected the Major's love of theatre. Homages to the sun, planets, Chinese emperors, great naval ships, ancient Greek wars and royalty, like King David, adorned every corner of the garden, supplemented with waterfalls, rockeries and mirrors. It was a wonder to behold and truly captured the Major's thirst for knowledge, drama and humour.

For the next couple of years, Playfair travelled extensively across Europe. In recognition of his military honours, he was presented with the Freedom of St Andrews in 1820, one year after his father died. The ball that night in the Tolbooth Town Hall on Market Street was a grand affair attended by over 100 guests. Today the outline of the Tolbooth can be seen in the cobbles by the George Whyte-Melville fountain.

In June 1827 he was promoted again to the rank of Major and ordered to take command of the 4th Battalion of Artillery at Dum Dum. For three years he again worked on improving the area and working conditions for the soldiers. Developments included a theatre, library, fines court, officers' mess, golf, cricket, bowls, gymnastics and more. The golf was in Dum Dum, which is the Royal Calcutta Golf Club today. The course had 15 holes, according to the *Oriental Sporting Magazine* of 1830, with some interesting hazards. Such was the influence of Playfair that golf was played in India long before many parts of the UK. It may be an overreach to call him the father of golf in India, but he certainly was one of the early protagonists.

Playfair created a fines court for errant soldiers, but this was managed by a jury of the soldiers themselves, so it actually empowered his men.

In July 1831 Playfair resigned from the 4th Battalion of Artillery and received many letters of gratitude from the soldiers themselves for the changes he had made. He was not the stereotypical, somewhat brutal British leader of that era, but rather he saw what was needed, what would improve morale, and simply made it happen.

Following 30 years' service, on 10 February 1834, Playfair resigned from the Honourable East India Company. It was a successful career and his passion for improving the life and standards of his men was noteworthy. In the *Memoir*,[5] it said, 'had his career been later by thirty years, his name would have been blazoned on the roll of fame with the Lawrences, the Outrams, and the Havelocks, who have become household words wherever honour, patriotism, and generous valour esteemed.'

By this time however, he had ambitions of a different kind – St Andrews.

Rumblings of change

When Playfair retired from active service in his forties, he came home to a town that had languished without investment for hundreds of years. Yes, the town council had funded some work but, with a dwindling population, they had less and less to spend. Many of the working classes lived in squalor and apathy at the end of North Street. Ballmaker, weaver, seaman and caddie seemed to be the town's primary vocations for the working classes. On the links, Davie Robertson's parlour at Sandyhill was the centre for all golfing needs. There was no such thing as a clubhouse – only Davie's parlour to store clubs.

Playfair was first elected to the town council in 1833 and immediately made an impact. His first step as a moderniser was to address the lack of a clubhouse. He rented rooms for the Archery Society, formed on 15 November 1833, of which he was also captain. He also supplied the society with a silver arrow for meetings. The membership fee was five shillings, and there were two annual meetings of the archery club – on St Andrew's Day and on the first Wednesday in August. In August members played on the Links to a target at distances of 50, 100 and 150 yards, for the silver arrow, to which the winner would attach a silver medal inscribed with his name and arms, much akin to golf's silver club and the attaching of silver balls to it, denoting the captain that year.

To become a member, you would have to be voted in. One black ball could exclude you. Entrance fee was set at £1. Given that Da' Anderson was paid £5 for tending to the links for the year, this was not a trifling amount.

In a modest building at the end of Golf Place, Playfair created a clubhouse for the Union Club golfers and, for a while, the archers. Based on the officers' mess that he created in Dum Dum, it accommodated the golfers' needs and was officially opened by Provost Dalrymple on 26 January 1835.

There were 45 members and Playfair was the secretary and treasurer. The Union Club had a reading room, billiard room and dressing rooms for the golfers. A small portrait of Playfair, presented by Mr Rodger, hung in the club.

Sergeant Ness was the porter, who tended to the member's needs including serving ginger beer refreshments.

In 1834, the Society of St Andrews Golfers changed their name to The Royal and Ancient Golf Club of St Andrews. They could not hold meetings in the Union Club and paid their own subscription for their own club. The difference was that the Union Club was a place like an officers' mess, where the golfers could relax, drink, change clothes, read the papers, etc. The Royal and Ancient Golf Club was there to play golf, much akin to the societies that do not have a facility in St Andrews today. Although many were members of both, the distinction was clear.

It was Playfair's diligence as secretary that saw the Union Club go from strength to strength. In 1853 it was proposed by John Grant, though not acted upon, that the two clubs should unite. In June 1853 the foundation stone was placed for the new Union Club building, on the land that the Society of St Andrews Golfers had been given in 1820 by the town council in return for their support for the feuing of links land. This right needed to be assigned from the Society to the Union Club. According to Peter Lewis,[6] it was agreed in the 1853 spring meeting that all members who had been accepted as a member of the Society of St Andrews Golfers would automatically become a member of the Union Club. In effect, they thus had the same memberships, but still distinct identities. This new arrangement eased the way for the transfer of the right to build a clubhouse.

On 13 July 1853 it sounded like a fine spectacle with a large procession of locals and members from outside Madras College to the land where the club would be built. John Whyte-Melville did the honours, striking 'the foundation stone with a mallet and called for 'the great architect of the universe to shower down his blessings upon the work'.[7]

It was thanks to Playfair's administrative skills that £850 from the Union Club was used for the new building, which was designed by George Rae. In 1854 the new Union Club clubhouse opened and a full-length portrait of Playfair by Mr Wilson of Glasgow hung in the large room. Wilson was the same artist who had painted the aforementioned William Playfair.

In that year Playfair was also given the honorary rank of lieutenant-colonel. All work in the building until 1877 was paid for by the Union Club. The Royal and Ancient Golf Club members had few rights, but in 1855 they were permitted to use the building for meetings.

In May 1876, largely thanks to the proposal at the Union Club Committee of Thomas Truman Oliphant, the issue of amalgamation of the two clubs came up again. A sub-committee was formed, to which John Whyte-Melville, Colonel Tod Boothby, Thomas Oliphant and Stuart Grace were duly appointed. They presented their proposals at the autumn meeting and the amalgamation was confirmed the following spring. The rules of the Union Club formed the basis of the new amalgamated club.

Playfair added comfortable seating to what he and other locals at the time would call Witch Hill, that is the Scores, and around the links, so the ladies could watch without being in any danger. It added to the spectacle.

With fears of the tides washing away the opening holes, Playfair erected an embankment along the opening and closing holes. This was the beginning of the West Sands land reclamation work that would continue up until the 1890s. It was the dawn of the first hole, and it is Playfair we must thank for the land of that easiest, and yet terrifying, of holes.

It was Playfair who created a tarmacadam road across the links from what we know as Grannie Clark's Wynd in 1849. Double pins on the greens were added for the first time from 1853–57, apart from the fifth, which had existed by the time the Chalmers' map was drawn of the course in 1836.

St Andrews anew

In *Memoirs*,[8] the author reveals that it had always been Playfair's greatest wish to spend his twilight years in St Andrews. In 1833 he started to involve himself in public affairs.

Playfair was elected provost on 4 November 1842 and the true revolution would begin at speed. Initially, he surveyed the town and noted what was needed to be done. The town's financial affairs were still in a mess, with dubious accounting. It was said that before Playfair, a £600 donation from the Convention on Royal Burghs was eaten and drunk, with the remaining £200 simply vanishing.

Funds needed to be raised quickly for the work, but this appeal was met by a wall of apathy. Three centuries of decay had dampened even the most modest of ambitions. In public meetings, Playfair was businesslike, and he certainly could be confrontational.

Playfair, however, appealed to the populace's higher selves, imploring the citizens of St Andrews to take pride in their town.

He cajoled. He nudged. He shoved.

Ultimately, his enthusiasm and sheer bloody-mindedness (or what some might call dictatorial tendencies) succeeded. Given the depression of 1847–48, Playfair frequently dipped into his own money to make things happen.

From the lowliest working class to the gentleman golfers, many took an interest in his improvements and this spirit of pulling together for a new St Andrews. The society ladies of the town created a sale of embroidered goods and raised funds that way. It was a whole town's effort – a rare feat indeed.

The first major public work was the paving of South Street from West Port to the archways by the cathedral. Humorously, the owners of houses did not want the pavement right up to their windows as they feared people might look in. Playfair's solution was to build the four-foot wide path, 14 feet from the windows. This gap quickly became a horrid dirt track and the locals themselves paid to fill the gap with paving, creating the wide pathway that we see today. Within a year there was continuous pavement the entire length of South Street.

The Tolbooth town hall sat in the middle of Market Street and was deemed an eyesore, not fit for purpose. In 1845 Playfair asked for donations to pay for its removal, with an appeal to vanity by saying a donation would perpetuate the name of the donor to future ages and secure the gratitude and blessings of generations to come. It took 13 years, but, in 1858, the new town hall's foundation stone was laid in South Street.

On 1 January 1846 he appealed again for donations with a not very subtle, 'To all who feel desirous of promoting the contemplated improvements in the ancient city of St Andrews, this memorial is fully addressed'. He tried to play to their higher natures, but, alas, this fell on deaf ears. Two months later, he issued another stern public note, saying that the town would suffer if he did not get the £252 to repair Market Street. It worked.

Irregular houses and porches that jutted out onto the street were removed, including the 'Principal's Nose' entrance porch that protruded onto South Street. Another unsightly porchway jutted onto the street where the tenant of the property was in arrears. Playfair promised to pay off his debt if he allowed him to remove the trees and porch. Handing over the money, the tenant went to bed to ponder on it all. When he woke, the porch and trees were gone, lest he change his mind!

At the West Port, working with John Grant of Kilgraston in 1843, he removed old buildings and had ornamental stone tablets, heralding King David, created and placed in the archway. A similar archway in North Street near Tom Morris' family home was removed in 1838, so that the entire street could be opened up.

Tenants who would not improve their own property found the property bought by Playfair and he made the improvements himself. Not one inch of St Andrews escaped the keen eye of Playfair. He built new fine houses at the corner of Castle Street and improved the old Black Bull Inn premises, which he renamed Victoria Buildings. To these new streets he added square lamps, and called it one of the best lit towns in the land. Finally, on South Street, he cleared the roads of old boulders, so that carriages could pass freely.

The harbour was cleared of old shipwrecks, widened and deepened. Roads, walkways and walls to the harbour were repaired. Piers were renewed and the eastern barrier erected. The old lighthouse at the end of the pier was removed and a new light placed there that shone for a distance of four miles out to sea.

On the north-west turret of the cathedral wall, the Turret Light was created, thanks to Playfair's request to the Commissioners of Northern Lights, and was kept alight, paid for by the town's funds. It was visible to mariners as a stationary white light. As his memoirs relate, 'On the evening on which the light was first exhibited, the 12th February 1849, a grand procession of all the seamen belonging to the city, accompanied by large numbers of tradesmen etc., took place by torchlight … the procession … headed by Neptune, moved from the Kirkhill along North Street, and then along South Street to Sir Hugh's residence.'[9]

Such was the glowing reception of the Turret Light that numerous letters and poems were written in honour of both Playfair and the lights. Naturally, there were a few dissenting voices to a light being placed on the ancient building, with one calling it, in the *Fifeshire Journal*, 'a desecration of the beautiful ruins'.

It would be a little rose-tinted to say that Playfair's reforms were universally welcomed. At every step of the way, there was someone in the shadows griping about the loss of this or that. Nevertheless, in his own indomitable way, he ploughed on.

In 1845 against the wishes of the house owners, Playfair insisted upon opening up a street, now called Bell Street, between Market Street and South Street. It cost him £2,000 and, for a while, the surface of the street was his own private property.

On what we now know as Greyfriars Garden, he was attempting to replicate the wonderful result of Bell Street, but one owner with an unsightly jutting porch had other ideas. Playfair's solution was to lay pavement as far as the porch. With pressure from the public, the porch was duly removed.

Market Street and North Street were paved, cleared of rubbish and all uneven mounding removed between 1846 and 1854.

Walks around St Andrews, including the Scores and Lade Braes, were beautified and all hillocks or obstacles removed. The cathedral burial ground was extended by the purchase of two additional plots, walks created, and ornate gateways added. Complaints about the pathways going over where relatives were buried stopped the construction work, but the pathways we enjoy today around the cathedral are Playfair's work.

Alas, the grave for Davie Robertson may have suffered accordingly and the only records of lairs in existence today are from 1860. We assume at this time that Allan's obelisk is somewhere in close proximity to Davie's and his father Peter's graves. On the new burial ground that Playfair purchased, he obtained permission for it to be appropriated for the poorer classes.

The change in life would have been noticeable for Allan walking around the cobbled stones of St Andrews. Playfair had rubbish cleared from all streets, removing centuries of foul odours. The fisherfolk tended to treat Playfair with caution and hesitancy. When he first went to their houses to gain an idea of what could be done, he was horrified to find that they retained rubbish in their attics and within walls. This would have led to all sorts of illnesses. Playfair implored them to improve their own lives. They were in charge. Facing obstinacy, he tried to instill Christian virtues, replacing health-destroying spirits with the joy of the Holy Spirit. The number of inns that were allowed to operate in St Andrews fell from 43 in 1842 to 27 in 1857, and the relative lack of drunkenness in the town was noted. The merits of clothing their children, rather than wasting money in a gin shop, was prevailed upon them with significant success.

Although not a big drinker, Allan would have witnessed the total abstinence campaigns in town, which largely fell on deaf fisherfolk and caddie ears. A school was created for them by Rev. Cook and a reading room replenished with books. The fisherfolk were not only being publicly noticed but actively being cared for.

The sale of mussels was a dying trade, but, thanks to Playfair's initiative, it raised on average £300 per annum. Playfair ordered that carts were to be provided for the wives of the fisherfolk who had for too long been carrying mussels from the Eden in sacks on their backs. Although again after some hesitancy, the mussels were soon carted from the Eden. There was not one element of their lives that he did not try his best to ameliorate.

He backed a public library and reading room, making it accessible to all. Madras College also benefited from his largesse; he paid for improvements, building on the £60,000 endowment left by Dr Andrew Bell when he died in 1832. Bell also left £10,000 in 3 per cent bank annuities for the moral and religious improvement of the city. A portrait of the founder Dr Andrew Bell was placed in the Trustee Room and a bust of him placed under the Blackfriars ruin. A huge performance stage and gymnasium were just two of the improvements that made Madras one of the most successful colleges at the time. It was too late a generation for Allan to benefit from the education, but, with the new college thriving, Allan could see his hometown rising from the ruins. Playfair used the bank annuity for the general improvement of the town, which raised a few eyebrows and was resisted until Playfair eventually and inevitably got his way.

Time and again, Playfair dipped into the Bell fund to get things done. Sometimes he bought property so that he could demolish it. One example of using his own funds was when he bought every house on the newly created South Bell Street (Bell Street today) for £2,000, knowing the town council would pay him back in time.

The university too benefited from Playfair's work in raising funds that covered the cost of the complete renovation of the university, including the snipping off of the principal's nose! This work complemented the 1827 award of £30,000 by the royal commissioners to re-build the United College, although only £10,000 was spent in St Andrews, the rest finding its way for political reasons to Marischal College, Aberdeen. St Salvator's Hall was knocked down and rebuilt. In 1856 the university awarded him an LL.D, Doctorate of Laws, in recognition of his support over the years.

Churches too, especially the college church, were improved with new pulpits. The street running alongside Holy Trinity church was changed from Kirk Wynd to Church Street and Foul Waste changed to Union Street.

Public lectures on an array of topics by phrenologists to mesmerists were created. However, on the date when McCarte's Circus came to town, one poor lecturer who had prepared to talk about the advancements of the electric telegraph walked on stage to a near empty room, despite the circus's poor reputation. Evening classes were arranged in Madras College. Just like Playfair's military days and his real improvements to the soldiers' lives, Playfair was looking to stimulate the minds of the St Andrews populace, including the fisherfolk. In 1859 he even brought in a whole variety of new sports, such as bowls, quoits, skittles, caber-tossing on the west of the links and football on the first fairway! He also created a St Andrews Annual Gymnastics Games and transformed the Bow Butts near the bandstand into a huge outdoor arena.

In 1848, the railway line came to Leuchars. Largely through Playfair and William Smith's work, the line was extended to St Andrews. This opened up the town to tourists and golfers like never before. Where the golfing visitor had been limited mostly to landed gentry, with the railway and also the new cheaper guttie ball, plus a Victorian enthusiasm for the outdoors, the game became open to all.

By the 1850s Playfair had contributed mightily to the modernisation of St Andrews. In recognition of this, he was awarded a knighthood in 1856. Allan's St Andrews was blossoming. Beautiful housing by Sir John Gladstone, George Rae and James Hope attracted wealthy families to live in the area. The father of photography, John Adamson (1809–70), his brother Robert Adamson (1821–48), David Octavius Hill and later John's protégé Thomas Rodger (1832–83) would add having a portrait to the attractions of a visit to St Andrews. Far from the decrepit St Andrews of Davie's era, Allan could enjoy the rise and rise of St Andrews. Tourists came from Edinburgh, Perth, Stirling, Kirkcaldy and Arbroath in numbers that Davie could only have dreamed of.

Thanks to Playfair's drive, St Andrews was re-born. Its fame spread throughout Scotland, and prosperity was once again possible in St Andrews. There was virtually no part of St Andrews life and townscape that Playfair did not work tirelessly to improve, be it the protection of the cliff-tops, the pends, ancient walls, clean water, unsightly houses, ruinous streets, Martyrs' Monument, the links, the town's first golf clubhouse, lighting the streets, University, town hall, Lade Braes walk. He was an incredible force of nature.

When we talk of a revolution of St Andrews, this is not an overstatement. He took a decaying ancient town, which could only dream of past riches and made it not only beautiful once more, but also profitable for many. The guest houses, the shoemakers, the bakers, the ball makers, the caddies, the restaurants, the carters, all had a major boost, including Allan.

With new housing came the middle classes and a desirable place to live once more. With that came jobs for carpenters like Hugh Philp and jobs as servants. The town's building trade knew no era like it. The improved university attracted more students. The railway drew in tourists and day trippers.

It was said that Playfair 'wiled, screwed, pinched, curried the money out of men'. In 1847 he talked about the prolific level of changes he had made to date and the people's reaction to his drive: 'Many of them are heartily sick of my services, and anxious for my promotion.' He was only half joking. Yes, Playfair upset a few people on the way, but his results are undeniable, and we are enjoying the fruits of his labour over 150 years later.

Grand National Golf Club Tournament

With the new double pins on greens to accommodate the burgeoning number of players on the links, according to Peter and Hugh Cleghorn's private letters, Playfair created a golf tournament between the best clubs of the day. It was called, like the racing equivalent, The Grand National Golf Club Tournament and started in 1857. Cleghorn noted that the event drew in golfers from all parts of the country and that never before was such golf seen. On the downside, Cleghorn lamented that it gave rise to much gambling!

And then he was gone

In less than 30 years, Playfair had re-built St Andrews, a town that had suffered since the Reformation, which was so destructive for its economy for over 250 years. It was a burden no more. St Andrews could look forward to pilgrims of a different kind and a brighter future.

It was in May 1857 that Peter Cleghorn, in his personal letters, wrote that Playfair had suffered an epileptic fit.[10] Rumours spread around town that Playfair had died. Cleghorn refuted this and noted his recovery was ongoing but slow. They had not moved him from the room where he was carried.

Playfair had a bronchitis attack in the winter of 1860. This was complicated, with the ongoing challenges of heart disease. With failing health, on 2 November 1860, just before he was due to come up for re-election as town councillor and provost, Playfair wrote to the police commission saying, 'I have neither the health nor strength left which would enable me to perform the various duties required of a member of the Town Council to my own satisfaction. My warmest and most grateful thanks I now render to all the members of the Magistracy and Council, with whom, for eighteen years, I have so happily and cordially acted – and by whose kind support I have enabled to carry on various changes – it may be thought by some, improvements – in our city.'

The councillors, however, did not want him to stop and implored him to take a titular position like before but with none of the requirements of office. Playfair obliged and was duly elected and was returned to the council on 9 November 1860.

It was not to last.

On 8 January 1861 the *Edinburgh Evening Courant* said that Playfair's health was giving his friends serious anxiety. Three days later, on 11 January 1861, the *Caledonian Mercury* stated that Lieutenant-Colonel Sir Hugh Lyon Playfair was gravely ill. The *Dublin Evening Mail* on 14 January noted that there was little hope of recovery.

While Playfair was said to have been in pain for a little while, this was mercifully short. Lieutenant-Colonel Sir Hugh Lyon Playfair LL.D. died, aged 74, on 21 January 1861 at quarter past eleven in the evening at his house in St Leonards. His death certificate put his death down to heart disease. It may have been a familial thing as his son, Captain Henry, died of the same cause some 22 years later, aged 40.

It was the end of an unprecedented reign.

Amid the intricate tightrope of St Andrews' politics, he had somehow managed to get things done, whether through his own pocket or sheer hegemony. *The Scotsman* described his as 'a most frank, unaffected … soldierlike manner'. It was this soldier's skillset that enabled his success where others had failed. His abrupt nature left some with a disagreeable impression of Playfair, but few doubted his noble aspirations for the people and town.

Obituaries singing his praise ran across Ireland and Britain. Phrases like 'he created the Scarborough of Scotland' filled columns. Seldom recognised for this, Playfair was noted by all the press obituaries for his passion for photography.

Playfair's dry sense of humour was recorded, alongside his multitude of achievements. Letters in the local paper from former students of the university called him a 'Provost-Magician' for what he had done to the town, comparing him to the town's first provost Maynard (Mainard) the Fleming, as he was known, around 1144.

One obituary in the *Edinburgh Evening Courant* on 23 February noted, 'And here let us pay tribute of one sentence to that able Lieutenant of the Major's – Allan Robertson the Champion Golfer, who died in September 1859. These two men, dissimilar in station, but akin in their genial natures, have done more for St Andrews than any school, or college, or storied tradition.'

Together, they literally changed St Andrews and set us on a path to the St Andrews we see today.

The paper added that the likes of Playfair would not likely recur in the burgh annals of Scotland. This was very true.

Allan would have witnessed Playfair's revolution. The crumbling town of his grandfather and father was a distant memory. New generations, like Tommy Morris and Jamie Anderson, would better reap the rewards of Playfair's work. They would not know the dirt tracks that were North Street and South Street.

Wide boulevards and straight streets greeted their generation. The eras of drinking water with a lead stripe were gone. After 1853, with the cleansing of the streets and the sanitary laws prohibiting street refuse, cholera epidemics dwindled. Income could be earned from scavenging, thus helping with the town's clean-up. It was just another clever idea of Playfair's.

The burgeoning of the town and university was largely thanks to Playfair. In lieu of being a town where only those who could not leave were stuck there, it became a choice place to live, love and golf. His vision that St Andrews would be a Metropolis of Golf and home to the middle classes was certainly achieved and more.

Playfair was buried on 27 January 1861 in St Andrews cathedral cemetery and a monument placed on the north wall, which is still there today, maintained by a long line of Playfairs including, today, his descendant Edward Playfair. All business in town stopped on that day and shops, including the golf parlour, were closed for two hours. The magistrates, town council, teachers and pupils of Madras College, principal, professors and students of the university, dressed in black or scarlet gown, attended. The Artillery and Rifle companies were there too. It was said the turnout of the general public was so large that every corner was occupied by sorrowing citizens.

A full-length portrait of Playfair was created in 1846 by artist Sir John Watson Gordon of Edinburgh (1788–1864) and presented at a breakfast gathering on 10 April 1847 in the old town hall of St Andrews. The great and the good of St Andrews were there, including fellow golfers and members of the Literary and Philosophical Society. Grace was said by the Very Rev. Principal Haldane, the owner of the Principal's Nose. Mr A.K. Lindesay spoke in wonderful tones about what Playfair had achieved and hoped that long would he continue his work. He need not have worried. At the end of his address, he unveiled the painting.

Provost Playfair in reply said, 'The honour you have conferred upon me on this occasion has placed me in a position much more prominent than I deserve to hold – a distinguished position to which few men attain in their native city, be their talents, their merits, or their deeds, ever so great. That picture is placed in the Town Hall, with the consent of the Town Council, as a mark of their approbation of the manner in which I have discharged the duties of the situation to which I was by them elected … It is now some forty years since my attachment to this city commenced. Throughout my career in life that attachment has never abated. To return to St Andrews in the evening of my days for years continued to be the most ardent desire in my heart … I hope my successors, when looking (at the painting), may be stimulated to devote a portion of their time to the objects which, for some years, I have pursued with an earnest to render the inhabitants comfortable and happy.'

The portrait still hangs in the town hall today. If you visit St Andrews, do try to see this painting. It is stunning.

Just like Allan Robertson and Tom Morris, inhabitants and visitors alike today enjoy the monumental and tireless work of this exceptional soldier, servant to the people, photography pioneer, occasional good golfer and all-round visionary, Lieutenant-Colonel Sir Hugh Lyon Playfair LL.D.

Eleven

WONDER YEARS

FROM the age of 15, during the 1830s Allan honed his skills on the links. They were playing the reverse links as we would know it, with single pins on the St Andrews greens. To Allan, that was the St Andrews links. The first green that Allan would aim for is today's 17th. His second was played to the today's 16th, which explains the location of Cheape's bunker and some of the other bunkers that seem to be placed randomly.

If a group coming inward on their back nine got to a green first as you were playing to the same green on the front nine, you simply had to wait. Given the low number of players, this was not too much of an inconvenience in the 1830s.

Allan's back nine used the same greens as we do today, albeit a little smaller then. The only difference is the location of where he would tee off from. A drop of sand placed a couple of club lengths from the hole on the green sufficed in an era when there were few courses in the country and manageable numbers of golfers playing.

Allan's clubs

In the early 19th century golfers played with mostly swan-necked wooden clubs that needed a sweeping shot. There was stigma attached to taking a huge divot and it would be deemed bad form if you did so. It was said that the ideal driver length then would reach from the ground to the pit of the stomach. The putter 'should be upright, perfectly stiff in the shaft, and vertical in the whole face; it must be a little heavier, but well balanced, with no feeling of deadness about it'.[1]

Allan had names for his clubs. His putter was *The Doctor*. Others included *Sir David Baird* (a present from Sir David, who was also the referee for the celebrated 1849 Dunns match against Allan and Tom) and *Thraw-cruck* (a throw crook was an instrument used for twisting, or thrawing, straw rope for bags or stacks of corn or hay). His niblick was called *The Frying Pan*, which was used to escape from bunkers around the green, and his cleek, his favourite, which he used so diligently around the green.

As a teenager, though, Allan played his featherie ball with wooden clubs. Eventually, 'Allan introduced the deadly loft "iron", which he wrought with miraculous accuracy. Instead of the putter for long-green approaches, Allan began to use the "cleek", unless he had some precarious putt to hole. No man could more scientifically miss a putt.'[2]

Dr McPherson said, 'Allan introduced the deadly approach-game with the cleek in 1848. Before that, the baffing-spoon was employed, so gracefully wielded by Sir Robert Hay and James Balfour; now it is obsolete. The iron is indispensable for short approaches, lofting bunkers, and stymies; but the shaft should not be strained by bunker-work, as a niblick iron is there more suitable. You cannot easily get two perfect handles for one "iron" in a lifetime, so long does it take to have its "sett" fixed by jerking; and no artificial "bend" can equal what it takes years to form.'[3] In other words, years of playing a wooden club would give the face the perfect shape for an individual player, and in time the player would come to know the swing rhythm that was best for the shaft.

This lofting shot of Allan's that McPherson talks about was an entirely new shot to golf, which was traditionally played low and running. It is probably why the club was called the 'lofter', and it was Allan who was known as the creator of the skilled shot.

On this last point, it should be said that artist Thomas Hodge, who knew Allan for the last five or six years of Allan's life and sketched him, said that Allan never played an iron club 'through the green'. Allan's obituaries and various commentaries by people who knew and played with him suggest otherwise. Perhaps he meant a full set of cleeks or a long shot with an iron to the green? That could be true, but Allan's skill with the unique high *Frying Pan* shot around the green was widely heralded.

The golfing exemplar

As a player, Allan was exceptional. Dr McPherson, who knew him and watched him play, said, 'One man mastered all: Allan Robertson. His coolness was almost miraculous; he was never known to "funk" (duff a shot under pressure) and he was *never* beaten. Unequalled in the world, the model player, none could approach him at the niceties. No gloved finger touched his club; he felt it as an artist feels his brush; he handled it with such marvelous dexterity that in the eyes of an ordinary player it seemed a magic wand.' He later added,

> Allan stands in front, facile princeps of golfers. Never was he beaten. He came of a golfing race, his grandfather and father being ball-makers and golfers. He played with toy clubs when a child, and when a youth he rushed out while the dew was on the grass of the undisturbed Links and practised with his coat off ... No-one who ever saw the champion can ever forget him. Frank and open to all, yet firm in his judgement, he was as polite as Brummel and as politic as a Metternich. Small of stature, thick-set, short-necked, he stored a tremendous amount of energy and pluck, but the humour never ceased to play around his happy features.
>
> His style was invariably elegant and faultless. He was exceptionally temperate; though kindly, he was firm ... Allan's game was pure, unadulterated science. He could not hold the candle to Dunn at driving; but his quarter-strokes [pitching] were deadly, his putting was perfect ... and he had it all his own way; he could play with the ball'.[4]

In *Reminiscences of Golf and Golfers*, H. Thomas Peter commented on Allan's game, 'Of the lot, I would place Allan, as a man, as the least powerful, but the most scientific. He could not play well on a rough green, for he used light clubs and balls, and a rough grassy green was too much for him; but on St Andrews with its unapproachable turf he was unrivalled. He was, we then considered, alike perfect in driving off tee, in his play along the green, and in his approach to, his putting towards and into the hole. Let me note that in putting he always took both putter and cleekin his hand – to be used according to judgment. He could take more liberties with the game than any one I ever knew, and his plan of just "snodding" his opponents at the Burn when he had an easy-going match became proverbial.'[5] 'Snodding' or 'snoddit him at the burn' or 'we'll snod them at the burn' meant closing out a match by 2 and 1.

At the conclusion in his book, he adds, 'it may be permitted to a veteran to give a few hints to young players, viz., to keep cool, avoid strong language, and never to forget Allan's golden rule, "Tak' it easy".'[6]

H.S.C. Everard wrote of Allan in *The Badminton Library – Golf* in 1890, 'All are agreed that Allan's style was easy and graceful; he played with light clubs, of all of which he was a thorough master, reducing golf almost to an exact science, and being able to heel [fade] or hook his drives at will. In his accuracy lay his strength, for he had no pretensions to the power of modern professionals; a charming partner and generous opponent, no amount of "cross accidents" could disturb his equable temper.' A lesson indeed for us all today.

In Allan's day, clubs were made 'more for skill than force. With what affection did Allan look upon his stock.' His clubs were made by Philp, but Allan 'reduced its weight to suit the thin handle until it looked like a toy'.[7] All the same, it was very effective.

In golfing terms, Allan was a strategic player. When he played the 13th, for example, he would play short of the bunkers, then with a short spoon over the bunkers to the foot of the hill, and then his third to the green, again with a short spoon.

Allan was short in physical stature, as many of the group photographs from the time show, but he was muscular and had strong arms, as well as being lithe and wiry. What he lacked in height he more than made up for in guile and cunning around the golf course.

If you consider that a long shot back then was around 180 yards, that might explain the high scoring of those days. Half-hit shots that came off the toe or heel were likely to go around the 150-yard mark, if not less. The wooden heads were not exactly forgiving. How long must the 14th hole on St Andrews have felt in the wind and rain? The amateur golfers, like Playfair in the 1820s and 1830s, were winning with scores of around 107 over 18 holes in St Andrews. Allan's shooting of a 95 in 1840 gives you an idea of the standard of play at the time.

The high scoring also points to the difficulty of the game around the green, as, by all records at the time, they could get close to the green in numbers not vastly different to golfers today, but it took considerably more effort for them to get the ball into the rough, hand-cut hole, without a tin cup and on a rough, natural green. As the ball and equipment improved, so too did Allan's scores.

Those who played with Allan describe his swing as rhythmical and forming a perfect arc. It was not uncommon for him to be outdriven, but the accuracy of Allan's second shots compensated for any deficiencies in length: 'with a wide sweep – always holding the leather by the very extremity – the little man came "whisk!" upon his 26 ball, it left like a rocket: or, when half-topped against the wind, it rose so gradually that at last it rest in the air before falling. Allan once struck a boy with his club who happened to be standing behind him; afterwards he instinctively cast his eyes behind before the stroke, however important the match was.'[8]

The genial soul

Allan was described by all those who knew him as a good-natured individual and pawky (a person with a mischievous sense of humour). When it came to playing golf, however, he was canny. Those familiar with Allan testify to his 'uniform geniality, thorough earnestness to win matches, and uncomplaining temper under trial'.

It was said that he 'possessed the best heart and kindliest feelings in the world. In the intricate dealing of the links, in the formation and playing of great matches, Allan was honourable, just and gentlemanly from first to last.'[9]

He was simply an immense talent, and respected by those fortunate to see him play. Children would watch him playing in grand matches and sneak behind mounds and try to imitate his rhythmical swing. It was said that after watching Allan and Tom defeat the Dunns, the kids who were pretending to be Allan felt like they could beat anyone on the links. Young caddies, including one named Punch, waiting by the golf parlour in the hope of being asked to caddie by a gentleman, would try to imitate Allan while hitting an old cork.

Such was Allan's fame.

'It was as a player, that I chiefly remember him,' said W.W. Tulloch in his biography of Tom Morris. 'His great reputation, together with his real kindness of manner and many admirable qualities, made him a hero to a youngster like myself. His wonderful feats, I was never tired of chronicling.'[10]

In 1899 *Golf* magazine said, 'Allan was what we should ordinarily call a little man, of stoutish build, sharp in his movements, with, if I remember alright, rather bushy whiskers, and of a cheeky, kindly appearance. I can now picture the little man in my mind's eye as he stood at the top hole of Musselburgh at the finish of the Musselburgh portion of the great foursome in 1849. He wore a round peaked cap, and a little red jacket, not the modern red golfing jacket, but a short jacket such as we used to wear when boys at school, and I can almost fancy I see him now, as I saw him then, gaily lifting his cap and giving a cheer with the big crowd, at the victory of his opponents.'

Even at the end of the round, at the conclusion of a bruising battle in Musselburgh where he and Tom lost heavily – and we will talk about the match in detail later – he still raised his cap and applauded his opponents. That was the spirit of golf, but it also tells us so much about Allan.

To date we have rested Allan's reputation on some barbarous poetry, or repeated readings into the word 'pawky', but Allan was so much more than this. Stories that portrayed him as conniving or stacking the deck in his favour are repeated and exaggerated on each re-telling.

The real Allan, as described by those who knew him, was kindly, friendly, magnanimous, funny and patient, as well as a scientist of the links. He was not some Fagin from *Oliver Twist* type character. He was universally popular. Allan's equanimity of temperament and easy-going, affable character are part of the reason why so many golfers of the time claimed he was the best.

This quotation in *Golf* also addresses the coat issue. If the Society of St Andrews Golfers wore red jackets, and the members were largely wealthy gentlemen, was working-class Allan, whose red coat is well known, not wearing the same clothing as the gentlemen? Despite the similarity of colour, there were important differences: his red coat was short, and theirs was an altogether grander, more formal affair. Over time, the trend of wearing red coats on the links faded, much like the use of a fore-caddie.

One might reflect on this final quote about Allan as a golfer, from Rev. W.W. Tulloch: 'I have recollections of seeing Allan Robertson putting. How he calculated every little mound and rough bit of grass in a long billowy "putt" is still a subject of admiration ... I have seen "the champion" ... hole long "putts" on very uneven ground with a certainty which makes one speculate as to what he could have done on the present greens.'[11]

A different outlook

From the many statements from people who knew him, a clear impression emerges about what sort of golfer Allan was, but what of his personality? What were his politics? The evidence here is less forthcoming. We therefore have to look at his scrapbooks to get an insight into what interested him. These were the clippings that he deemed worthy of capturing and retaining.

The very first scrapbook entry is a clipping from the *Chambers Journal* dated 7 December 1833. Allan was just in his 18th year. The article, which he includes in full, is called *Bad Times.*

The essence of the article is that although times were hard, they had been much harder before. It details that only 50 years previously, many houses were made of mud, peat and thatched porous roofs. It laments the complaining of all classes, and encourages a positive outlook based on a reality of the better times in which they were living. Comparing the soft furnishings of the modern 1830s household to that of Peter Robertson's generation and his grandfather's was one tangible way to show how things had improved. Even the very roof over their houses had been enhanced.

> If the middle classes knew how poorly, in comparison, their predecessors lived – if the labouring classes knew what unutterable hardships and discomforts were endured by those who have gone before them in the same humble but useful walk-in life – there would be much less of this standing charge against the present age.

This clearly resonated with Allan. It would not be too much of a leap of faith to say that the 18-year-old boy, whose father was evidently industrious and a business owner, saw the merits of the argument. The mere boy, who would be a business owner himself within two years, and an employer, clearly came from an ambitious family.

This was not the norm. The Piries were never employers; nor were the Andersons.

All of those working-class caddies at the links saw their life and its perceived limits. They caddied, and often spent most of their working time at the handloom. They were wabsters. They picked the crops at harvest time. Employers were 'them' and the workers were 'us'.

This was not the Robertsons' ideal.

They were ballmakers.

They were the crack, champion golfers.

They were the serial keepers of the links.

It is not that they didn't feel working class. They certainly would have. Allan was a member and captain of the artisans club, The St Andrews Golf Club, in 1853. It is just that they clearly had ambitions. Davie's deal, selling clubs made by McEwans from Edinburgh, did not just fall from the sky. He clearly was the best St Andrews golfer in the 1820s and early 1830s. Davie saw there was a demand for clubs in St Andrews and, one way or another, negotiated a deal to sell McEwan clubs.

That entrepreneurial way of thinking also explains how the Robertsons' Sandyhill started off as a mere house, was expanded, took in lodgers, and then ended up as a hotel for Allan's brother David. Even during Allan's time, there was always a lodger in residence.

If any further evidence was needed of Allan's thinking, a clipping from a few pages further on in the scrapbook is entitled *A Chapter for the Industrious.*

While we have no direct evidence of Allan extolling the virtues of the 'power of oneself' or in support of a 'just do it' approach, the evidence of his father developing a business from scratch and he himself being an employer shows at the very least that Allan was commercially minded. This was an era of 'self-help', and this was the embodiment of Allan's approach. He was canny and prudent too.

When we come to discuss the guttie-ball argument with Tom, we will see that it is the power of money – the mighty pound sterling – that eventually wins the argument over the centuries of the Robertsons' tradition making featheries. It was simply, contra to his fears, good for business.

The Royal and Ancient Golf Club of St Andrews

The Society of St Andrews Golfers itself was growing. In September 1831 they introduced a handicap system to help make their meetings more appealing, rather than just for the best golfers playing for the Gold Medal. The committee included, among others, Whyte-Melville, Holcroft, Messieux and Patullo, 'to frame such regulations as they may deem proper'.[12] The North Berwick handicap rules that typically included the same players, given how few links there were, divided golfers into five classes. Class 1 gave two shots to the next class, three to the next, six to the next, and eight to Class 5.

The rules in St Andrews would have been broadly identical. Allan was, like his father, the natural arbiter of fixing the odds when asked. It is also said that Davie himself, in fixing the odds, would only play matches that he thought he could win. Although the temptation would be to look at a similar trait, with Allan refusing to play Willie Park some 20 years later, it was very different as we shall see.

It was also in 1833 that the idea of a name change for the Society of St Andrews Golfers came to light. From the 1830s onwards, so many global innovations, fashions and even the influence of Playfair would transform the sport in St Andrews. Golf ball, railway, changing appetites for travel, tourism and the overall lowering of the cost of the game, would all play a part in the revolution. By gaining royal support, the eminence of the game grew too. King William IV became patron of Perth Golfing Society and gave permission for it to become the Royal Golfing Society of Perth in 1833, largely through the work of Lord Kinnaird.

At the autumn meeting of 1833, Major John Murray Belshes of Invermay proposed that he approach the king's secretary, Sir Herbert Taylor, to request that His Majesty become patron of the club and for it to be called henceforth The Royal and Ancient Golf Club of St Andrews. Although the resolution was passed, there was the odd dissenting voice. Belshes felt the make-up of the society of noblemen, gentlemen, and high ranking military officers gave the society a strong case, especially as the king was Duke of St Andrews. Sir Herbert replied that the name change was acceptable to the king, but he initially refused to become patron. Belshes' reply letter to Sir Herbert is a diplomatic work of art:[13]

Invermay 19th January, 1834

My Dear Sir Herbert,

It was particularly gratifying to me to find by your kind letter of the 15th Inst. which I this morning had the honour to receive, that His Majesty had been graciously pleased to accede to the wish of the members of the Golf Club of St Andrews, in so far as to approve of that Society being in future styled 'The Royal and Ancient Golf Club of St Andrews' which distinguished mark of His Majesty's kindness and condescension I shall not fail to communicate to the members at their earliest meeting.

I am extremely sorry, however, also to find by your letter that circumstances prevent His Majesty becoming Patron of the Club and I trust I am not taking too great a liberty in soliciting you to be so good as to avail yourself of a favourable opportunity of explaining to the King, that when I made the request that His Majesty would become our Patron, I was not aware that His Majesty had laid down any rule relative to applications of a similar nature, and at the same time to express my deep regret in having done so. In fact I would not have ventured to make such a request, had not Lord Kinnaird last year communicated to the Royal Golfing Society of Perth, that at an audience which his Lordship had with the King, His Majesty had graciously consented to become the Patron of that Society and to approve of its being styled 'Royal'. That being the case and under the peculiar circumstances of His Majesty being Duke of St Andrews, it appeared to me that if any preference was to be given to a Society of that description, perhaps the Golf Club of St Andrews of the two was the best entitled to it; not only from the above circumstances, but from its being nearly a century older, and from its members being entirely composed of a great portion of the nobility and Gentry of Scotland, many of whom are in different quarters of the world; and although most gratifying to every member of the Club, yet to those far distant from their native land, such a mark of honourable distinction conferred upon them by the Duke of St Andrews, their Sovereign, would be received with sentiments of the greatest pleasure, and with feelings of the deepest gratitude.

Permit me to apologise for again troubling you on the subject, and to request you will accept my most grateful thanks for the very kind manner in which you have been good enough to forward the wishes of the members of the Royal and Ancient Golf Club of St Andrews. Believe me ever to be with great regard and esteem.

My Dear Sir Herbert, Yours etc. etc. etc.
J. Murray Belshes.

What a remarkable letter. It is not unsurprising that the king responded positively within a week, assenting to their wish that he become patron. How much history hinges on that pivotal moment? In the autumn meeting of 1835, Belshes was elected to be captain. He is the only captain to reign for two consecutive years, as he was also elected for 1836.

Another fine Robertson ballmaker

As mentioned in the previous chapter, in 1836 Allan's father died and suddenly Allan was on his own. The 20-year-old Allan was suddenly the primary earner for his brother David, who was 11 years old, and his mother Ann. Together they lived in Sandyhill.

Davie had not left them destitute. He had handed over a comfortable golf business that made featheries, offered refreshments and sold clubs. Few of the working-class weaving and ball-making families could have left such a bounty. Davie was held in high regard but, alas, the eldest cad was gone. His death would have been lamented. Although never covered in the papers, one can imagine how the gentleman golfers of the newly named The Royal and Ancient Golf Club of St Andrews attended the funeral or raised a glass to Davie, for years their go-to St Andrews professional and town golfing hero.

It is very possible that many of the older golfers could have looked to the young Allan and wondered if Davie's business and level of service would continue. They need not have worried. The golf parlour at Sandyhill would be just fine.

Under Allan's stewardship, players continued to leave their clubs at the parlour. Among the many who left their clubs to be stored in a box locker was Principal John Tulloch, father to Tom Morris' biographer Rev. William Weir Tulloch.[14]

Allan Robertson was not only famous for his prowess as a golfer, but he was recognised as the pre-eminent golf ballmaker of his time, along with Musselburgh's John Gourlay and Tom Alexander.

The small kitchen in Sandyhill was Allan's place of operation. He sold his golf balls out of the side window facing the links. The front of the house faced Golf Place and the back garden, with flowers and bushes (planted by Allan and Tom), just behind it. In those first few years without Davie, Allan and his younger brother David were largely on their own, except for the occasional support of their cousin Lang Willie (Robertson).[15] In time that would change.

Allan was never actually a clubmaker. Almost all of the golf professionals were claimed to be clubmakers from Allan's day through to the 1920s, such as Harry Vardon and Ted Ray. In actual fact, they assembled clubs to meet the requirement of their customers, and themselves. Fitting a shaft to the head, adding a grip or finishing were the sum total of their manufacturing, albeit a valuable service to the golfer. None of this work was ever a part of Allan's setup. He was a traditional and very much acclaimed feather ball maker. There was an art to making a featherie and Allan simply had that gift.

It should be said though, given that there were 40 golf clubs of assorted kinds in Davie's will, it would not be surprising if Allan also sold Philp clubs.

The art of ballmaking

In 1837, according to H. Thomas Peter, the only clubmaker in St Andrews was Hugh Philp and the only ballmaker Allan Robertson. He remembered Tom Morris and Allan 'pounding away at the stuffing of feather balls, which were the only ones we had at the time'.[16]

The making of a featherie golf ball was no easy task; in fact, it was arduous, and not a particularly healthy pursuit. Consumption, an old term to describe tuberculosis, was said to be a common complaint among the ballmakers, as they breathed in the micro-fibres of the goose feathers. A good deal of strength was necessary to make a leather golf ball.

Thomas Mathison's poem *The Goff*, written in 1743 says:

> The feathers harden and the leather swells;
> He crams and sweats, yet crams and urges more,
> Till scarce and turgid globe contains its store.

As noted in Chapter 2, the ball is made from three pieces of leather. Some ball historians say that the leather was boiled in water and alum to soften the hide. The alum supposedly also helped repel water when the ball was complete. While malleable, the leather pieces are shaped, and holes punctured to allow stitching with a curved needle and waxed thread easier. After stitching, the ball is turned the right way around, leaving the stitching inside the ball and a small hole by which boiled goose or duck feathers could be inserted into the ball. This task was intricate and only the most skilled could finish it well.

When nearly filled, the ballmaker would use a blunt tool, known as a brogue, which he placed on his chest to force more and more feathers into the ball. When complete, a final stitch was made to seal the feather ball. After drying, the ball would be painted and receive the maker's mark.

Allan Robertson marked all of his golf balls, fcathcrics (and gutties), simply with the imperious title of 'ALLAN', all letters uppercase. The golfing world knew, or would come to know, who ALLAN was. It also offers an insight into the internal confidence of this industrious working-class man.

That is also why the much-expanded Sandyhill building is now called Allan Villa. Ball-making was painstaking and time consuming, and therefore these golf balls were not cheap. There would be a variety of second-hand balls available, too, like what we see in the second-hand shops in St Andrews today. Trade in second-hand balls was a useful income stream for local children, who would hunt for them among the heavy whin that covered the fairway of what we know as the front nine, or delve in the Swilcan Burn, hoping to find a ball in decent shape that might earn a shilling. It is said that the boys would deliberately muddy the waters, so that golfers couldn't find their balls. Golf in Scotland was always a game for everyone, but there were definitely marked differences in standard.

An experienced ballmaker like Allan would aim to make around three balls a day. One of the very few competitors to Allan in the high-quality ball-making market was John Gourlay (1815–69) of Bruntsfield Links and Musselburgh. The price of a featherie was dependent upon the reputation of the maker. In the 1850s a featherie would likely cost around two shillings each, a price charged by the Gourlays. Allan charged 1*s.* 8*d.* for each ball (£1 per dozen), although that may have been a concessionary price to a regular customer or a bulk purchaser. Allan's shop and the expanding staff numbers are reputed to have produced, for the home market and export to the colonies, 1,021 balls in 1840, 1,392 in 1841 and 2,456 balls by 1844.

The song, *In Praise of the Gutta-Percha*, famous at its time and first sung during the autumn meeting at Innerleven Golf Club in 1848, gives us an idea of Allan's featheries:

> When Gourlay balls cost half-a-crown,
> And Allan's no' a farthing doun,
> The feck o's wad been harried soon
> In this era of taxation.

Remarkably, the featherie performed very well and could be hit reasonable distances. Having tried one, I would compare it to a balata feel on the putter.

However, as H. Thomas Peter wrote in *Reminiscences of Golf and Golfers* in 1890, 'Golf was rendered expensive in those days, not by the clubs, which were cheaper then than now, but by the balls. Their prime cost was high and their durability not great. On a wet day, for example, a ball soon became soaked, soft and flabby; so that a new one had to be used at every hole in a match of any importance. Or, on the other hand, a "top" by an iron in a bunker might cut it through. This I have frequently seen occur.'[17]

Balls with a loose seam would lead to showers of feathers. According to H. Thomas Peter, those that started with a 28 pounder could finish a wet day with a much heavier 40 pounder!

The longest drive recorded with a featherie golf ball was a mere 361 yards in 1836 by the Swiss golfer, Mr Samuel Messieux. A St Andrews resident and well-known practical joker, Messieux was a medal winner in 1825 and 1827. On the day, the fact that it was blowing a 'hooley' and the ground frozen hard could well be the reason for this anomaly.

The gutta-percha was an improvement on the featherie ball, with some modest performance advantages, not least because it was more durable. This will be taken up in later chapters, including Allan's storm-in-a-teacup row with Tom.

For now, in the 1830s, business was good and Allan's golf was getting better and better.

Twelve

THE KING

ALLAN's life of his twenties in the late 1830s was gradually improving. On 16 May 1837 he married his first wife, Helen Elliot, in St Andrews, with the service provided by Rev. Thomas Aitken. Helen was 21, having been born on 3 August 1815.[1]

According to local historian David Watkinson, Rev. Aitken was a 'minister of the United Secession Church in North Street. This was located where No. 52 (council flats) is now. It was built in 1826 and replaced in the 1850s by Hope Park Church (now St Mark's). What little is known of Aitken is to be found in T.T. Fordyce's history of Hope Park, published around 1994. Aitken came to St Andrews in 1829 and left in 1838, having fallen out with his congregation, and emigrated to America.' Fordyce's co-authors on the book were D.E.R. Watt and Betty Willsher.

The champion in golf from 1830 to 1835, as noted in the press, was Allan's father Davie Robertson. Young Allan, from the age of 15, would have seen his father being acclaimed as the best golfer in Scotland and therefore the world. When Davie was beaten by Tom Alexander in 1835, how did the teenager Allan feel to see his father lose? Did they plan a re-match? Sadly, it did not happen as Davie died the following year.

After Davie's demise, the Piries became the golfers to beat in St Andrews. In 1837, the day after his 22nd birthday, Allan partnered Sandy Pirie, his senior by 20 years. It was the old guard partnering with the new, a pattern Allan would himself repeat, first with Tom Morris and then with Andrew Strath when Tom left for Prestwick. St Andrews best, side by side.

It is only one line in this press clipping but it is Allan's first and so poignant. It said, 'On Thursday morning, the inputs were won by Sandy Pierie [sic] and Allan Robertson beating Tom Alexander, Marshall (David), Geddes (Thomas) ...'

How exciting was it for a young Allan to see his name in the press? The best players in St Andrews beating the exalted Tom Alexander, David Marshall and Tom Geddes – the crack players from Musselburgh. 'Inputs' is an old term that used to denote medal play. This would have been a good pay day for Allan, while the golf parlour was left to others to look after.

Please remember also that the shop then was not inundated with tourists like the shops, such as Auchterlonies, are today. There were only around 30 folks playing in an autumn meeting. Caddies loitered around Allan's hoping to get to carry clubs (no bag) for a golfer. There was no real worry about both locals and gentlemen playing to the same greens with one little pin. It was a much quieter, sedate affair in St Andrews at that time.

How moving it was that the first time Allan is mentioned, he is part of a team that defeats the very man who vanquished his father. They had beaten the reigning champion.

How much did Allan learn from Sandy? Was that typical stoical caddying for which Sandy was so renowned evident on the links? Sandy gave his clubs names like the fierce 'instruments of war'. This was something we know Allan did too.

Sandy took Allan under his wing. Together, they also set out links, such as those at Monifieth in 1845. Allan was learning from Sandy. This was the start of Allan creating course layouts, which we will look at in the Appendix, but it also sets a pattern, which Allan would replicate with Tom. Later generations of best-known golf architects like C.B. Macdonald would, in turn, spend time with Tom. Each generation learns from the one before it, and when we look at the combined influence of all those architects, who spread golf throughout the UK and then the world, it is astounding. Hundreds upon hundreds of courses worldwide are due to the guiding influence of a few great men.

When Allan won his doubles match with Pirie in 1837, was he counting the days until a grand match could be lined up? He was a mere 22-year-old youngster, a golfing maverick who had lived and breathed golf since he was first able to walk. Certainly, his golf would have been well known for the great Sandy Pirie to choose him as a partner. Sandy and his brother David were the crack golfers in St Andrews.

In 1838 Allan had a hole-in-one at the short eighth. The following year, he drove a ball 250 yards, which would be his longest drive and certainly a good 50 yards farther than the best players at the time. In October 1839 the *Perthshire Courier* reported that Allan won the inputs. Of records extant at time of publishing, this was his first recorded victory when playing for himself.

With the increasing number of golf matches pulling him away from business (although it could be argued that his inputs winning golf was a business), and with three other people to feed at home, Allan needed help in the shop.

Tom Morris – the apprentice ballmaker

One of the most historic partnerships in golf started in 1839, when Allan took on his cousin John Morris' teenage son. Tom was 18 years old when Allan employed him to help with the making of featherie balls in the golf parlour. Tom, by his admission, was drifting. He talked in interviews about how the plan had been for him to be a carpenter's apprentice. This would be in contrast to working like his father and grandfather, working the weave. His father John was also a letter carrier. They were a respectable, working-class family and both his father and grandfather were on the town guild, which was a committee of the representatives of the town's tradesfolk.

Speaking around New Year's Day in the 1880s,[2] reflecting on his youth and life, Tom said, 'An' it hadna been for gowff,' he said to the patron who greeted him in the customary form for the first day of the year, 'I'm no sure that at this day, sir, I wad hae been a leevin' man. I've had ma troubles an' ma trials, like the lave; an' whiles I thocht they wad hae clean wauved me, sae that to "lay me doun an' dee" as the song says – lookit about a' that was left in life for puir Tam. It was like as if ma vera sowle was a'thegither gane oot o' me. But there's naething like a ticht gude gowing mautch to soop yer brain clear o' that kin' o' thing; and wi' the help o' ma God an' o' gowff, I've aye gotten warsled through somehow or ither. The tae thing ta'en wi' the tither, I haena had an ill time o't. I dinna mind that iver I had an unpleasant word frae ony o' the many gentlemen I've played wi'. I've aye tried – as ma business was, sir – to mak' masel' pleesant to them; an' they've aye been awfu' pleesant to me. An' noo, sir, to end a long and maybe a silly crack – bein' maistly about masel' – ye'll just come wi' me, an' ye'll hae a glass o' gude brandy, and I'll have ma pint o' black strap, an' we'll drink a gude New Year to ane anither, an' the like to a' gude gowffers.'

Translation (by Dita Stanis-Traken, Chair of St Andrews Pilgrim Foundation):

'Had it not been for golf, I'm not sure that I would, sir, be alive today. I've had my troubles and my trials [difficulties] like the rest [everyone else], and for a while I thought they would leave me so completely enfeebled that I might just "lay down and die" (as the song says) and it looked like this was all that was left in life for poor Tom. It was as though my very soul had entirely left me … but there's nothing like a tight good golfing match to clear your brain of that kind of thing, and with the help of God and of golf I have always struggled through, somehow or other.

The two things taken with the other (i.e. life's difficulties juxtaposed with God and golf), I haven't had so bad a time of it. I cannot remember that I ever had an unpleasant word (ie. wasn't on the receiving end of poor manners) from any of the many gentlemen I've played with. I have always tried – as my business was, sir – to make myself pleasant to them, and they have always been awfully pleasant to me. And now sir, to end a long and perhaps silly story – being as it is mostly concerned with myself – you'll just come with me and you'll have a glass of good brandy, and I'll have my pint of black strap (light beer), and we'll drink a good New Year to one another, and likewise to all good golfers.'

It was caddie Sandy Herd, who suggested to Tom that he try Allan for work. It was probably the best advice Tom ever received.

How important to all of us and to golf is that seemingly inconsequential advice?

Tom freely admitted that it was golf that saved him and straightened him out at difficult times. By extension, it could be hypothesised that it was Allan who saved Tom and gave him something (and someone) to focus on and look up to.

For four years Tom worked with Allan as an apprentice ballmaker and for five more years after that. This wasn't Tom starting to work for a stranger. Age wise, they were only five years and ten months apart. They were first cousins once removed and, in all likelihood, they had been playing golf together for years by that stage and had already formed a bond.

In a 1907 interview covered by the *Lancashire Evening Post*, Tom said, 'During my lifetime I have seen three eras of golf balls: the feather, the gutta and the rubber-core. I ought to know about balls, for I was a maker of them in my youth, first in the workshop of my friend and partner in many a foursome, the famous Allan Robertson, and afterwards on my own account. When I first started, of course, it was with the feather balls, and as the art of making has gone completely out of existence, it may be interesting to briefly explain how they were made. The cover was in the form of a little bag or pouch of bull's hide, specially cured and prepared with alum, and into this we put as many feathers as we could; these little bags held a wonderful lot of feathers when tightly packed; then, when the cover would hold no more, we sewed up the opening, and the ball was complete.'

In an 1895 interview with H.S.C. Everard,[3] Tom said 'When I was seventeen or eighteen; though I'd played many years before that. Allan Robertson was giving me half-one when I was eighteen, but I soon knocked that off.'

In time, a half-one, or a shot every second hole, became a third. In Tom's own words, they were soon playing an equal par game. What an education it must have been on the links to see Allan play close at hand. Teenager Tom now had a stable job and someone to learn from. What a different world this would be compared to the one in which he had believed at times that he could have just laid down and died.

The two men were friends. In an interview with H.S.C. Everard and others, as above, Tom continually referred to his 'friend' Allan. It would be the dawn of an enduring friendship, which would hit a few guttie-shaped bumps on the road but ultimately lead to one of the most powerful foursomes teams in the game's history. Allan and Tom were a tough team to beat, akin to other historically successful foursomes partnerships; at times they seemed almost to know what the other was thinking on the links.

Allan Robertson (image courtesy of The Royal and Ancient Golf Club of St Andrews).

A sketch of St Andrews links in 1846, with Allan's house, Sandyhill, at the top of the links, and the Union Club across the road. The photograph below also shows Sandyhill, *c.*1840s.

This map art by Joe McConnell places the 1820 John Wood map over the links today. Notice the difference between the shoreline of Davie's links and our own. From this it appears that the original first green, called Old Golf Hole on the map (circled in red), was approximately in the garden of St Andrews Golf Company or behind where the Auchterlonies shop stands, on Golf Place. The final hole was moved to pretty much where it is today, although that spot would have been both closing green and the tee for the first.

The garden where Tom and Allan planted bushes was built over in the 1860s. This photograph shows the first Golf Hotel. If you look carefully, you can still see traces of the signage. The arched windows also remain.

A ball made by Tom Alexander, Champion Golfer, *c.*1837 (image courtesy of Christies).

Undoubtedly one of the best golfers in his day and an elder playing partner to a youthful Allan, Sandy Pirie was frequently called upon when a challenge match came in from Musselburgh. He also set out the holes at Monifieth in 1845, with Allan assisting. This painting of Pirie is by Charles Lees (1847).

ABOVE Note how near the closing green is to the edge of the shore. If the ball went on to the sand, it was simply played as it lay. With steep banks, it was described as a deep hazard, akin to Shell bunker.

LEFT Sir Hugh Lyon Playfair sitting beside a photo of the new town hall, which was just one of the many improvements to St Andrews.

BELOW Playfair's stunning home is now St Leonards School, one of Scotland's finest, that teaches both primary and secondary pupils.

Members of the Union Parlour: 1. Ogilvie of Inchinnan; 2. Campbell of Saddell; 3. Unknown; 4. James Ogilvy Fairlie of Coodham; 5. Campbell of Schichallion; 6. Colonel Hunter; 7. Professor Ferrier; 8. Sir Hugh Lyon Playfair; 9. Unknown; 10. Edward Ellice MP; 11. Samuel Messieux; 12. Unknown; 13. Unknown; 14. Maidstone Smith; 15. Unknown; 16. Dr Adamson; 17. Unknown; 18. Mr Jackson; 19. Grant of Kilgraston.

A pre-sketch of Allan Robertson by Charles Lees, *c.*1844.

These grips were also of Allan's era and akin to the ones he used.

Allan kept a scrapbook of *Chambers's Journal* articles that covered such topics as Christmas traditions, golf and the economy.

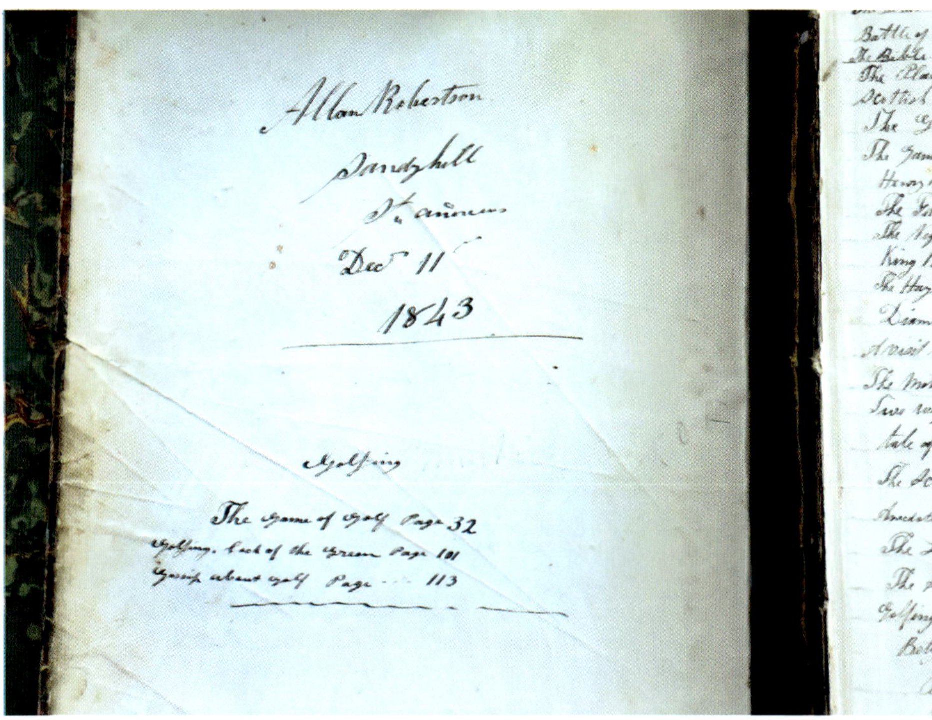

The clubhouse for the Union Club opened in 1854. It would be a further 20 years or so before the amalgamation with The Royal and Ancient Golf Club of St Andrews started to be discussed.

Allan Robertson's featherie ball, allegedly used by him to hole the links in 87 strokes in 1842 (image courtesy of The Royal and Ancient Golf Club of St Andrews).

Allan wearing his famous little red coat in a photograph by Thomas Rodger. It is said that in a grand match, wearing his red coat, and with serious money backers, he was unbeatable.

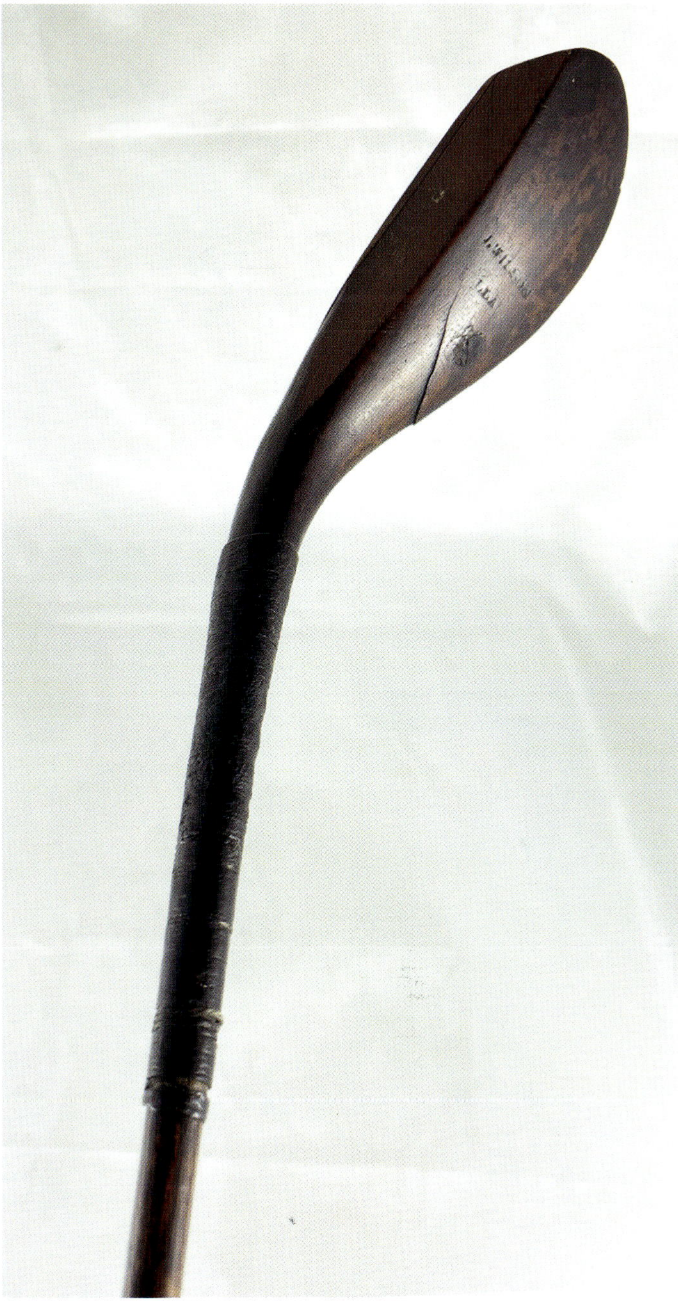

Allan's beautiful driver, made by James Wilson, has been cracked and repaired crudely with a screw. This was typical of the time and must have kept the club playable (image courtesy of The Royal and Ancient Golf Club of St Andrews and Pehr Thermaenius).

This photograph, taken in the early 1840s by David Octavius Hill and Robert Adamson, shows Allan second from left, with Tom Morris beside him. Charles Lees used this image to create some of the poses in his painting *The Golfers*.

Allan and Tom v. Dunnie and Park Snr in a staged photo by Thomas Rodger. There were three images taken that day. They were the giants of the game in the mid-1850s. From left to right: Jamie Wilson, Bob 'The Rook' Andrews, Willie Dunn (driving), Willie Park Snr, Allan Robertson, Daw Anderson, Tom Morris, and Bob Kirk.

In later life, Tom Morris frequently talked about Allan in cordial tones. This photograph is very similar to the painting by Sir George Reid PRSA (1841–1913) that is in the Big Room of The Royal and Ancient Golf Club of St Andrews. It was unveiled to 'great acclaim' at the spring meeting of 1903, according to Peter Crabtree and Dr David Malcolm in the opening pages of *Tom Morris of St Andrews, The Colossus of Golf, 1821–1908*.

The Principal's Nose was both a pair of tricky nostril-like bunkers and a porch of the University Principal that jutted out onto South Street. Playfair soon cut off the latter.

Allan Robertson and Tom Morris immortalised on Cope's Golfer's Cigarette Cards, made in 1900. As card expert John Morton noted in conversation, these cards are the only ones to denote the Cathedral in the background. None of the others in the collection have such. By 1900, Allan was long gone and Tom Morris was approaching his 80th year. He was golf's Grand Old Man. These are two of the most sought after of Cope's Golfer's Cigarette Cards.

Willie Dunn Snr (1821–78) was a hugely talented and likeable golfer. Born in the same year as Tom Morris, they sometimes played as partners and issued challenges in the years after Allan's demise. That the St Andrews, Prestwick and Musselburgh crack golfers played together in one team shows us that the rivalry between the great golfing capitals is perhaps overstated.

Allan's grand obelisk reflected his popularity and skill. It is just off the path, as you walk towards the graves of Tom and Tommy Morris, and a mere 20 feet away from those of Jamie Anderson, The Dempsters, George Bruce and Willie Auchterlonie.

David Robertson (1825–64) was one of the first pioneers of golf in Australia, where many of his relations reside to this day (image courtesy of Matthew Smith).

In 2025 a plaque was unveiled on Allan's house beside St Andrews links by the chair of the St Andrews Pilgrim Foundation, Dita Stanis Traken. Jack Nicklaus honoured Allan by making him the 2026 Memorial Tournament honouree. Allan is today celebrated as one of the finest who ever held a golf club – a king of the sport.

You cannot help but get the sense that Tom looked up to Allan and that, in return, Allan deemed Tom likely to be the most talented golfer of the next generation. Together they were almost unbeatable. Although they lost the odd Musselburgh battle, they were never beaten in the overall war. We shall look at this relationship closely in the next chapter.

For now, in the late 1830s, 18-year-old Tom and around 23-year-old Allan were working in the shop making high-quality featheries, while Tom was working on becoming as good as Allan on the links. He certainly would want rid of those charitable shots.

The path to the king

It was 1840. Within ten years, Charles Dickens, having finished *Oliver Twist* in 1839, would pen among others *A Christmas Carol* (1843) and *David Copperfield* (1849). For Allan, it would indeed be the best of times and the worst of times. From his mid-20s in the 1840s, Allan would enjoy great highs and success but also much personal pain. Allan's star was rising, but first he had to defeat the man who vanquished his father Davie, Musselburgh's Tom Alexander, the champion golfer for five years.

In 1840 Tom Alexander married his second wife, Hannah Galvin, and then, at the October meeting, came Allan's opportunity. Sadly, there are no detailed reports of that day in St Andrews. There are no poignant moments of drama when 'The Doctor' came to Allan's rescue against the champion golfer, Tom. However, H. Thomas Peter noted that he remembered Allan beating Tom Alexander in St Andrews: 'Tom Alexander was not a great driver, but capital at the short game. He had great confidence, and, though considerably behind, backed himself freely, and, indeed, with bluster. But Allan beat him'.[4] It is recorded that Allan beat him by four holes over 36 holes, scoring a 95 during one round.

In a similar twist to Davie not having the chance to avenge his defeat, Tom Alexander too would die within a year of losing the title, aged only around 38. It was a colossal loss for golf for Alexander to die so young. Would he have gone into battle again with Allan and perhaps the title of champion return to Musselburgh? With Willie

Dunn coming through and Willie Park thereafter, the story of golf could have been so very different. Musselburgh could have been the home of champions, and certainly had their fair share of Open winning players.

Alas, poor Tom Alexander never had the chance.

Reports of Tom's demise say that he was out and about in February 1841 at Musselburgh and Leith, and then returned to his home, Golf Cottage (Golf House) near Musselburgh Links. For the next three days, he was in some pain but still seen outside. According to the *Perthshire Advertiser* of 18 February, when the local Dr Moir was called on the Sunday morning Tom was found to be 'moribund, and almost pulseless, with his eyes sunk, and his features collapsed; but he continued occasionally to talk with his usual nerve and cheerfulness. In the course of the day, he seemed to revive a little, but suddenly expired at midnight. His death was found, on examination, to have proceeded from the bursting of an aneurismal sac in the aorto [sic] or great artery of the heart. In all branches of golf, Tom was proficient, and the turf is not soon likely to see his equal again. *Sic transit gloria.*'

Another later edition added, 'He was equally proficient in the making of balls and in the use of them, those of his own manufacture bringing generally one shilling a-head [per ball], above the average price, and there is no doubt that when genuine they were worth the additional price.'

In 2023 retired surgeon and golf historian David Hamilton said, 'No doubt that it was a fatal rupture of a balloon-like weakness in the main aorta in the chest, just after that big artery left the heart. There was a small leak first caused by usual aging process.'

The *Perthshire Courier* of 18 February 1841 said, 'As an artiste, in the laborious handicraft of ball-making, he held the highest rank, as a golfer, for nearly twenty years he had no equal in skillful execution of the nicer subtleties of the game; and his unexpected decease (from aneurism of the heart) has occasioned a blank in the golfing community not likely soon to be filled up.'

After five years, it was the end of the old champion's era.

St Andrews' Davie Robertson had won and then lost the title of champion to Tom Alexander. These two were the giants of the game and they dominated the sport for ten years, if not more. One would expect portraits to remember our champions, but alas there are none. Photography was just about to take off in St Andrews, and we are fortunate to have images of Allan, Willie (Dunnie) and Jamie Dunn, and Tom Morris, but for the preceding generation, we only have Carnegie's poetry and the glowing reports of those who witnessed them on the links.

Unfortunately, Davie's headstone may also have been demolished when Playfair added his neat pathways to the St Andrews Cathedral cemetery.

Nonetheless, for a time, the heavy betting was on our game's heroes Davie Robertson and Tom Alexander.

Willie Dunn (Dunnie) of Musselburgh

Allan restored the title to the Robertsons and St Andrews. Although Allan was *de facto* champion golfer and the betting favourite, he still had to prove himself.

His new rival from Musselburgh was Willie Dunn Snr (19 August 1821–14 February 1878), nicknamed Dunnie. Born almost six years after Allan (and the same year as Tom Morris), there would be matches in 1843 (two), 1844 (two) and 1846 (one) to settle the question once and for all, who was the champion golfer of Scotland, and thereby the world.

Dunnie and his twin brother Jamie were born in 1821 in Musselburgh to plasterer Thomas and Janet Hodgson. The twins had an older sister Catherine, born in 1817, and an older brother Thomas, born in 1819.

Dunnie served as an apprentice ballmaker to John Gourlay. He would move to Blackheath in 1851 to become the keeper of the green there before returning to Scotland in 1864 to work for the Thistle Golf Club at Leith Links. While at Blackheath, he created the guttie ball-making and club-making business, Dunn of London, and was also in demand to set out links.

Married to Rebecca Duncan, they would have two sons, Tom and Willie Dunn Jnr and one daughter, Catherine. The sons would all be ball and club makers and Catherine's four sons would become professionals in America. Willie Jnr would do well in the US Open in 1895, coming second, and designed and redesigned links, including

Shinnecock Hills. The Dunn family's influence and spreading of the game globally, including in France, is quite remarkable. There are numerous articles in *Through the Green* archives covering this remarkable golfing family.

In the Open, Dunnie would have three top-10 finishes, the best being in 1861, but, despite being a favourite, he never won. It should also be noted that his best era was the 1840s. The Open did not start until 1860, by which time he was in Blackheath.

It was said that Dunnie had a huge following and was extremely popular. Covering the Open in 1866 the *Fifeshire Journal* said, 'It is a pity that Willie Dunn's success does not bear any proportion to his personal popularity, else he would be crowned perpetual champion. He can afford, however, to console himself by resting on his past laurels as one of the most accomplished professionals who ever swung a club.'

In the 1868 Open, *The Sportsman* on 26 September said, 'The veteran [47-year-old] Willie Dunn was most unfortunate, but as is his wont, took his ill luck with a good humour eminently characteristic of one of the most successful golfers, in his palmy days, who ever lifted a club. It must be so far consolatory to him that in the person of his son the family reputation is still likely to shine.' Palmy days here means the days when he would be earning good money and funds would pass into his hand.

Aged only 56, Dunnie died on 14 February 1878 at 8 Millhill in Musselburgh, which was the same street and a stone's throw from champion Tom Alexander's house at number 39. Dunnie had epithelioma of lip, which is a painful form of skin cancer. He was buried in Inveresk parish church graveyard in Musselburgh. His wife Rebecca was the witness.

In his time he was a crowd favourite and, outwith his matches with Allan, he was one of the finest exponents of the game and certainly one whom the boys of Musselburgh were likely to try to emulate.

The grand matches

At this stage in our story, Willie was only in his twenties and, after Tom Alexander's demise, the crack Musselburgh golfer. Dr McPherson captured him as that player when he wrote,

> Of the brilliancy of Willie Dunn's style no language can give any adequate description. He stood more straight up than Tom (with his half-bunker) or even Allan (with his long flat clubs). His driving was simply unrivalled, without any forcedness to detract from its sweetness.
>
> Tennant of the Glen so admired Dunn's style that he was determined to get his flat clubs (long for his short stature) made more upright. Old M'Ewan looked at the little man and the long club, and told him that this was impossible. 'What?' asked Tennant, 'can't I have my clubs altered and made more upright like Dunn's?' 'It wu'd be oncommonly oonconvenient,' answered the pawky club-maker. 'Why?' 'Because if ye played wi' them mair upright, without cuttin' the handles, ye wu'd need to play aye on a stool.'[5]

In *Reminiscences of Golf and Golfers*, H. Thomas Peter said, 'Willie had a particularly graceful style. He was taller than the other three (Tom, Allan and Jamie Dunn), very supple, and swung the club with great agility and power'.[6]

He surely was a wonderful player and intimidating too with his long driving. When it came down to it, to find the champion golfer, there had to be a match between Willie and Allan. More than that, there needed to be a series of matches – one that could show that, by winning again and again, one of them was the undisputed champion.

From 1840 to 1843 Allan played many singles and foursomes matches, which only added to his fame, having beaten the champion golfer Tom Alexander. It was not only on the St Andrews turf that he was reigning supreme. On Montrose links he beat Mr James Calvert Jnr in 1842, shooting 99 to Calvert's 102, a feat he repeated in St Andrews the following year. Between 1842 and 1859, he would knock 20 shots off his scores. He also beat Tom Morris 2 and 1 in 1842 with a score of 93 in St Andrews.

In October 1842 the *Chambers Journal* referred to 27-year-old Allan saying, 'There is a ballmaker, Allan Robertson by name, who besides having the highest character for his wares is reputed to be the best player at St Andrews and consequently in Scotland – I may as well add, in the world. This is an eminence which golfers must needs admire and, in the little world of the links, men of estate and title will be heard speaking of worthy Allan as if he were a kind of King amongst them.'

He was in many St Andrean's eyes already king and had reigned happily since 1840.

Such was the belief in Allan's skill that at times he was forbidden to play. After the R&A meeting in 1842, where Tom Morris won with a 92 and his father John came second, the *Fifeshire Journal* noted that Allan was 'prohibited by his brethren from competing for these stakes on account of his superior play, it being their impression that they would have no chance in any contest in which Allan took part.'

Allan was indeed golfing royalty, but Musselburgh believed their best should be king.

The order of the two matches in 1843 vary but the winner is always the same – Allan. We shall follow the clippings in Allan's scrapbook.

If Willie wanted to take Allan's title that Allan had taken from Tom Alexander, Willie would need to beat him on Allan's own turf.

A grand match was duly arranged in St Andrews for July, and would be a huge spectacle. It would be for 36 holes a day for ten consecutive days, except Sundays. That was an eye-watering 360 holes. The money on the match was incredible for the time, equivalent to 20 years of salary for a keeper of the green. This is Jack versus Arnie or Tiger versus Phil. Before the Open era began, this would be the battle of the kings.

A clipping in Allan's scrapbook adds, 'The playing was masterly on both sides – Allan taking one round at 87 strokes. The manner of Dunnie's playing is particularly elegant. Allan is a little light-made lad; Dunnie is the head taller and of a lithe make. Allan plays with ease – Dunnie with grace; Allan's play seems the result of long practice – Dunnie's as if he was to the manner born; Allan often exceeds your expectation – Dunnie never falls below it; Allan's play is conventional; Dunnie's is original; Allan's teestroke goes its length in a plain common sense-like fashion – Dunnie's ball seems endued with mind; Allan is an artiste – Dunnie is a genius.'

Poet Carnegie is said to have sung,

> Ten days they were fighting, ten days, ten days.
> Complete at their weapons, always, always,

With club, cleek, and putter my Muse cannot utter,
A millionth part of their praise, their praise!

It was a remarkable, exhausting match and for the players more of an endurance test. Allan certainly tired after the first three rounds.

Although Allan came out triumphant, it was not a walk-over. There was just enough of a glimpse of Dunn beating Allan to whet the betting appetite. It was a bookie's dream.

In September 1843 what would become The St Andrews Golf Club was created by 11 golfers, including George Morris, Tom's brother. It was a club for the artisans, the working classes, and was called The St Andrews Mechanics' Golf Club. Mr David Todd, a painter, from 13 South Street, was proposed as captain by the cabinetmaker, Mr A. Carstairs. The name changed to The St Andrews Golf Club in 1851. In time, this would be home of 12 Open champions and is still today a players' club, with hundreds of members below five handicap.

The darkest hour

Amid the highs of beating Willie Dunn and thereby cementing his hold on the title as the champion golfer, Allan suffered terribly when his wife Helen died on 2 September 1843. This must have been a real blow to Allan. She was only 28. We do not know if it was during child labour or an underlying health condition, but for a relatively young Allan it can only have been a true hardship.

On 11 December 1843 Allan starts his scrapbook of *Chambers Journals*. Inside there is a poem called 'Death' and it is heavily pencilled.[7] The second verse says,

Joys are like summer flowers,
And soon the blossoms of their beauty fall;
Clouds gloom o'er both: brief are of both the hours-
Death ends them all.

For Allan and Dunnie, a re-match was lined up, according to press reports, for October. This time it would be over a gentler 36 holes. If Dunnie thought he was getting to know the St Andrews links and might get the edge on Allan, he was mistaken. Dunnie lost 8 and 7. Allan shot 88 in the second round, ten shots lower than his winning score against Calvert the previous year.

Allan would face James Calvert again and Robert Lindsay before the year end, beating them both in St Andrews, but, in truth, the year ends on a low ebb.

Upstairs at Sandyhill was used for tenants, such as one listed as David Campbell. After Helen's demise, the house would be filled with only Allan's mother and brother. That too would be all too fleeting as, on 15 March 1844, Allan's mother Ann died, aged 56.

Suddenly, it was just the two boys, Allan and David.

Allan's world was changing dramatically. Alongside the loss of his loved ones, the whole townscape of St Andrews was being remodelled by Playfair. In December 1843 the populace was introduced to the characters Scrooge and Tiny Tim, and the joys of Christmas-time festivities with family and friends. If Allan had read it, he would have seen parallels of his own life and Scrooge's, who felt alone in the world when loved ones passed.

Playfair became town provost in November 1842 and gave its inhabitants an injection of belief in their future, but for Allan it must have been a bitter-sweet time. Even young David, who was noted in the 1841 census as a clothing merchant, aged 16, would soon be leaving for Australia and be one of the pioneers of golf there.

Amid all of this, the gambling gentlemen were likely to have been pushing for another match with the game's finest, Allan and Dunnie. I doubt either player had much of an appetite to repeat the 360-hole marathon.

The third match came together in May 1844, this time consisting of three matches of 36 holes on three different courses: St Andrews, then the neutral links of North Berwick, and finally Dunn's home links of Musselburgh.

With his wife and mother gone and Allan at a low ebb, Dunnie must have thought his chances of beating the king were considerable. If ever there was an advantageous time to go up against Allan, surely this was it.

Thirteen

GOLDEN REIGN

THE Factory Act in 1844 offered a new beginning of sorts for the working classes. Adults were only allowed to work up to 12 hours a day. Children aged six to thirteen were permitted to be working for six hours a day. Although the idea of a child labour such as this fills us with horror today, it was a sign that attitudes towards child labour and the conditions people had to deal with were slowly changing. Public health in urban areas was poor, with dirt, unclean water and lack of sanitation resulting in periodic outbreaks of deadly cholera in particular.

It was also the year when Robert Chambers Snr, writer, publisher and St Andrews inhabitant, with a grand residence on the Scores as we now know it, would pen the groundbreaking *Vestiges of the Natural History of Creation*. It set out the theory of natural evolution for the first time, which would have been shocking to a Christian world that believed we were all made in God's image. It was so controversial at the time that it was published anonymously. It is said to have influenced Charles Darwin in his writings, especially the 1859 *On the Origins of the Species*, which was published to a society slightly more open to the controversial theory.

It was against this backdrop that the third great match with Dunnie loomed. This time the money men wanted the match to be played over three links. Not the exhaustive 360-hole challenge, but 36 holes on St Andrews, neutral North Berwick and then Musselburgh – a mere 108 holes. With Allan having beaten Dunnie comprehensively in their last gathering in St Andrews alone, it was deemed only fair to have the match over those three links. James Ogilvie Fairlie backed Allan and John Campbell of Glensaddell backed Dunnie.

Fairlie was one of the most important figures in golf.[1] Not only was he a regular playing partner of Tom Morris, but in 1851 he invited Tom to move to Prestwick to re-design the pre-existing Prestwick links. Fairlie was also the driving force behind the creation of the Open with the Earl of Eglinton. It gives an idea of the prestige of this grand game that Fairlie was a backer in the match, which was for £100 a side, and such was his belief in Allan, that he backed him.

John Campbell of Glensaddell was a familiar face in St Andrews and owned the house by the cathedral, called The Priory.[2] He was well known for his betting, and it would not be the first time that Campbell bet against Allan.

It is not hard to understand that Allan probably would have had the wind knocked out of him by the loss of his wife and his mother. It would be a huge loss for any of us. We tend to see images from the 1800s in sepia, non-emotional tones, but the reality would have very different and all too human. Many would have locked themselves away with their grief or lost their appetite. When four times champion Tommy Morris' wife died during childbirth at 1 Albany Place, St Andrews in September 1875, he was said to have gone into a dark stupor for weeks. He eventually came back to golf but broke down on the links when he and his father Tom were five holes ahead. His match against Arthur Molesworth from Westward Ho! in December that year was played in woeful conditions, with snow covering the links and their golf balls painted red so that they could be found. Weeks after the match, Tommy died in his sleep at 6 Pilmour Links, due to an aneurysm in his lung. This is very likely, according to David Hamilton, to be a result of tuberculosis. Tommy shared accommodation with Davie Strath and almost all the Straths were taken by tuberculosis. Tommy effectively bled to death in his sleep. Such a tragedy for one to die so young – a mere 24 years old.

Allan would not get to see any of that. Tommy was born in 1851 and, to Allan, he would be Tom's keen little boy who lived with Tom in Prestwick and only occasionally came back to St Andrews.

Allan and Dunnie's third match came barely a month or so after his mother's passing in May 1844. This match was a new format, but the money-men had a huge hit on their hands with the best players.

Also, by spreading the game across more courses, they could potentially make even better returns.

The first game was in St Andrews, which, despite all the difficulties in his life, Allan won. The second game at neutral links North Berwick was a half. It all boiled down to the final match in Musselburgh, where Dunn was strong favourite.

The *Perthshire Courier* of 6 June 1844 carried the story of the match. 'Saturday week, the last of a series of interesting matches at this ancient and national game, between Allan Robertson of St. Andrews [sic], and William Dunn of Musselburgh, was played over the Links at Musselburgh. The match was made some time since, and besides a stake of £100 a side, for which the parties were backed by their respective friends, the result was understood to settle the title to the championship between the players on the north and south sides of the Forth. It was arranged to play on three different golfing grounds, the winner on the majority to be victor. The first match came off at St Andrews, and was gained in gallant style by Robertson. The second was played at North Berwick, when the parties came off equal. The concluding match at Musselburgh excited great interest and drew together a large field of sporting gentlemen and others. At starting, the betting on the result of the day's play was even, but after some fluctuations Robertson shot ahead by three holes, when 2 to 1 was freely betted upon him. Dunn afterwards pulled up, catched [sic] his opponent, and finally won by two holes, thus tying this great match, and entitling each party to draw his stakes.'

With one hole to go at Musselburgh, Allan was one down and lost the closing hole to be beaten by two holes. What a close game over 36 holes in Musselburgh – a course that would be relatively unfamiliar to Allan. The phrase, 'entitling each party to draw his stakes' simply means that the backers can get their initial stakes money back.

Although Dunn had managed to tie a match with Allan, the champion, he had not been able to wrest the title from him. Allan was still the reigning champion golfer.

A new game was quickly arranged for early July by the same backers for the same stakes. It must have seemed to backers, caddies and golfers alike that the wind was in Dunn's sails, especially as the first game of the fourth match was arranged to be in Musselburgh. This was only fair after the first two matches had been in St Andrews, and the third had begun in St Andrews, tipping the scales to the king each time.

The fourth match

The fourth contest was in 1844, at a time when provost Playfair continued with his work in protecting the links.[3]

The 'Town Council employed David Steele several times from 1844 to 1849 to widen the area by building a brick wall on the boundary alongside the 1st hole and filling in the gap with rubbish, remnants from building constructions and soil, then seeding the area. Over time, the stones would be taken away and, with more dumping, the wall would disappear altogether, increasing the links further. The wall was known as "Mr Steele's barricade" or the "sea walls". In 1854, Steele was paid again for "levelling down a large quantity of rubbish that is laid down from time to time by carters in the West Sands and forming a breakwater with stones got out of the rubbish and sowing it with grass seed". He was paid a princely sum.' This would be the start of the creation of the flat land that the first hole today is played on, but to Allan it would have been mere piles of building rubble on the beach to protect the first and 18th holes.

Something unexpected also happened on 10 June 1844. Allan got married at St Cuthbert's church to 31-year-old Jane Kyles from Leith, who was born on 23 January 1813. Her father David, who had died prior to the marriage ceremony, had worked as a sailor and married Jane's mother, Jane Duff, on 24 August 1812. Jane's grandfather Alex was a witness to that wedding, and his profession was noted as a cutler, an artisan who made domestic knives, scissors, razors and other sharp instruments.

How did Allan meet someone from Leith? Was it while golfing in that area of Scotland? Did it happen on his last foray to Musselburgh to play Dunnie?

Allan was not yet even 30. Jane was a little older, at 31. It had been a horrible year, but finally there was some joy to behold.

Those were not the only wedding bells to ring that month. Eleven days later, on 21 June 1844, 23-year-old Tom Morris was married by Reverend Dr Willie Ferrie to Agnes 'Nancy' Bayne in St Mary's

Kirk, Market Street, St Andrews.[4] As well as being the minister at Kilconquhar, Reverend Dr Willie Ferrie was also chaplain to the Society of St Andrews Golfers, The Royal and Ancient Golf Club of St Andrews, and held the chair of Civil History at St Andrews University.

Nancy, as she was known, whose father worked as a coachman in Kincaple, worked for Captain Broughton at 91 North Street as a domestic servant, which was only yards from where Tom lived on North Street. It must be said though that Tulloch places Broughton at 2 Playfair Terrace. Nonetheless, the two houses are in close proximity on the same street.

It is this captain who bet against Tom on the links during a friendly game. Tom got into trouble in the High Hole bunker and the good captain said that he should just lift his ball out. Tom joked that he thought he could hole it. The captain said he would give Tom £50 if he did. Sometimes when golfing you can just see a putt and no matter what you do, the ball is going into the hole. Such was that moment with Tom as he duly holed it. It was said that the captain came into the parlour the next day with £50 for Tom – this was ten years of salary, but Tom refused it saying the bet had been made in jest. This gives us an insight into the character of Tom, as there are not many who would have refused such a lifeline.

With Allan aged 28 and Tom just turned 23, these young men continued making featherie balls in Allan's house. How they must have laughed in the golf parlour as the two crack golfers in St Andrews were married around the same time. It was certainly a good cause for celebrations after months of grieving.

The fourth match with Dunn was lined up for late June. The first game, on Tuesday 25 June, was over 36 holes on Musselburgh.

James Ogilvie Fairlie and John Campbell of Glensaddell were the backers once again, for £100 each, and there was heavy betting recorded on both sides, both on the match and on the individual games throughout.

It is a little romantic, but it is tempting to think that Allan got a spring in his step once more. He certainly had broken the run of bad news and the sense that all his loved ones were gone. On the links, everything lay in the balance. Would he lose to Dunnie and let the title return to Musselburgh, or would he maintain his grip on the crown?

The final round of the grand matches would be played in St Andrews on Wednesday 3 July. Allan was the bookies' favourite. That did not stop many betting on Dunnie. The lure of good odds may have won over some wishful punters.

The match was reported to be followed by huge crowds. Press clippings lamented that they did not have the result at time of printing – such was the interest in the game.

Dunnie did not let his backers down and won convincingly by 3 and 2 on his home turf. At North Berwick on Thursday 27 June, which was deemed the neutral ground, Allan took the honours, winning by the same margin, 3 and 2. It all came down to the final match, but, with Allan on his own ground, he quickly took any element of doubt away and won with a dominant 6 and 5 victory.

Allan was the undisputed king of golfers.

He and Dunnie had played four times, and Allan had won three matches and halved the other. Hundreds of pounds had been won and lost in the games, but there was little doubt who the reigning king in 1844 was.

A king without clubs is still king

There was one more game that year, against Captain David Campbell, in St Andrews when Allan won with an 87 and that was not considered of any merit, but it is probably worth noting here that if Campbell had won, he would not have been thought of as the champion golfer, merely that he had beaten the champion golfer. Allan would still retain the title.

There is a match reported in Baxter's *Golf In Perth.*[5] Allan and his frequent partner on that links, Sir John Muir Mackenzie, were beaten by James Condie and Tom Patton of Glenalmond. At the dinner afterwards, Condie, who was known for his sense of humour, teased Allan of having a lot of good clubs but 'a bad player behind them'. A match was arranged for the next day for the opponent's clubs, so if you won a hole, you took away one of the other's clubs. By the last hole, Allan had only his driver and putter left, but alas he lost the hole and his driver. They played one extra hole and Condie won that too.

'Surely you'll let me take one club home!' pleaded Allan.

'No,' replied Condie, and Allan's clubs remained in Perth, at least for one night.

This also did not make Condie champion. To earn the title, there had to be backers and a formal match, when it was known to all that the title was being played for. This was at best a fun (albeit not for Allan) bounce game.

This issue would come up again when Willie Park Snr challenged Allan, and also when Prestwick challenged Allan, placing Tom in a somewhat awkward position.

One further point of note from Baxter's anecdote is that Allan, the professional working-class golfer, dined with Sir John and others after the match. It shows that golf was back then, and is still today, the great leveller. There is no them and us; there is only us – the golfers.

How did Allan feel with those educated gentlemen, when he had barely schooled? His collection of *Chambers Journals* would have helped keep him informed of global matters. With his own business, and clippings pasted into his scrapbook that heralded the power of self-determinism, he may well have been perfectly able to hold his own in the dinner conversations with the Perth gentlemen golfers.

There is one other minor match worth mentioning, played in September 1844 and reported in the *Fife Herald*. At the autumn meeting in Innerleven after the medal, Allan, the noted champion of Scotland, and Tom played against each other. This is the first time a match between the two friends is mentioned in the press. Unfortunately, the report does not provide the result, but does praise their skills. When the challenge to Allan's crown comes from Prestwick, this match is not included in either side's evidence of their respective cases. I doubt there was anything unusual in the result, or the report would have included it, but it certainly was not a match where anything like the title of champion golfer was on the line.

Changing times

After two hard years, 1845 was quieter, as both he and Tom settled into their new marriages. Allan never had any children. There has never been a noted reason for this. Tom's wife, on the other hand, was pregnant around September that year. Their first son, Thomas, was born on 15 May 1946 and christened by Rev. Dr Haldane, on 1 June.

With Jane Kyles now a new Robertson in the Sandyhill residence, Allan's two-storey house doubled up as a golf parlour to meet the golfers' needs and as a boarding house upstairs.

Tulloch shared his fond memories of Allan, saying, 'How well I remember him, his wife, and his house and shop – his going in and out of the Club-House, his matches on the links. After all these years I see quite vividly that … bewhiskered, humorous and smiling face.'

Quoting from an H.B. Farnie article in 1859 following Allan's death, Tulloch said, 'Who that has once seen the Champion Golfer can ever forget him? Let us try to help the picture which every player will oft in fancy draw. Our scene is the St Andrews Links [sic] on a genial summer's day. Allan's house crowns the summit of the slope; down towards the sea – the blue, beautiful sea – lies the white Club-House, with its gravelled terrace. It is not yet eleven, that great hour of cause on the Links. Groups of caddies are prowling about; a clash and rattle of clubs are heard as you pass the club-makers' shops [possibly Philp, Forgan or Wilson]. One or two golfers are idly putting at the starting hole with their burnished cleeks, trying some impossible putt, which, if they had only done but yesterday, would have put a very different finish on a certain match. Suddenly a golfer appears at the Club-House door; he looks about for somebody who is evidently lacking. "Where's Allan?" – the cry is repeated by telegraphic cadies [sic] right up to the champion's little garden. A minute lapses, and down comes the champion in hot haste to the Club-House. He is, as you will recollect, oh golfer, not of much stature, compact, rather robust indeed, with a short stoop, and short-necked. His face is pleasant to look at – rather Hibernian, indeed, with its habitual drollery, which has almost given the stalward golfer one or two dimples. He is dressed, as you must remember, in his favourite red jacket. And carries a cleek (a pet weapon) in his hand. But now the match is arranged. Allan has evidently got to nurse an elementary golfer. It is a foursome; Allan and his protégé against two rather good hands. Remark how pleasant the little man is; no miss of his partner causes a shade to habitual good nature, and, ten to one, when the match comes in from their round, but the new player swears by Allan, and gives his adhesion to golf for once and all'.[6]

Although a fictional narrative, this was Allan's daily life.

Times were slowly changing for the better. It was in 1845 that the Poor Law (Scotland) came into effect, imposing on towns a duty to take care of the poor. Under the new law, parochial boards assumed responsibility at a more local level. Parishes in Scotland could create poorhouses and raise taxes locally to cover the cost. Locals could apply for some money to support them, known as outdoor relief, and could appeal if refused, unlike the similar but different workhouse system in England. Poorhouses were to house local paupers, and this was called indoor relief. If children went to the poorhouses, they would receive a little classroom education but would also be expected to work several hours a day.

Parishes could join together to create one large poorhouse. In Scotland, in the poorhouses, health care was free, although there were strict terms of admission. This explains why three-time Open champion Jamie Anderson went to the poorhouse in Thornton, shortly before his stroke and death in 1905. Dickens famously railed against the harsh conditions in English workhouses, but the Scottish poorhouses did not garner such a bad reputation, and did act as both sanctuary and hospital for the poor and destitute.

This Poor Law system would last until 1911. Due to historic abuses within the system, it was replaced by the National Insurance Act. In 1946 came the National Health Service Act, which was the start of today's National Health Service and this was followed by the National Assistance Act 1948.

In this ever-evolving Scotland, Sir Hugh Lyon Playfair was continuing with his vision to transform St Andrews. In March 1846, he wrote an open letter to the citizens of the town,

> LADIES AND GENTLEMEN,
>
> You have done much in contributing to the Improvement of your City, but something more remains to be effected. The Market Street should be supplied with FOOT PAVEMENT on both sides, from Union Street to Bell Street. It is for you to determine whether this shall ever be accomplished. The City of St Andrews, through the Town Council, have this day subscribed £50 towards the object, in their anxiety to increase the comfort

of the people, and the beauty of the city. If other Public Bodies will imitate this example, and contribute according to their ability, this great purpose may be accomplished. The Ladies, by a SALE OF WORK, might do much. The Householders in Market Street will, of course, lend their utmost aid, and it is expected that other Inhabitants will assist them, as they did when called on to subscribe for the South Street Pavement.

The amount required is £252. If this sum is subscribed the work will be commenced – or not subscribed the amount guaranteed by the City will be withdrawn, and the Market Street will remain in its present deplorable condition, much to the discomfort, may we venture to say, much also to the discredit of the Inhabitants of our venerable City and its Vicinity.

ST ANDREWS, 14th March 1846

He was successful.

To show the town's gratitude for their endeavours, a portrait of Playfair was painted by Sir J. Watson Gordon, from Edinburgh. This was unveiled on 10 April 1847 at a public breakfast in the town hall, which was attended by many of the subscribers to his efforts in resurrecting the town and the painting itself. Attendees also included Sir David Baird, Allan's acquaintance, playing partner and occasional match referee, and, from the university, the Very Rev. Principal Robert Haldane.

The final Dunn match

The fifth and final Robertson–Dunn match was set for April 1846. Once again, huge bets were placed and crowds followed each game. The format was game at Musselburgh, and then St Andrews. If the score was tied at that stage, they would toss a tuppenny bit to see what the next course would be.

They played on Musselburgh on Wednesday 8 April 1846. The following Tuesday, the *Fife Herald* reported, 'These celebrated players are backed by gentlemen interested in the game, and bets to a considerable amount depend upon the result … Yesterday Dunn, after eleven holes were played, came in seven holes a-head of his opponent, with five holes to play. The eleven holes taken by Dunn at 53, and by Robertson at 64 strokes.' It is assumed that the match was over 36 holes. Either way, this 7 and 5 result was a resounding victory for Dunn. Remarkable play against the king.

The second game came a week later on Wednesday 15 April in St Andrews in woeful weather. Allan nevertheless won 5 and 3. Press reports talked about the huge following and the large sums again being bet on the outcome.

With the match tied at one apiece, it left the outstanding issue of the deciding course. At the outset they were merely going to toss a coin for it, but the *Edinburgh Evening Post* on Wednesday 22 April 1846 reported, 'The terms of the match were, that if each won a game, they should toss up for a choice of the green for the third game. It now, however, appeared clearly, that by following out this, the toss of a halfpenny, and not golf-playing, must decide the match. The parties, therefore, with consent of their backers, agreed to play a deciding game on a neutral green; and that was Innerleven, namely Dubbyside [sic], was fixed upon, where the match will be decided on Wednesday first. The result continues to excite the highest interest amongst golf-players, and numerous bets are depending upon it.'

This neutral ground is where Allan had played the year before, so it was not completely unfamiliar to him. The Innerleven links, known as Dubbieside, no longer exists. It was founded on 29 February 1820, 'when 15 golfers drew up their first rules. Initially, the name of the club seems to have been Innerleven Golfing Society, referring to the old name of Innerleven. Originally, members were required to wear a jacket of King Charles tartan when competing for any prize. By 1866, the name had become Innerleven Golf Club. The first captain was R. Black. They played on Dubbieside, which was on the south west of the River Leven, and does not exist any more. Dubbieside initially consisted of five holes but was soon extended to nine, though play for the silver medal was over 15 holes. The members also drew up 12 rules of play.'[7]

As mentioned earlier, it was at Innerleven in 1848 that the song, *In Praise of Gutta-Percha*, was sung at the spring meeting.

On 29 April 1846 Allan and Dunn set out on what would be their last match for the title of champion golfer. The *Fifeshire Journal* carried a full report on 30 April.

> The last game of this match, the best of three, was played on Wednesday on Dubbieside Links, Leven, between Allan Robertson of St Andrews and Dunn of Musselburgh, when the former gained by 6 holes, and 4 to play; thus winning two out of three games. A great number of gentlemen interested in the game of golf, beside those interested in the match, and who had taken bets upon it, were present from both sides of the Forth.
>
> As we have before stated, Dunn won the first game at Musselburgh, by 7 holes, and 5 to play; and Robertson the second at St Andrews, by 5 holes, and 3 to play. It may be worth mentioning that in all the 3 games of this match they were won by two holes each more than there were to play. – Allan has now been successful in all his matches against Dunn, viz. – 4 great ones, where large stakes and heavy bets were depending, besides also several smaller ones. We were the first, we believe, that lauded Dunn's elegant style of playing, and at one time scarcely hazarded a doubt respecting his superiority; but now as these two men have been pitted against each other on almost every links in Scotland, and the result having been uniformly in one direction, we can have no hesitation in asserting, what everyone conversant in this very difficult games admits, that Allan has proved himself the best golfer extant; and we are glad to add that we understand a number of gentlemen have made arrangements to present him with a handsome medal as champion, and well he deserves it, for he is not only the best golf-player, but is also a capital ball-maker, and withal a quiet, hard-boned, wirey little fellow, as always cool as a cucumber, and may be depended upon as doing his best at all times.

The king had won again.

It was indisputable and beyond a shadow of doubt that Allan was the best player in the world. How they must have heralded their king in St Andrews on his return. It had been a long few years with much pain, but by the end Allan was the champion golfer of Scotland. By the end of the year, he played one more match against Captain Broughton, winning with a score of 95 in St Andrews.

Tom's father John Morris died, aged 68, on 22 December 1846, and was buried on Christmas Eve. How traumatic for Tom that he would find his own son dead on Christmas morning 1875. Each year, when the Christmas bells were ringing at Holy Trinity, his thoughts must not have been too far away from lost loved ones.

Throughout the late 1840s and 1850s, Allan played many single matches, which he largely won with ease, but there would be no more grand matches. He had had his fill of those, but it would be quite wrong to say that his match-playing career ended after the final match in 1846. There would be no more challenges to Allan from Musselburgh for a good few years, but each time he came up against the best golfers of the day, he won.

In September 1848 he played against the best of the best – Dunnie and Tom Morris – over two rounds at Innerleven links. Allan beat them both, shooting 80 against Tom Morris' 87 and Dunnie's 91. At 33 years of age, he was untouchable.

In his whole playing record, noted in the papers from 1840 to 1859, outside of his matches with Tom, there was only one occasion, against his friend Sir Thomas Moncrieffe, he would lose, having given him six shots, so Sir Thomas' 91 beat Allan's 88. That is why Allan was feted as golfing royalty – he was virtually unbeatable on the St Andrews links.

Around 1854 Allan founded the Juvenile Club in St Andrews and provided prizes for their two competitions every year. The winner with the lowest score won the silver medal which, to commemorate the 1815 Battle of Waterloo, was named the Duke of Wellington Medal. James Kirk won it in 1854, then a 13-year-old Jamie Anderson, who went around the links in 111 strokes, won it in 1855. It is wonderful to think of Jamie's first medal being presented by Allan – a hero and inspiration to many young golfers.

It was in that same year that Allan headed to the Balcomie links in Crail, which was a short, rudimentary course back then. The Crail Golfing Society tended to use the Sauchope links more. Today, the Sauchope links is a mobile homes site, but you can still see the land of Crail's first links before they moved to Balcomie, which Tom would then add to. David A. Lindesay from Wormiston presented the Crail Golfing Society with a medal in 1830, which was open to all golfers.

In 1855 two rounds were played over the Balcomie links. Allan won by seven shots, shooting a 55. Such was the nature of the infrequently played links that Mr John Bowman walked with the first group to show them where the holes were. There were no GPS devices and no yardage markers, just pure golf and judging distances by sight.

The event was reported in the press, 'We may mention a fact which will likely take not a few by surprise, for as many great matches as Allan Robertson has played he never before competed for a medal; this then is his maiden medal! The ball with which the match was gained was presented to Miss Crombie, Kilminning Farm, Crail, by whom no doubt it will be kept as a trophy ... The party returned to Crail where an excellent dinner was prepared for them by Mr Dickson of the Golf Inn. Allan was called to the chair and Mr Patrick, captain of the Leven Club, acted as croupier. The mirth and jollity was kept up to nine o'clock fully, when they had to break up, each to seek their own home. It is pleasant to see such harmony of sentiment existing between the St Andrews and Leven Clubs, each meeting seems to cement it, and why not? New life seems to have sprung up within the St Andrews Golf Club; it has lately suffered much from emigration, but now its ranks are rapidly swelling.'

Interestingly, it was Allan's first medal and it came at a time when challenges were coming in against him loudly.

His period of dominance had begun way back in 1840, when he beat Tom Alexander, and for the next 19 years it was truly a glorious golden reign. He was simply the best player in the world, renowned as the king of golf, and rarely beaten on his own links.

Allan had one final flourish that demonstrated his dominance, but we will save that for our closing chapter. Allan, in the late 1840s, was the irrefutable champion. It wouldn't be long before Prestwick had their eyes on his crown and one new extraordinary young golfer from Musselburgh would be issuing challenges in the press, but what is also coming is nothing short of a seismic shift in the game. Allan would perceive this evolution of the game as a threat to his family history. Hundreds of years of Robertson ball-making heritage would end on his watch, and he was far from happy about it. It would sever his working relationship with Tom Morris and lead to Allan acting less than rationally in forlorn attempts to stem the tide.

It was now the era of the guttie ball.

Fourteen

DAWN OF GUTTA PERCHA

IN 1847, but more so the following year, the gutta-percha golf ball, also known as the 'guttie', ushered in a new era of golf, offering a cheaper ball that went as far, if not a little farther than the featherie.

The origins story of how gutta-percha came to the UK is subject to many claims. On 15 November 1845, an article in the *Railway Bell and London Advertiser* said, 'A very curious and interesting substance has lately been introduced into this country from India, by Dr Montgomerie, of the India Company's service … In many respects it strongly resembles caoutchouc or india-rubber, and is, like that substance, obtained from a tree, from which it exudes at certain seasons of the year; the substance has, we believe, not yet been subjected to a critical chemical examination, such as its extraordinary properties would warrant … At the temperature of the atmosphere, it is hard and almost entirely unelastic, but at the temperatures of boiling water, it softens becomes pulpy, and may readily be moulded into any required form, which it retains perfectly when cooled.'

The *Manchester Examiner* on 28 September 1847 offered more details on the Scot who brought gutta-percha to our shores. Dr William Montgomerie (1797–1856) was a Scottish military doctor for the East India Company. In 1843 he was assistant surgeon to the presidency at Singapore. The *Examiner* reported,

> We had yesterday an opportunity of inspecting, at the office of Messrs. Samuel Statham and Co., Brown Street, who are the agents for the London patentees, a great variety of useful and ornamental articles formed of gutta-percha.
>
> Scarcely had caoutchouc [rubber] been shown to be capable

> of being applied to a hundred purposes never dreamt of by our forefathers ... was fortunately discovered by Dr Montgomerie in Singapore; and although this discovery was only made in 1843, the 'applicative genius' of Englishmen has already devised several hundreds of uses to which it may be with great advantage devoted. From an article in *Chambers' Journal* of June last, we learn that the tree from which gutta-percha is procured, is found in abundance in the island of Singapore, in some dense forests of the Malayan peninsula, and in parts of, if not all over, the island of Borneo. The tree is very large, and the gutta-percha, which is contained in the sap, exudes from the lacerated surfaces in the form of a milky juice. On exposure to air, the juice quickly coagulates.

After discussing its rock-hard consistency below 50 degrees, the article continued:

> A ball one inch in diameter was completely softened by boiling for ten minutes and it regained its hardness entirely in half-an-hour. It is an important fact, that these processes may be alternated any number of times without injury to the material ... The patentees, of whom Messrs. Statham & Co., are the Manchester agents, have been at work on this novel material for about two years; but it is only about twelve months since they introduced their manufactures into this town [Manchester]. Surgical instruments, whips, golf and cricket balls, cart covers, cord, cloth, in fact, about 150 distinct articles have already been patented.

Thus, we know for sure that golf balls were being manufactured by 1847, that they were impervious to water, and that they could be put in boiling water, softened and re-shaped without degradation.

The 'concrete juice', as it was called, was nothing short of a scientific revolution, used on everything from the soles of boots to the cornices for grand houses. Although locals in Malaya had been using it for handles for some time and it had already been used in Europe, it was unknown in the UK and Montgomerie is credited for its introduction. In fact, he first came upon it in 1822 during his first tour to Singapore from 1819 to 1826, but could not get a sample of it until he returned 20 years later.

From 1843 onwards there were many experiments by the various scientific societies, including in Dublin. In 1845 Dr Montgomerie was awarded the gold medal by the Society of Arts (which became Royal in 1847) for his introduction of gutta-percha to the British people, and gave lectures on it.

In the same year invitations were sent out by The Gutta-Percha Company, based at East India Chambers and created by Charles Hancock and Henry Bewley, for applications for patents.

In the article, *History of The Introduction of Gutta-Percha Into England*, written in the Caledonian US Club Edinburgh on 26 October 1846 and published in *The Mechanics' Magazine* of October 1846 and also in the *Pharmaceutical Journal* of February 1847, Dr Montgomerie said,

> Having in many late numbers of the *Mechanics' Magazine*, seen frequent notices of the patents taken out for the application of the new substance, gutta-percha, to various purposes, and its extensive usefulness becoming daily more apparent, it has occurred to me as I was the person through whom the substance was first brought to the notice of the public, a few observations from me regarding it, might be valued by many of the readers of your highly popular and useful journal.
>
> I may not arrogate myself to the actual discovery of gutta-percha; for, although previous to my introduction of it, it was quite unknown to Europeans, still it was known to a few of the inhabitants of certain localities of the Malayan forests; but even the most native inhabitants of the towns and villages near those localities, to whom I showed it, did not know what it was, and it was likely to have remained unknown … as far as I could ascertain, [it was] only occasionally used to make handles for parangs [wood choppers].
>
> As far back as 1822, when I was in Singapore as assistant-surgeon to the residency, I had obtained the name of it, while making inquiries relative to *caoutchouc*, of which there are several varieties and some fine specimens were brought to me,

> particularly one called *gutta-girek* and I was told of another variety called *gutta-percha*, and sometimes *gutta-tuban* … but none of it was brought to me at the time, and I lost sight of it, having returned to the Bengal presidency ... At Singapore in 1842, I … observed in the hands of a Malayan woodsman the handle of a parang, made of the substance which appeared quite new to me. My curiosity was excited, and on enquiry I found it was made of the *gutta-percha*, and that it could be molded into any form by dipping it in boiling water until it became heated throughout, when it became plastic as clay, and when cold regained, unchanged, its original hardness and rigidity.

Dr Montgomerie goes on to say to whom he spoke to, his experiments with the concrete oil and his recommendation for moderate farming of it, but finishes with, 'Allow me, now, to correct an erroneous mode of pronouncing the name, which I have observed used by many gentlemen with whom I have conversed on the subject. The word is a pure Malayan one, *gutta*, meaning gum or concrete juice of a plant, and *percha*, the particular tree from which it is procured. The *ch* is not pronounced hard like a *k*, but like the *ch* is the English name of the fish *perch* … if one of them were to enquire of a Malay for *gutta-perka*, he would be told the thing was unknown, when perhaps plenty of *gutta-percha* might be available. As an application of it of minor importance certainly, but one very general usefulness, it has been suggested to me that it would be found useful in stopping decayed teeth.' Today gutta-percha is still in use in dentistry for root canal work.

So this provides a theory about who brought gutta-percha to the UK, but who was it who developed the idea to use the material for the manufacture of golf balls?

Looking through the British Library archives shows that Charles Hancock took out numerous patents – nos 11032 (1844), 11208 (1846), 11575 (1847), 11874 (1847), and 12143 (1848) – including for gutta-percha corks and *balls*, although the documents do not mention golf specifically. It was all-encompassing patent that set out that gutta-percha could be moulded into balls. It was the use of moulds that he patented in 1846, so that the gutta-percha would achieve any shape desired. In that year Thomas Hancock patented the use of magnesium oxide to stop the gutta-percha from sticking to the mould. In July 1848 Charles took out a patent for the improved apparatus and machinery for making balls. It was the industrial era, and it was likely very apparent to Allan, who could by all accounts only make three featheries a day (or nine if all the staff were engaged), that if guttie balls succeeded, it would not be long before factories could be making golf balls.[1]

This, therefore, was something of an industrial revolution for golf balls. The demand for the art and skill of the featherie ball maker was coming to an end.

Guttie balls

There are a few tales of how the guttie came to the attention of golfers. *ScottishGolfHistory.org* relates: 'The traditional story of their creation relates that, in 1843, Robert Adams Paterson, a divinity student at St Andrews, received a package from Singapore of the God Vishnu packed in gutta-percha, which is dried gum resin from guttiferous trees especially of the Malaysian sapodilla tree. It was not uncommon to make things from this gutta-percha packaging, and Paterson tried heating and moulding it to make golf balls. His early experiments were not successful. After he graduated and emigrated to America, where he died in 1904, his brother worked on to create an acceptable prototype, which he stamped "Paterson's Composite – Patented" golf ball. The patent only existed in his imagination, as none was ever patented.'[2]

H.T. Peter's *Golfing Reminiscences by An Old Hand* fills in the detail about how he came across the ball.

> I believe I may with justice claim the credit of having first brought them to the golfing world, and this at the spring meeting of the Innerleven Club in 1848. The previous month, when on my way home from a two years' stay in France (where, by the way, golf was unknown), I chanced to see in the window of a shop down a stair in St David Street, Edinburgh, a placard bearing the words – 'New golf balls for sale'.
>
> I found them different from anything I had seen before; and was told by the shopman they were 'guttie-perkies!'

> 'Guttie-perkie! What's that?' I asked, for I had never heard of it.
>
> 'It's a kin' o' gum like india-rubber.'
>
> 'What kind of balls does it make?'
>
> 'I ken naething aboot that – best try yin yersel!'
>
> I bought one for a shilling. It was not painted, but covered with a sort of 'size'. Which, after some practice with my brother James, who was a good golfer, I saw reason to scrape it off … I then determined to try it upon the Innerleven Links, against David Wallace … a golfer who always beat me … The upshot of our day's play was that I beat him by thirteen holes – a thrashing, he said, such as he had never had in his life.

This mispronunciation of *gutta-perkies* gives more credence to Peter's tale after what we have learned from Montgomerie. It was obviously commonly mispronounced.

Peter also noted the first time both Allan Robertson and Old Tom Morris saw this new ball.

> I won the silver medal [against Wallace] in April 1848; and it was at this meeting I showed the new ball to Allan Robertson and Tom Morris. It was the first time either had ever seen a 'gutta'. I told them of its great superiority to 'feathers', and that the days of the latter were numbered; but Allan would not believe it. At my request, he tried the new ball; but instead of hitting it fairly, struck it hard on the top in a way to make it duck (which by the way, no one could do more deftly than Allan).
>
> 'Bah!' he said, 'that thing'll never flee!'
>
> I, however, struck it fairly, and, to Allan's disgust, away it flew beautifully!
>
> For a long time Allan persisted in this opposition to 'guttas'. He has often told me, when I wanted him as partner in a foursome, that he would not play unless I used feather balls – condition to which I, of course, acceded.[3]

In Tulloch's book, Charles Anderson remembers a similar incident. Anderson 'was following a match of Allan's when he told old Bob

Kirk to tee one for a trial shot. Allan took a full swing, deliberately topped the ball, and remarked in pretended disgust, "Ach, it winna flee awa'." "Fell, d—n ye," cried out old Bob, "nae ba' cud flee when it's tappit."'[4]

The details of John Campbell of Saddell's claim to having brought the guttie to the attention of Scottish golfers was covered by James Stewart Lindsay, when he said in *Golfiana Miscellanea*, 'In the spring of 1848, Mr Campbell of Saddell (we believe), brought a few experimental gutta-percha balls from London to St Andrews. They were not first-rate, to be sure; were not hammered, and flew heavily. Still, the material was unquestionably good and adaptable, and consternation on every face, Allan's included … It is even related that Allan would gladly buy up all the gutta-percha balls found in the whins, etc., and actually attempt to destroy the obnoxious interlopers with fire!'[5]

Referring to their playability, H.T. Peter in his *Reminiscences* said that gutties' only disadvantage was in the wind and that they could not hold their course. As an aside, he also admitted that he, with his brother, took to adding lead to the ball and that all his victories were due to leaden balls. This is the very thing that Hugh Philp complained about, with golfers coming to his shop with broken hickories due to the lead added to guttie balls.

A good golfer could hit a featherie between 170 and 200 yards, and the guttie was not particularly longer. However, when the ball was put into play and hit with an iron club, chips to the smooth surface occurred and surprisingly the ball performed aerodynamically better. The producers of gutta-percha balls began adding hammer lines to the sphere, which elevated its performance above the featherie and it was much cheaper to buy. The days of the featherie golf ball were numbered.

In 1891 Dr McPherson offered a little detail on the types of guttie available, when discussing how the balls evolved from the initial smooth shaped to the time-consuming hammering of lines into the ball, 'The "Silverton" ball is made of a better kind of gutta-percha; and the "Eclipse" a composition of less density, is more elastic for driving but less accurate in putting. Balls of different weights, according to the clubs used, varying generally from 27 to 30 grams; but the 28 is the favourite of strong players. Even the uninitiated eye recognised a striking difference between the 26 of Allan and the 30 of Robert

Clark – almost as marked as the difference between the toy-driver of the former and the putter of the latter.'[6]

Allan's reaction

Tom Morris was slowly starting to make a name for himself, with his name appearing in clippings. In February 1846 Tom was labelled the de facto no.2 golfer. When noted as playing the links in the dark as a fun experiment, he shot 108, which may have beaten some of the gentlemen golfers at their best.

He had worked with Allan since 1839 and together they whiled away the hours stuffing and stitching featheries.

Tom would be there observing Allan as he sorted out the odds for games. Tom was there when Allan carried out any links' remedial work or to set out holes in Carnoustie. It was a thorough education. As Allan became champion golfer in Tom's first year of employment, Tom watched as the former thereafter defended again and again his title in the grand matches with Dunnie. Allan's well-known phrase was 'Tak' it easy', but Tom would have known what he really felt when the doors were shut.

As the days ebbed towards another grand match, Tom saw how Allan prepared. Watching Allan do it so successfully must have helped when Tom himself faced the same pressures against Willie Park Snr. These were very public spectacles now.

Throughout the 1840s Tom was there at key moments in Allan's life. When Allan's wife died, Tom would have been a witness to Allan's grief. When Allan married again, Tom married Nancy weeks later. Each step of the way, they were there for each other, which makes what happens next over the guttie ball very awkward.

With the game naturally evolving, why was Allan so upset? It is worth considering that featherie ball-making was part of his family traditions going back centuries and that he had continued that heritage and made a living from being a recognised, excellent ballmaker. It was not an easy task, but those who excelled in the art of the craft would have seen their livelihoods flashing in front of their eyes. Allan also was an employer. Lang Willie and Tom Morris were both his relations and staff, so he may have felt that additional pressure.

When the guttie came along, therefore, it is not surprising that we find Allan less than enthusiastic. Generally speaking, Allan was considered a popular, congenial, mild-mannered individual, but when it came to the gutta-percha ball, uncharacteristically, Allan was prone to otherwise unseen outbursts of temper and disdain. His easy-going manner and coolness of character were nowhere to be seen.

Unquestionably Allan perceived the new ball as a threat to his livelihood and those who worked for him. To him the gutta-percha was, at the very least, a menace to generations of business. All that rich heritage – and make no mistake, he was evidently proud to be another Robertson ballmaker – was all about to end on his watch. It was also the death knell for the ball with which he had become champion golfer and had truly mastered.

There is something intriguing too, that Allan, who was the king, did not take the Prestwick role in 1851. Was he even offered it? How big a coup would it have been for Prestwick to have Allan as their new keeper of the green? He certainly had an acquaintance with James Ogilvy Fairlie for him to be his backer in the matches against Dunnie. In the context of family bereavements and threats to his business, Allan's repeated caution and hesitancy to change is surely understandable. Not only had be lost his father, mother and first wife Helen, but his brother David had emigrated and was noted in 1849 in *Bell's Life*, Sydney, as being a golfing pioneer in Australia. Instead, it was Tom – in 1851 – who headed to Prestwick, leaving Allan to fight for his business. With everyone having left or leaving, bar his new wife Jane, the golf parlour business would be all he had.

The fear of being a pauper king would not have sat well. That is why his reaction was so much more extreme than mere anger over a ball: it was about his heritage, his family and his business and, consequently, born of fear of an uncertain future.

James Balfour stated in his book *Reminiscences of Golf* on St Andrews that in 1844, four years before the gutta-percha came on the scene in any great numbers, Allan's kitchen factory was producing 2,456 featherie balls. This would have generated a handsome revenue for that time. In addition, producing a featherie golf ball involved far more skill than the new guttie ball. Allan was one of the few making the featherie golf ball well, which gave him a semi-monopoly in St Andrews.

What Allan did not realise at the time was that the cheaper and easier to make guttie would attract overwhelming numbers of new golfers into the game. A cheaper game, combined with the advent of the railway across the Forth Bridge and the new railway line into St Andrews, would create an unprecedented boom in golf.

The lower price of the new ball would lead to much lower profit per ball, but this was more than offset by the higher volume of sales: Allan's economic model adapted but was far from destroyed. Far from compromising his heritage, it would enrich it and offer a prosperous future.

The demise of the featherie golf ball took about three years after the gutta-percha became freely available in 1848. Fellow ballmaker John Gourlay, who always claimed that Sir Thomas Moncrieffe (Allan's frequent playing partner) brought the ball to him from London, is said to have adapted to the changes with ease, in sharp contrast to Allan. Gourlay's business accounts show the sharp decline of featherie sales to Douglas McEwan, clubmaker at Bruntsfield Links and Musselburgh. David Malcolm and Peter Crabtree, in their book *Tom Morris of St Andrews, The Colossus of Golf*, state that those sales to McEwan had dropped by 75 per cent in 1847 and were zero in both 1850 and 1851.[7]

In time all the established featherie golf ballmakers, such as Dunnie, Gourlay, Tom and even Allan Robertson himself, switched to making guttie golf balls. Allan came to realise that he could make around a dozen gutties in the time it took to make one featherie.

Nevertheless, the gutta-percha was not common knowledge everywhere in 1847 and 1848. As Rev. T.D. Miller observed in the *History of the Royal Perth Golfing Society*, it was not until 1850 that the guttie made its way north of Fife and East Lothian, 'In 1850, a notable member of the Aberdeen Club, Mr Duthie, of the firm of Footdee shippers and shipbuilders, received by one of their frigates, a present from the Far East of a handsome ewer and basin moulded in gutta-percha, and being both an expert engineer and golfer, fashioned a golf ball mould and converted the domestic utensils into the first guttas seen upon the northern links of Aberdeen sands'.[8]

A brief falling out

With Allan as the undisputed king of golf, and Tom gaining his own reputation as a crack golfer, Allan, in 1848, was at the stage in his life of despising the guttie balls, burning them and hoping that they would not last. His business was looking like it could fail.

This was the stark backdrop to Tom's 1848 game with John Campbell of Saddell, which ended Allan and Tom's partnership. Three holes from home, Old Tom's last featherie ball burst. Tom told the rest of the story in Tulloch's biography, 'Allan couldna abide the sight of the new ball at first. One day I was out playing with Mr Campbell of Saddell, and I got stint of balls. Mr Campbell gave me a gutta to try. Coming in, we met Allan, and somebody told him that I was playin' a grand game with one of the new balls. Allan said nothing at the time, but I saw he didna like it, and when we met in the shop we had some words about it; and this led to our parting company, and I took to making balls on my ain account.'[9]

Allan would have seen this as an act of treachery. After everything he had done for Tom, how could he play with the unmentionable ball? What was Tom to do? He could hardly just walk off the course: both he and Allan were too cognisant of golf etiquette even to consider that as an option. Also, Tom may have felt like he would have been quite rude to refuse Campbell.

When Tom was interviewed in later life, he repeatedly talked of 'my friend Allan'. With Tom around 27, having spent nine years or so with Allan, it was perhaps time to set up on his own. He immediately took over a small, white, shed-like building at what today is 15 The Links and started to sell clubs and balls.

Yes, he had a good education from Allan, but with an open mindset about guttie balls and about other subjects, such as ladies' golf, it seems that it would have been only a matter of time before Tom forged his own way. Remember, neither Tom Morris nor Allan were from the very lowest classes. Their parents were letter carriers and business owners, so therefore had a brighter outlook than the average working-class workers and socially a world apart from the often drunken caddies.

It was the end of a business relationship. That is all. It certainly wasn't the end of their golfing partnership.

The little contretemps blew over very quickly. In September 1848 they shared a carriage ride to Innerleven, where H. Thomas Peter was a member, to play around the time of the autumn meeting. Allan was against Dunnie and Tom in a strokeplay event. He beat Tom by 7 strokes and Dunnie by 11, still using his trusted featherlie.

Allan re-affirmed his dominance of the game, and they all moved on. Maybe it was because they were second cousins? Maybe they were simply just very good friends? Whatever the case, their golfing partnership went from strength to strength, and they became unbeatable.

Fifteen

THE INVINCIBLES

It was 1849 in St Andrews. Provost Playfair was continuing his revolution and fulfilling his vision for the town. St Andrews was not only undergoing a grand physical renaissance; it was also having a moral upgrade. In December Playfair posted all around the town new rules for the people of new St Andrews, covering the discarding of rubbish; the cleaning of slaughterhouses; fish-curers and the storage of dung on streets; the supplying of liquor to under 14s; the regulation of second-hand goods tradesfolk; the naming of lodgers in guest houses; the removal of turf from the Scores and the links; the riding horseback on public walks; and the imprisonment of parents for unruly children if they could not afford to pay their fines.

As a token of the town's gratitude for his acceptance of provostship for the third time, two lamps with the city arms painted on one side were placed on each side of Playfair's entrance gates at St Leonards. These were paid for by local donations.

THE LAMPS OF HONOUR AT ST. LEONARD'S GATE.
A New Year compliment to the Provost for 1849
By the Author of 'The Major'.

A novel Theme the Muse selects at length,
Stretching her pinions doubtful of her strength.
'Rise Honest Muse and sing,' in verse elate,
'The Lamps of Honour' at St.Leonard's Gate.
In bright and pleasing colours there we view
The City Arms, and eke the Provost's too;
Type of the pleasant amicable mood

'Twixt Folk leagued only for the Public Good.
Long may these lamps in rival beauty stand.
And coloured splendours dart on ev'ry hand;
Through many a Lustrum destined to proclaim
St. Andrew's Gratitude – its Provost's Fame.
Hail Ancient City! once 'Of Steeples' named,
But now for Comfort as for Learning famed;
For health and social pleasures thine the meed,
'Mong Britain's Cities northward of the Tweed.
Happy St. Andrews! without row or storm,
To reap each real advantage of Reform!
Long may thy patriots with ready zeal,
Their Cash contribute for the Public Weal.
May feuds political, sectarian strife,
Ne'er vex the tranquil current of their life;
And not a trace of rivalry be seen,
Save friendly contests on the Golfing Green.
Here's to ye, Provost! may it prove your Fate
To wield the Civic Sceptre long and late.
Still may St. Leonard's Lamps of Honour show
Your Popularity with high and low.
And may a lustre brighter far than theirs,
Illume your lengthened path exempt from cares.
Diogenes, in Athens, searched each street
With lamp in hand – an honest man to meet;
St. Andrews hails an honest man in you,
And lights you up not with One Lamp but Two.

Amid these times of great change golf continued apace, attracting the best players, and matches that were arranged by the bookmakers and betting men. The records of Allan and Tom's matches are not complete, for not every match was recorded. Games with not much riding on them, including friendlies or those without money at stake, were usually recorded only if they were worthy of comment. What we do know is that Allan and Tom's four grand matches definitely were detailed in the press and books of the time, and their record was incredible.

To say they were never beaten is not quite true, but in terms of these four grand matches, the title 'The Invincibles' is well deserved.

The first foursomes grand match was against the Dunn twins, Willie and Jamie, in July 1849. The match was over three courses, with 36 holes on each links, for £400, which was a colossal sum in the 19th century. The first was set for Musselburgh, then St Andrews, and finally at the neutral links of North Berwick. This exciting match would be between the pairing of champion golfer Allan and Tom, whose star was now on the rise, and the famed Dunn twins. This was as exciting as it could get.

It should be said that it was highly unlikely that Allan and Tom would have been using a guttie for this match. By all accounts from that time, it was not until the early 1850s that Allan relented and started to use the guttie. He would also insist on his playing partners using the featherie ball too.

On Thursday 5 July 1849 the *Caledonian Mercury* gave the details of the first match: 'Yesterday, the first of three games, on different greens, was played on Musselburgh Links, between four of the best golf players in Scotland, and of course in the world – namely, Wm. and James Dunn, of Musselburgh, and Allan Robertson and Morris, of St Andrew's [sic], all golf ball makers. Thirty-six holes was the game but the Dunns beat their opponents by thirteen holes a-head, and twelve to play. The next game comes off, we believe, next week at St Andrew's, where if Robertson and Morris should win on their ground, the deciding match will be played at North Berwick. Besides the stake, we understand that considerable bets are depending on the result.'

Interestingly, they do not appear to have known Tom's full name. At this stage of his life, he was the new crack golfer. Also worth noting is that beyond the £400 bet there were a multitude of other bets placed.

This was the biggest drubbing of Allan's life and no doubt a painful pill to swallow. Matches in Musselburgh were always a losing game, be it Allan or his father, but never to this extent. With Allan being the captain of the team, he may have endured the brunt of the blame.

The *Dundee Advertiser* on Friday 13 July picked up the story of the second match. 'The second match between the Messrs Dunn of Musselburgh, and Messrs Allan Robertson and T. Morris, of St Andrews, came off on Wednesday, on St Andrews course. The first match was played on Musselburgh course, and the Dunns were winners by 13 holes, with 12 holes to play. On Wednesday however, the St Andrews men won by 3 holes, with 2 holes to play. The play was very fine on both sides. The first round was done by the St Andrews men in 96 strokes, and by Dunns in 94. In the second round, two holes were left unplayed, the match having been decided at the sixteenth hole; but, allowing the two to have been played at a fair number of strokes, say 11 – the St Andrews men would have holed the round in 91 strokes, and the Dunns in 94. The third and deciding match is to be played at North Berwick, which is neutral ground to both parties. The stakes played for are for £200 a side, and there are other sums by private parties depending on the issue. This is perhaps one of the best matches ever played at our great national game. We believe no such four players could be pitted against one another in the world. It has created great interest in the golfing world. On Wednesday, about three hundred admirers of the game accompanied the players round the course, but the most perfect order was preserved, and not the slightest interruption occurred to affect the play.'

What once had been a quiet, serene game had started to grow in the public eye, increasing the throng of spectators. For 300 people to be following the game was quite unprecedented, if one considers that spring and autumn meetings of the Royal and Ancient Club were garnishing a fraction of that. It was also the first time that the issue of crowd management was raised. How far removed from the boisterous match between Tom and Willie Park's at Musselburgh, which was so bad that Tom had to walk off into Mrs Forman's and refused to continue.

It points to the excitement that the four golfers created.

Allan was not playing well, and he knew it. The burden of the match weighed upon him. It is to these moments that we should look when wondering why he was a lot less prolific in the 1850s compared to his champion winning ways of the previous decade. He would sit in silence for hours pondering on the match, labouring on what was to come.

The final game of the match was at North Berwick, which had seven holes. So, they played five rounds and one more hole. H. Thomas Peter, captures that day beautifully:

The finest foursome of all that I remember was that between Allan and Tom against the two Dunns in the final at North Berwick. It created intense interest in the golfing world of that day, and crowds flocked to North Berwick to see it. I crossed over from Leven [Fife] with my brother James and remember it well. When I awoke at five o'clock the rain was pouring, and I got up and told my brother so, and that it would be unwise to go. However, in short time afterwards he came to my bedroom and said, 'Man, Tom, I see a wee glint of blue sky! I think we should gang [go].' 'All right!' I said, 'I'm up.' And in due time we arrived at North Berwick.

On meeting Allan, I said I had come to see him win. He replied that he hoped so; but he had a dejected look about him, and I got the impression that he was doubtful of the result. The match was one of thirty-six holes, which required five or seven rounds (I forget which) of the North Berwick Links at that time, and one hole more.

The match started amidst the greatest enthusiasm. The weather had cleared up, but the wind blew pretty strong from the south-west. Each party had its own tail of supporters, those for the Musselburgh men predominating – for which, of course, the proximity of that place to North Berwick might account. They were led by Gourlay, the ball-maker. I never saw a match where such vehement party spirit was displayed. So great was the keenness and the anxiety to see whose ball had the best lie, that no sooner were the shots played than off the whole crowd ran, helter-skelter; and as one or the other lay best, so demonstrations were made by each party.

Sir David Baird was umpire, and a splendid one he made. He was very tall, and so commanded a good view of the field; but it took all his firmness to keep even tolerable order.

The early part of the match went greatly in favour of the Dunns, whose play was magnificent. Their driving, in fact, completely overpowered their opponents. They went sweeping over hazards which the St Andrews men had to play short of. At lunch time the Dunns were four up, and long odds were offered on them.

On resuming the match, the advantage went still further to the credit of the Musselburgh men, and everyone thought that victory was theirs; but one never knows when the tide at golf will turn – and turn it did. Allan warmed up and got more into his game; and then one hole was taken and another and yet another; and I remember Captain Campbell of Schiehallion, with whom I was walking, saying in great glee – 'God, sir, if they take another hole they'll win the match!' And, to be sure, another was won, and so on until the match stood all equal and two to play.

How different the attitude of the Dunns' supporters now from their jubilant and vaunting manner at lunch time! Silence reigned, concern was on every brow, the elasticity had completely gone from Gourlay's step, and the profoundest anxiety marked every line of his countenance. The very Dunns themselves were demoralised!

On the other hand, Allan and Tom were serene, and their supporters as lively as they had been depressed before. We felt victory was ours!

When the tee shots were played for the second last hole, off we flew as usual to see whose ball lay best! To our intense dismay Allan's lay very badly, whilst the Dunns' lay further on beautifully. Should the Dunns win this hole they would be dormy – they might win the match! Our revulsion of feeling was great, and as play proceeded was intensified, for Allan and Tom had played three more with their ball lying in a bunker close to and in front of the putting green!

But, on the other hand, the Dunns' ball was lying close to the back of a curb-stone on a cart track, off the green to the right! First of all they wished the stone removed and called to someone to go for a spade; but Sir David Baird would not sanction its removal, because it was off the course and a fixture. The ball had therefore to be played as it lay. One of the Dunns (I forget which) struck at the ball with his iron but hit the top of the stone. The other did the same; and again the same operation was performed and 'the like' played. All this time the barometer of our expectation had been steadily rising and had now almost reached 'Set Fair!'

> The odd had now to be played, and this was done by striking the ball with the back of the iron on to grass beyond the track. Had that been done first, the hole might have been won, the match also; but both men had by this time lost all judgment and nerve and played most recklessly. The consequence was the loss of the hole, and Allan and Tom were dormy.
>
> We felt the victory was now secure; and so, in fact, it turned out, and Allan and Tom remained the victors by two holes.
>
> I think it only just to say that, in my opinion, the winning of the above match was due to Tom Morris. Allan was decidedly off his game at the start and played weakly and badly for a long time – almost justifying the jeers thrown at him, such 'That wee body in the red jacket canna play gouf,' and such like. Tom, on the other hand, played with pluck and determination throughout.[1]

How exciting it must have been to be there. With crowds chasing after their ball, it must have been an intense atmosphere.

Speaking to H.S.C. Everard in 1895 in the article, *A Haver with Tom Morris,* Tom talked of that day at North Berwick. We join the conversation with Tom talking us through the closing holes:

> The Dunns were four up and seven to play … their principal backer was Mr Nixon, he lives at Westward Ho! now: he left us and didn't go the last round, but went up the town, he was so sure he would win. When it was all over he met Mr Peter of Leven, and said, 'I suppose it's all over?' Mr Peter said, 'Yes, but I'm afraid it's [gone] the other way for you.' Mr Nixon's face did change! Mr John Watt made a pile of money; he took all the odds he could get at 15 and 10 to 1. I heard 20 to 1 offered to the late Sir David Baird, but he refused. He thought no odds were good enough, but ye see facts are dingin' things! Mind ye, Allan the nicht before was as quiet as pussie; he wouldna speak. At other times he was a great talker. When we'd won the match I said, 'Why were you so quiet last night?' 'I just thought that if we lost the match you would get the blame for it.'

This gives us one of the great insights into the mindset of an all too human Allan. It was not the match he was overly concerned about; he was worried that Tom would get the blame for failure as the weak link. That speaks volumes. The weight of these matches was a burden on Allan. This line also explains why Allan's own scrapbook was so full of clippings about Tom. On the other hand, Tom had no such fears adding, 'I told him those who saw the match would have been able to put the blame on the right man'.

About the match itself Tom said, 'There was a tremendous crowd from Edinburgh, for the railway had just opened; the crowd would not keep in bounds, and Sir David said if they did not behave, he would order the players to lift their balls. Allan and I played quite steady, as well as we would play; and the Dunns just fell awa', and the match turned. The stone in the road at the last hole [on the course but the 35th hole in the match] did not make any difference, for we were dormy and would have won in any case.'

At 74 years of age old Tom's memory may have been a little off. They went dormy after winning the 35th hole and one to play. Everard then asked him, 'Do you think you ought to have won that match?'

'Well, they looked the strongest, and were a more dashing lot; they had fine driving. Willie Dunn was a splendid driver … but all the same I think they had the pull of us on the whole.' In other words, Tom thought his opponents were stronger.

The papers hailed the match as one of the greatest ever. The *Montrose Review* on Friday 10 August 1849 said: 'The match from the first excited great interest, which was, if possible, increased on this occasion, the links of North Berwick being crowded by numerous and fashionable assemblage of both ladies and gentlemen. The ladies seemed to take fully as great an interest in the game as the keenest golfer amongst the gentlemen, almost every one betting her gloves in favor [sic] of Musselburgh or St. Andrews, according to their respective predilections. The play was excellent, which may be understood by the result – the St. Andrews players winning only at the last hole. Before commencing the last round, the Messrs. Dunn were five ahead, but on this round they lost every hole, which decided the match against them.'

Of those five rounds over the North Berwick course, newspapers reported that the first round was tied; the second the Dunns went four-up; and the third was tied, so the Dunns remained at four up, at which time the players went in for lunch. It was a welcome break as the sun was beating down on the golfers. It was here that backers offered odds of 20–1 against Allan and Tom. During the fourth round they went to five up, but were pegged back to four up with one round to go. Of the last seven-hole round, Tom and Allan won the first, second, fourth and sixth, drawing back to all-square. The match dynamic had completely changed and the St Andrews men were now on the march. It was said that the contest had all the 'animation of Derby Day when the little cluster of favourites approach the winning post'. This was a tenacious turnaround: seven holes to play and winning from four down. Allan had a 'never give up' reputation and this would only have added to that standing.

It has been hailed as one of the most keenly contested games of golf ever played in Scotland. The Invincibles certainly had ridden their luck, but, at the end of the day, the winners were the winners, regardless of how they got there.

The 1850 re-match

It was a remarkable match in 1849. Allan and Tom would have been the toast of St Andrews and, whether in Tom's little shop down at where 15 The Links is today, in Allan's golf parlour, or in the Union Club, the story of the match would have been replayed over and over again.

In town Playfair had radically developed the commercial side of the mussel scalp business and turned what had been making £25 per annum for the town into £400. In light of this success, another tribute was paid to the reformer at a dinner in December and a large silver mussel snuff box, made by jeweller David Smith, was presented with the inscription, 'Presented by the Town Council of the city of St. Andrews, to Major H.L. Playfair, provost of the city, as a small mark of their gratitude for his great assiduity in protecting and bringing to perfection the mussel scalps, and thereby greatly increasing their value and importance, 1850.'

In his 1884 volume *Wrecks and Reminiscences* Local George Bruce has an altogether different take on Playfair's work (or as he called him, Play-false or Play-foul), lamenting, 'But, no doubt many of the older fishermen and women would think it a "gey change" frae the "days o' auld lang syne," when they were driven from the bed of their chartered river, imprisoned in Cupar, and taken to the Court of Session, for taking the mussels belonging to the citizens on the north as well as the south side of the Eden; their very numbers limited, hampered, and restricted by Rules, Regulations, and Police Bye Laws ... fined for putting mussel shells on them, or even setting down a basket or creel, or sitting on a stool or chair on the streets of this wonderful Tradeless Town, nor even allowed to carry home their mussels on their backs from Eden, for fear bare legs would corrupt the morals of the clean and virtuous golfers!'[2]

In a long-heated tirade against Playfair's damage to the fishing industry and the poor fisherfolk, he makes abundantly clear his opposition to Playfair.

Against this backdrop, Tom Morris and his wife Nancy faced their own tragedy when their first boy, Thomas, died. According to the death register, he passed on 17 April 1850 and was buried on the 19th in what would become the Morris family plot. According to the birth register, Thomas had been born on 26 May 1846, and therefore would only have been three years old when he died.

Errors on tombstones, including Allan's, were commonplace at the time. On the headstone it said pitifully,

> In the silent Tomb we leave him,
> Till the Resurrection Morn
> When his saviour will Receive him,
> And Restore his lovely Form.

Alas, we do not know how he died. Tulloch, as a sign of the times, mentions the births of other siblings, but does not touch upon Thomas' passing. It was tragic.

A re-match of the 1849 victory would have been all too pressing. Perhaps it was Tom's private tragedy or perhaps it was Allan refusing to play yet another grand match, but the second time they played a match against the Musselburgh twins was not at the spring meeting, but at the R&A autumn meeting in October 1850, which was always the larger of the two meetings and remains so.

The 36-hole match on St Andrews links had a fund of £50 a side. Tulloch was there and captured the end of the game in his book, saying that when they 'were equal at the hole before the Eden coming in, Allan off the tee put Tom in the bunker just facing the hole. Tom, playing the like, took the ball out of the bunker, but just on to the edge, leaving a long putt over sandy ground of about five yards. Allan had to hole out for a half: he did it with his putter. I had been standing at his back, and after play was finished, said to him, "My man, Allan, you never had a narrower squeak for a hole all your life." "Man," he said, "I bid [had] to do it. You see, I put Tom in the bunker."'[3]

Once again, we see Allan's thoughts for Tom.

Tom and Allan closed the game out at the Burn hole, winning two and one with a score of 88. It was a hard-fought win, but it only added to their reputation as being unbeatable. The fact that it was on their home links is another matter.

Calls to Prestwick

The papers do not record any foursomes for Allan and Tom in 1851. It was a change of gear for Allan as all his foursomes matches that year were with or against gentleman golfers of the town. After the huge singles matches and the boisterous foursomes, matches with gentlemen golfers would be a recurring theme for the next decade.

It was a time of change too for Tom. His second son, also called Thomas but known as Tommy, as was the tradition of the time, was born on 20 April and christened by Rev. Dr John Craig in the Holy Trinity Church on 10 May 1851. Tommy would become champion golfer four times and, to this day, is still the youngest winner of the Open. To Allan, though, he was Tom's new baby boy, whom he knew until the age of eight. Tommy learned his golf at Prestwick and won all his Opens there, in 1868, 1869, 1870 and 1871. He would be 13 when Tom eventually returned to St Andrews.

Around the time of Tommy's birth, Tom was invited by Colonel James Ogilvie Fairlie to move to Prestwick, to re-design the existing short links into a more substantial course and be their keeper of the green.

Tom and Col. Fairlie got on very well. Speaking to Tulloch, Tom said, 'No better gentlemen ever lived than Colonel Fairlie; I'm perfectly certain o' that.' Bringing golf at that time to life, he added, 'In those days we used to take our luncheon on the green [i.e. golf course], and the Cornel [Colonel] would give me a ceegar [sic]. Then he gave me a pipe and I had to buy tobacco. I never smoked till I was thirty, but I've made up for it since ...'[4]

In other words, he took up smoking around the time of moving to Prestwick. What is also interesting to note is that golfers who played together in the mid-1800s, and who took some sustenance, ate together, regardless of class or position. This is very much in keeping with Allan's games at Perth, where he dined with aristocracy, or at Crail Golfing Society, where the founding members in 1786 included both lords and the local innkeeper.

It was a daunting request for Tom in many respects. Gone would be the relatively busy St Andrews links, but, more importantly, Tom would be bidding farewell to his golfing partner and friend, Allan.

Although we have no words from Allan about how he felt, it would be very human to find the combined effect of the loss of his parents, first wife and also his younger brother, who had moved to Australia, a little hard to take. The links would have felt a little quieter without his family and now his friend and playing partner Tom. They were most definitely friends. In countless interviews Tom gave in later life, he referred to Allan as 'my friend'. Not my boss, my employer, my mentor, nor even my golfing partner – it was almost always 'my friend'.

The Prestwick club were seeking to elevate their status, and they would have been keen to attract Allan. That he did not go, I think, comes down simply to Allan's status as the king of St Andrews. His fame, his parlour and his business were working well in St Andrews, and I do not get any sense that Allan was a gambling man. He had a sure thing in St Andrews and the thought of going to the west of Scotland, to a links that would have seen a fraction of the traffic of St Andrews, would not have been so enticing. The other reason is simply, and to put it starkly, there is no evidence that he was even asked.

Colonel Fairlie was kind to Tom. He was his friend and playing partner. Tom's life, with one child dead and another just born, was in a place where a change of scenery, a steady job and a chance to design his own links would have been attractive.

There is a poem called *Separation* in Allan's scrapbook of *Chambers Journals*. As it is heavily pencilled all around, it clearly resonated with Allan.

Separation

Severed soon will thine image be
From one who loves to look on thee,
Not with the fitful feverish glance
Of passion, nursed by warm romance;
But with a fervent searching gaze
Which sees each hidden charm, each phase
Of the light thy beaming eyes express,
Radiant with mental loveliness.
Yes, severed 'tis my doom to be
From the form I regard so tenderly:
And thy words, that win a life and grace
From the beams of thy smile-illuminated face,
No more shall charm my raptured sense.
Yet memory, wi with a grief intense,
Shall treasure those when last we met,
Which bid me fly – despair – forget.
Though my love, which is now my misery,
Unblest has been by one smile from thee,
I repine not; for, with forward mien,
I pressed fond hope, where scorn has been.
Farewell! May these pangs – the sleepless eye –
The oft-heaved, deep convulsive sigh –
Never o'ercast *thy* happy lot:
I obey – I despair – but 'forget' thee not.

This poem could have made Allan think of his late wife, his parents or a lost friend.

When Tom arrived in Prestwick, how did he feel? When he looked over the wild barren links, did he feel excited by the prospects? This would be the first full course he would set out himself. It wouldn't be Allan's. It would be his. Being labelled an apprentice or undercard at the age of 30 must have also grown a little tiresome for Tom. The chance to do something for himself must have been very alluring.

The links would have been very quiet apart from spring and autumn meetings. Tom would have enjoyed the space to design the 12-hole course without much interruption.

Tulloch noted that they were very happy years for Tom. 'Prestwick was a delightful residence. It had known golf for ages, for it was not on these links or hard by that in pre-Reformation times, to settle some deadly feud, a match at golf took place on "Ye linkes atte Air for his nose between a Monk of Crossraguel and a Lord of Culzean". The links were the property of the club, whose servant Tom was, and he was virtually lord and master of the situation.'[5]

Tom's work of creating the 12-hole course was heralded a triumph. As Tulloch noted: 'He superintended the layout of the magnificent links, and played many matches on them. Even in Tom's day, Prestwick was celebrated as perhaps the best 12-hole course known – magnificent turf, splendid hazards, with beautiful views of Arran, Ailsa Craig, and the Heads of Ayr. And no doubt it was owing very much to Tom's good care of it that the links became one of the champion courses of Great Britain. It had several characteristics too, notably its own. "The course," says Mr H.G. Hutchinson, "went dodging in and out amongst sand-hills. The holes were, for the most part, out of sight when one took the iron in hand for the approach, for they lay in deep dells amongst sand-hills, and you lofted over the intervening mountain of sand, and there was all too frequent excitement, as you climbed to the top of it, of seeing how near to the hole your ball may have happened to roll."'

The standout hole on the Prestwick Links was the first, which was 578 yards. It would have been a monstrous hole for golfers who were on average hitting the ball around 150 yards. It makes Tommy's 3 there in 1870, while on his way to winning his third Open and retaining for good the Champion's Belt, truly remarkable.

A frequent visitor

Tom did not just retreat to the links at Prestwick and return 13 years later. He returned regularly with Fairlie for autumn and spring meetings.

This may have been largely due to the journey being simplified by the new railway line to St Andrews.

First discussed in 1849, the town applied to Parliament in 1850 for permission to extend the line from Leuchars to St Andrews. The cost was £21,000, which was raised quickly, thanks to Playfair. The directors of the St Andrews Railway Company were Messrs. Meldrum, Aikman, John Brown, R. Haig, W. Smith, A. Briggs, Walter Fogo Ireland and, naturally, Hugh Lyon Playfair.

The St Andrews Railway Company Act was passed and, in July 1851, received royal assent. Work began in September that year with engineer Thomas Bouch in charge. It was his unfortunate miscalculations that led to the Tay Bridge Disaster of 1879. The railway was officially opened on 29 June 1852. The station master's house was built at the time of opening and is today's Jigger Inn.

At the 1851 autumn meeting, a mere few months after Tom had left for Prestwick, he returned. At Hastie's Cross Keys Hotel at the annual R&A dinner, Fairlie retired as captain and welcomed George Whyte-Melville as the new captain.

Tom and Allan hosted their own dinner for the caddies in Mr Ritchie's Golf Tavern. According to the *Fifeshire Journal* of 23 October, they spent a glorious evening with 'about thirty of the fraternity present – Mr Thos. Morris occupied the chair, and Mr Allan Robertson, the "cock o' the green" croupier. Thomas Morris arrived in the beginning of the week with his patron, Captain Fairlie, and has had several days on his native Links, and among old associates.'

Tom was back, on a night out with Allan, and still very much part of the St Andrews scene. He was no stranger. He simply came home and it was like nothing had changed. There was no mention in the press of them playing together. Allan played with a Mr Campbell of Achalader on two occasions against Sir Thomas Moncrieffe and Robert Anderson, losing the first and winning the next on the 17th that started at the Ginger Beer hole. They played down the last hole for £1 and Allan's team was victorious. He also partnered with a Mr Montgomery and played against Jamie Dunn and a Mr A. Wood, beating them by three holes. After the excitement and exhaustions of the previous ten years or so, it must have been a welcome relief with a lot less pressure riding on matches and fun soirées thereafter.

The third match

Allan and Tom's next grand match of note was once again in St Andrews. In 1852, at the autumn meeting, they faced Mr Robert Hay and Dunnie for £100 to £50. We assume the money disparity reflected the fact that Hay was a lesser-skilled amateur and the others were deemed professionals. Quite possibly it also meant that Hay stood to win no money. It would be quite wrong to portray Hay as being lost in such vaulted company. In the year of this match, Hay won the gold medal at Prestwick. He was widely known at the time as being one of the finest amateurs.

The match garnered much interest. It would have been an exciting occasion to see Allan and Tom playing together again. It had been almost two years since their last match. The relationship would have been evolving too. Tom was slowly but surely becoming an independent force in his own right.

In Allan's scrapbook, the 1852 match is documented. Capturing the excitement of the prospects of the match, it said,

> 'Now comes the day, the great, important day, big with the fate of Allan and of Tom' as was parodied on the occasion by a humorous member of the Royal and Ancient ... The atmosphere was clear and sharp, and a slight breeze out of the west ... The afternoon was looked forward to with great anxiety, being the time for a struggle, replete with interest in many ways, between Mr Hay, the lion of the week, in conjunction with Willie Dunn, against the pride of St Andrews – the invincible firm of Allan & Tom. The betting was extreme – the latter party giving two to one ... Half-past twelve was the hour of the cause, when set-off from the first hole took place, and then and there, had collected an exceedingly numerous company to escort the actors, and view the proceedings in this all-absorbing trial of dexterity betwixt St Andrews and Musselburgh. The game was almost totally abandoned for the afternoon by the other players, and the course presented a fair-field and no favour. Beside stranger and resident golfing gentlemen, in themselves a host, the match was witnessed by doctors, lawyers, and divines (young ones at least

> of the latter profession), professors, bankers, railway directors, merchant's clerks, tradesmen, workmen, Madras boys and other youngsters, as well as a goodly sprinkling of general idlers. All the attention of the city was concentred [sic].

In an era without television or internet, this was a grand spectacle. Outside of the R&A medals, it would have been one of the highlights of the meeting.

'The crowd followed the players closely, observing with great excitement the effect of each stroke. The putting greens especially were places where the utmost concern was displayed as each and all looked on in breathless suspense. Mr Lees' picture of "The Golfers" can best convey an idea of the sight.' With bets being placed one way and another, it must have been quite daunting, for Hay in particular, lining up with the Jack, Tiger and Rory of the day, never mind the large crowds. This clearly did not show in his play.

'Mr Hay and his partner began the battle with a great prestige of success, capturing the first two holes. We fell in with the match at the "Hole O' Cross", travelling inward the first round. At that time the star of St Andrews seemed to be in the descendant. The state of the poll was that the Musselburgh men had a majority of four holes. They had played an almost unexampled game in the outward half of the round. Mr Hay was reported to have been driving tremendously long balls, and with the most unerring precision, and Dunnie showing himself to be a worthy mate; both also holing their balls at all distances in the green. This was too grand to last. On the other hand, Allan and Tom had been doing well – gone out in forty-six. Allan had shown his wonted first-rate play but Tom, it was insinuated, was at his old trade of "funking".'

Alas, Tom was having an off day with his putting. Funking can also mean duffing a shot or fluffing a putt in a pressure moment.

'The St Andrews folks at this juncture were desponding a little, and some quaking for the renown of their men. But the "Hole O' Cross" was the crisis in the conflict. Allan and Tom's good time was fast coming – neither of their right hands had forgot its cunning. Their never-failing pluck and characteristic uniformity under the adverse game began to tell, for they immediately commenced to apply the process of subtraction to their adversaries, by taking the "Ginger Beer" hole at six to the others seven, ditto with the next, by five to six. Driving off at the succeeding one, Dunnie bunkered in the "Principals Nose". Allan drove a wide ball the second shot, which Tom skillfully redeemed, but after all Dunnie seized half the hole by a wonderful put [putt] at two more. Allan failing to put [putt] in his at one off two. The Hay party still two holes ahead, but they lost the next by seven to five. The home hole was divided – Allan narrowly missing taking it all, which would have placed them on an equality.'

So, after the first 18, The Invincibles were one down, but were finding their rhythm. The crowds were said to have been bigger for the second 18, swelling to hundreds following the game.

'After a brief interval the battle was renewed … and the excitement augmented. Hay and Co., it will be noted, were a hole ahead, but Dunnie aiming at over the burn the second stroke, set his ball to water, while Tom cautiously drew short on the east side of the hazard and accounts were immediately squared. Next hole did not alter matters, but at the third Allan plumped his ball into the Principal's beak. Tom scooped it out, but it rolled into a sheep track, and Hay and Co. got for the last time ahead. Allan and Tom retrieved at the fourth hole, and now that the tug of war has come, they began to assert their supremacy. They took the fifth hole at five, and the sixth at four. The high hole was next, which was then played admirably. A long tee ball of Allan's shot far ahead of Mr Hay's corresponding one; indeed, one could hardly conceive how Allan's little body could propel a ball so far. At second strokes, Tom swiped past the hole, and Dunnie's was caught in a bunker, which Mr Hay did not eject, Dunnie doing it in his turn, while the other ball was at its destination in four to seven. Hole eight was halved. Hole of return went to Allan and Tom, but they owed to a stymie.'

One gets the sense that the wind was in their sails. This was Allan and Tom at their best, where they were in tune with each other once more and almost unbeatable. Any golfer who plays a winning foursomes will relate to the feeling.

'Homeward bound now, with four in favour of St Andrews men, to which was added one next hole, cancelled at high hole by Hay and Co., the second only they had won in eleven. The hole of Shell ran

Allan's side up to a five once more. Playing off here, Mr Hay sent his ball astray, and Dunn could not make much of it, but Mr Hay made a splendid swipe next, landing in the green at three, the same as the opposite one, but not so near the desired point by some yards. Allan made the decisive putt – tumbling the ball in at a long distance – and instantly a spontaneous cheer signalised the success of Allan and Tom by six ahead and five to play. The remaining holes were contested for a minor bet, we believe, but these need not be particularised. It was supposed that Allan and Tom in going over these – their success being declared – intentionally gave advantages by driving wide and being careless, but we don't think this was the case, suffice it to say, that at the thirty-sixth hole Allan and Tom's side was four holes in advance. In the progress inward, some boys removed the flags for guiding to the holes from their positions, and held them aloft in the procession, giving it the appearance of a triumphal entry. Such a scene has not been on the links for many years, the last of a similar kind was, if we rightly remember; in the summer of 1848, when the two Dunnies tried to pluck the laurels from the brows of Allan and Tom. The combined prowess of the firm still endures, and they remain the cocks o' the green. Long may they hold that honourable elevation. St Andrews for ever!'

Another journalist reported that the only expression of feeling that was vented was a cheer when the match was decided, saying that 'in every other respect, no expression was made of sympathy one way or another'. With flags waving, and cheers ringing out from the exuberant crowds, how wonderful it must have been to see the pageantry of it all.

How enjoyable it must have been for the St Andrews golfers to be hailed once more. That cheer when Allan's long putt went in would have rung in his and Tom's ears for years to come.

As mentioned previously, not every single match of Allan and Tom's is noted in the press. One must think that they played more minor matches for and against gentlemen golfers. With Willie Park Snr on the rise in Musselburgh, Allan would see his king status challenged repeatedly and hear whispers of 'funking' or avoiding matches grow louder.

Little could he have known or expected, that the first public challenge would come from his own close friend and golfing partner.

Sixteen

PAPER WAR

It was 1853. The railway was operational. Allan would face a year of matches with his gentleman partner Sir Thomas Moncrieffe, including a 62-hole marathon against Captain Maitland Dougall and Robert Anderson, which they won by three matches and 12 holes.

Sir Thomas (1822–79) was just about six years younger than Allan, and they played many matches from 1853 to the end of Allan's life. Sir Thomas was born at Moncreiffe House in Perthshire. When his father David died, Sir Thomas became the 7th Baronet of the Moncrieffe baronets. A first-class cricketer, he served in the Grenadier Guards and Royal Perthshire Militia, attaining the level of honorary colonel. He became a member of Royal Company of Archers in 1837 and was Captain of The Royal and Ancient Golf Club of St Andrews in 1844, just after Sir David Baird; both were Allan's supporters.

Golf was growing in popularity, and Allan spent his time with the golf parlour business and with these matches with gentlemen, which mostly came up during spring and autumn meetings. At these meetings, Allan would also give out the odds, in other words, handicaps. Simply, he was central to the burgeoning golfing life in St Andrews and was respected as the champion golfer of Scotland, and therefore the world.

By and large, Allan's life seemed to be heading for a stress-free year. Tom himself explained what happened next in his 1895 chat with Everard. 'Lord Eglinton … got Sir Thomas Moncrieffe to approach Allan and ask if he would play me. He said he would not play a single, but he would take me on his side and play a double. I dinna ken why he would never play me a single. They said if there had been more money on our two singles, Allan would have won.'

So, it was Lord Eglinton who instigated the idea of a challenge match and not Tom. The aim would be for their new Prestwick professional to be the holder of the champion golfer title. It was, however, up to Allan to decide when or if the champion golfer title would be played for and, like a champion prize boxer, he did choose his fights. That was in the gift of the champion, and the champion chose not to play against his friend and relative, Tom. He possibly could not bring himself to think of Tom as a foe, unlike the Musselburgh or Perth golfers.

At the next spring meeting Allan and Sir Thomas faced Tom and Col. Fairlie (1809–70). Col. Fairlie was the oldest in the group, aged 44. Allan's team won the first match by 2 and 1. Two days later, they met again with the first round tied; they played a second, with Tom's team winning by 2 and 1. As honours were even overall, they decided to play out to the High Hole and, on reaching there, Allan's team were two up. They assented to extending the game and it ended in a half, largely thanks to Allan being stymied on the last. They were obviously very closely matched, not just Allan and Tom but Col. Fairlie and Sir Thomas.

An incidental spring meeting note in the *Fifeshire Journal* on 12 May 1853 reported that on Monday, 'The weather … was of the same description as the Saturday. The hail and rain showers both longer and stronger. A small residue of the stranger golfers appeared on the ground; the great majority departed on Saturday. Allan and Tom encountered each other in single combat with clubs and balls – a rare occurrence – some little cash depended on the issue, which Allan – strange to say – lost, Tom surpassing him by 3 holes on the round, which he performed in 90, Allan in 93, notwithstanding the storm's adverse influence.'

The paper then went on to discuss a minute of the town's Finance Committee regarding the ground to be feued to the Union Club for a clubhouse. This was the origins of today's R&A clubhouse. It detailed the dimensions of the new club, 119 feet in length from east to west and 117 feet from north to south.

There was little to no reaction to Allan's loss. Why should there be? It wasn't a grand match. Yes, they had played a match, but it was just a friendly game, played at the end of the spring meeting when most, including Col. Fairlie, had since departed. It was therefore somewhat of a surprise that it would lead to a challenge to Allan's kingship.

Almost a month later, on 9 June 1853, the *Fifeshire Journal* reported that in Prestwick, 'The links are in beautiful order and have been much played on for some time ... To-day, Mr Joseph Hume and Mr Gillon have engaged Mr Thomas Morris to play a match, the terms of which we have not heard, but the odds must be long, as Tom is "the king of Scotland", and reflects the highest credit on Prestwick. Mr Hunter's (of the Red Lion) luncheon was in his usual good style.'

King of Scotland?

The shock of the claim was immediately addressed by a Fife journalist, in brackets, directly below the above copy in the paper and said in very clear terms: 'Our St Andrews correspondent has to take exception to part of the above paragraph ... Mr Tom Morris, who is titled "King of Scotland", was imported to Prestwick from St Andrews. The real "King of Scotland" in regard to golfing, reigns in St Andrews, and is well known as Allan Robertson; all others taking that dignity are usurpers, and guilty of high treason. Allan is the legitimate and indisputable King of Clubs.'

It did not take long to garnish a reaction from the west coast. In the Communication to the Editor section of the *Fifeshire Journal* on Thursday 23 June 1853, a letter dated 21 June by 'A Loyal Prestwickian' set out that Tom had vanquished Allan on their last encounter.

> It might have been painful to your correspondent's feelings to think of the palm of victory, which has so long reposed in quiescence in the sombre shade of old St Rule, gracefully waving, as it now does, in the 'westlin' breezes by the shore of Kyle ... But now that the healing influence of time and reflection must have come to his aid, it is to be hoped that he will gracefully concede to 'Tom' the honour claimed for him as 'King of Scotland' ... But in case your correspondent should still refuse to own the 'soft impeachment', and to set the question of supremacy again at rest, I have the imperial command to put forth the following
>
> PROCLAMATION OF WAR!
>
> We, Tom, King of Clubs throughout Scotland, by right of conquest most indisputable, in a convocation of our most loyal

golfing subjects, holden within our Royal Lodge at Prestwick, shire of Kyle, taking into our royal consideration that certain treasonable discourses or writings hath appeared and been promulgated in and through a printer paper styled 'The Fifeshire Journal', and that said discourses or writings appear to have been devised through or on behalf of our trusty and well-loved cousin Allan, chief or governor of our golfing province of St Andrews in the east and that the indulgence in such treasonable discourses or writings, if not speedily prohibited, may tend to stir up in the breasts of our loyal subjects a spirit of insubordination, and lead to the formation of plots to deprive, depose, or suspend us from the style, honour, and royal name we at present enjoy of 'King of Clubs': And further, taking into our royal consideration that our said trusty and well-beloved cousin Allan would moreover, and notwithstanding our last royal combat with him, in which we were victorious, still seem to claim (at least said discourses and writings claim for him) jurisdiction, power, superiority, pre-eminence, and authority over us, by taking upon himself the style and title of 'the real, legitimate, and indisputable King of Clubs.' We, in our wisdom and clemency (suppressing our royal 'dander' at such treasonable compassing of our royal prerogatives), have resolved again to satisfy our doubting subjects in our province of the east, that to us exclusively pertains the style and title of 'King of Clubs;' and for that purpose, and to secure at same time the peace and wellbeing of our ancient Kingdom of Clubs, do hereby, by and with consent of our loyal Prestwickian subjects, announce to our doubting subjects in the east aforesaid, that we are prepared to peril our right to the kingly honours and dignities we now enjoy in a contest (in friendly mood) with our said well-beloved cousin Allan, and by the ancient and chivalric ordeal of single combat (but with clubs and balls); and have accordingly commanded our faithful knights, squires, and caddies to hold themselves prepared to consider, arrange, and conclude such a cartel of combat as may befit our imperial dignity – we reserving only the power of fixing the single proviso in said cartel, that in the event of our being right royally 'floored' in said contest, the imperial and pleasing duty be accorded unto us of transferring the wreath of victory from our own royal brows to those of our said well-beloved cousin Allan, forasmuch as, in the performance of said duty, we shall simply feel that we are crowning our other royal self. Save the King!"

Hoping that you may find it convenient to give a place in your next issue to matter so important as the above, I remain, &c.,

A LOYAL PRESTWICKIAN

One can presume that there were several authors of this reply and, given its tone, they may have included Lord Eglinton or James Ogilvy Fairlie. How they must have laughed as it was being composed. The audacity and the faux solemnity with which it is written would have been quite hilarious at that time.

It is not sinister. It is not aggressive. Its sheer pomposity shows that it was intended in good humour. However, the reply did not retract the claim and it proffered that a match should be played. Worse than that, their proviso suggested that if Tom lost, they be allowed the honour of passing the title back to Allan. It was not theirs to give or take, for that matter!

The following week, on 30 June in the *Fifeshire Journal* came the robust reply. Allan must have had a hand in it as it knew minute details of his journey to becoming the champion golfer.

'THE CHAMPIONSHIP' – THE PRESTWICKIAN AGGRESSION. UNFOUNDED ASSUMPTION OF TITLE.

THE KING versus TOM.

The Prestwick colony is in open rebellion against the liege lord of golfers – the bona fide king of clubs – Allan. The manifesto which appeared in last Journal displays, firstly, unrighteous appropriation, and then teems with rampant treason to the true and rightful sovereignty by conquest of all golfing territories within the realm. We little anticipated that the few lines appended to the Ayrshire Golf Meeting report would have proved a bombshell in the Ayrshire camp, and produced such a potent blast from the trumpet of sedition. By the way, we have to mention that the writing of those said few lines was not instigated by Allan, but was purely voluntary on our part.

After talking about the origins of George Glennie, as Prestwick were also claiming his victories as their own, the repost then addressed the King of Clubs title, 'Let us now turn to the main point – the title set up in name of the Pretender, for whom Prestwick has renounced allegiances to king Allan. The sole foundation for this open attempt to disturb his Majesty in the possession of his crown and dignity is the circumstance recorded in our account of last St Andrews May meeting, and quoted by Prestwickians, that Allan and Tom had a single-handed match, which the latter gained by three holes. But the collateral circumstance was omitted to be stated at the time, viz., that the match was a private one, over one round only, in which no public interest was taken, played on a forenoon, with a fierce northerly wind blowing, accompanied with rain and hail. Who would have conceived aught so preposterous as that this insignificant match should be seized, and a claim to the "championship" constructed upon it, by any one conversant with the usages of golfing. But that is the "tottle of the whole" upon which Tom's claim to the kingly dignity is reared – a precious groundwork truly whereupon to build a superstructure of the sort, but quite in keeping with the castle in the air which the Prestwickians have erected upon it. Verily, Ayrshire must be an airy region, with the 'westlin breezes by the shore of Kyle', and the windy character of the inhabitants, if we in the east may judge of the latter from the specimen which has reached us with such an amazing puff.

But we beg to announce to the Prestwickians what is thought by golfers here of the relative merits of Allan and Tom. The universal opinion is that in a regular pitched battle of properly testing length, and with anything worth fighting for depending on the result, Tom has no chance with Allan. Golfers everywhere who are acquainted with them will, we are sure, at once concur in this judgment. Every one who has attended the grand contests for supremacy which have come betwixt Allan and Tom and the brothers Dunn, knows that it was Allan's pre-eminent dexterity and never-say-dieism that turned the tide of victory to him and his coadjutor. Allan never perpetrates a bungle nor declines in his imperturbable coolness; at the losing game he blenches not, but outshines all the others engaged in dexterity in the use of his tools, and as the excitement increases as the crisis approaches, so surely does his and his partner's success. It is therefore but justice to Allan to say that in these interesting strivings the victory chiefly rests upon his play in the estimation of all who know the peculiarities of both players thoroughly. We repeat what has often been alleged in these columns, that the pair are invincible, they having amply proved this – and will 'lick' any other couple in creation. But the union is the power.

When Tom is out of leash with Allan and adventures on his own account he finds a superior. Allan is the right hand of the pair, Tom the left. 'Allan and Tom'. Allan's name, be it remarked, justly goes first as leading member. But setting aside Allan (one can safely do so, as he is the premier golfer admitted by all, bating unknowing Prestwickians), how does Tom's claim to be king stand in comparison with other professionals? We would not have subjected him to this test had not Prestwickians traitorously attempted to get him enthroned. Tom has been twice vanquished on St Andrews Links by William Dunn in regular drawn engagements with heavy bets on them, which matches were looked upon with great interest here, and in golfing circles generally, and we believe held as decisive (the last especially) of who was the better player. The first was in October 1850, when Dunn prevailed by one hole only. The second was in May following, and ended in Dunn's favour by two holes. Bob Anderson, a player of note here, has also beaten Tom twice, and these the only occasions they ever engaged.

These facts abolish any claim for Tom to be held as King of Clubs, quite independent of Allan. Tom and Dunnie are splendid players, they may be either positive or comparative respectively, but Allan is superlative, and we will now show this unquestionably as regards Dunn by recounting briefly some of the grand matches these two have had which produced and established the celebrity of Allan. In 1843, they had a match over our links of two rounds – 36 holes – where Allan whipped his opponent by 8 holes. On this occasion Allan holed the second round in 88. In July the same year they entered the lists and continued playing for ten consecutive days (Sunday excepted of course) at the rate of two rounds per day. On the tenth day, at concluding round eighteenth, Allan was a round a-head, and, taking the nineteenth round, placed the laurels on his brow by 2 rounds in advance, and 1 to play. In 1844, they had a series of contests forming one match – 1st, on Musselburgh links, where Dunn gained; 2nd at North Berwick links, where Allan was victorious; and 3rd, at the final and decisive trial at St Andrews he also won, and again got the palm, having the best of three. In April 1846, they again took up a match on three separate links, vis, Musselburgh, where Dunn beat Allan by 7 a-head, and 5 to play; St Andrews, where Allan won by 5 a-head, and 3 to play; and he also triumphed at Leven by 6 a-head and 4 to play – so this also went to his credit. Moreover, in September 1848, Allan, Tom, and Dunn had a competition – who would dispose of 2 rounds of Leven Links in the least strokes. There Allan eclipsed his rivals: he took 80, Tom 87, and Dunn 91. We don't imagine that Allan's right to sway the sceptre of golfdom was ever doubted by the many who know he has discomfited all who have challenged him; but we have made these details to endeavour to convince darkened Prestwickians that their braggadocio on Tom's part is but sounding brass.

Let the western cocks crow on their own dunghill, and plume themselves on having Tom among them. He is a right worthy export from St Andrews, and, like the prophet, receives greatest honour in a foreign country. Prestwick may fulminate treason, but it is laughed to scorn by Allan's numerous loyal subjects, who know him to be, and glory in his being, the best golfer extant; and, as such, the 'real, legitimate, and indisputable King of Clubs'.

Though the Prestwickians have not the King of Clubs in their pack, we must accord them the credit of possessing the knave of that ilk. In olden times, Kings were wont to keep jesters at their Courts, but at Prestwick they have a true jester and a false king. His jestership writes rank treason, but his humourousness is worthy of a better cause, and in classic quotations we must deplore our unreadiness to return him in kind, even though we live in the vicinity of academic bowers – under 'the shade of old St Rule'. We cannot dazzle like this bright occidental star, but we are bound to employ our pen in the service of our King as we best can. The document emanating from the illegal Court of the Pretender is termed a 'Proclamation of War', but his ministers are evidently ignorant of royal formalities, else they would have known that war is a matter that should be declared. Peace is proclaimed; war is declared.

Diplomatic relations being at an end between King Allan and his Prestwick dependency, he has commanded his royal will and pleasure to be expressed in the following terms: –

Allan R.

Allan, by his might and skill, of all golfing territories in the known world, and more immediately of those in the country called Scotland, King as well de jure as de facto, to all and sundry to whose knowledge these presents shall come, greeting –

Whereas we are apprised that in that portion of our dominions called Prestwick, a conspiracy hath arisen against our lawful … and undoubted sovereign, by the same being claimed as pertaining and belonging to one Tom, who was in time bygone a noble of our royal court at St Andrews, and to whom we have formerly extended our royal favour and condescension, inasmuch as we have permitted him at sundry times while he attended our court aforesaid, to be our companion in arms in doing battle against aspirants to our crown, for his knightly conduct in which encounters the said Tom became qualified and fitted for the government of said part of our realm called Prestwick.

And whereas the said Tom having allowed his allegiance to me to be turned away by evil and ignorant counsellors inhabiting Prestwick aforesaid, and hath instructed or permitted publication to be made of a writing impugning our said right to our said crown and asseverating that the 'same doth truly belong to him'. Be it therefore known to all our true and loving

> subjects that it is our royal purpose and intention, upon the said Tom being apprehended and brought to our royal residence at St Andrews, tried by his peers, and found guilty of unlawful usurpation of, and treason against, our throne, to thrash off the head of the said Tom through the instrumentality of driving club, long spoon, short spoon, click, iron and putter, and by means of such other like implements as may be requisite, and that in right royal fashion, after the manner and custom of golfers used and observed in like cases in all points; as the just punishment demanded by the great crime of the said Tom, as an example to deter all others in time coming from following rebellious practices identical or akin to that above described, under the pain of a similar fate.
>
> Given at our Court at Golf Bank, St Andrews, the twenty-eighth day of June in the year one thousand eight hundred and fifty-three. – Save King Allan.
>
> To recur to ordinary phraseology, Allan will meet Tom, and have a battle royal with him, providing and declaring that the match shall be lengthened adequately to the important effect its result may have, and on condition that it shall be such as to awake the interest of the golfing fraternity in the way that Allan's numerous and successful tilts with William Dunn did. Preliminaries to be arranged, if the affair is spiritedly entered into, by the members of the different clubs.

At this point there appears to be the potential of a grand match brewing, but in the papers for the next three months, silence. The bravado, the genteel and somewhat friendly aggression and the acceptance of a challenge led to, well, nothing.

On Friday 15 September, Allan was elected as captain of the newly named The St Andrews Golf Club, formerly The Mechanics Golf Club. At the same meeting, George Bruce was elected secretary.

The autumn meeting came in October. Allan's dog Tell passed away and was a big enough celebrity on the golf scene to warrant a notice in the *Fifeshire Journal* on 13 October, which noted, 'Died at St Andrews on Monday last, "Tell", the sagacious and handsome Newfoundland dog belonging to Mr Allan Robertson. "Tell" was well known for his quaint behaviour, sagacity, and dignified deportment, and his familiar face will be missed by the frequenters of the links.'

It is notable that the passing of Allan's popular dog would be considered of interest to readers, yet the death of Allan's wife Helen ten years earlier had not warranted a newspaper correspondent's consideration. A sign of the times, rather than any slight, one thinks.

In the old Union Parlour, a challenge was posted: 'Prestwick Golf Club – Challenge. We are requested to state that two players, presently at Prestwick, will be in St Andrews next week, and will there play any two in the world in a match of two rounds.' The two players were Tom and, unusually, Dunnie.

Allan played with or against Sir Thomas Moncrieffe, Captain John Stewart, and John Campbell of Glensaddell, but no singles match with Tom. The papers said, 'Although a lot of first-rate professionals were in attendance, none of them were pitted in single conflict against each other, but they figured in some doubles matches'.

The Prestwickian claim to the throne seems to have vanished in the ether. Lord Eglinton had started it; journalists had fuelled it; and both Allan and Tom had played their part engaging in a paper war, with language akin to an ancient medieval jousting challenge, which Lord Eglinton would know only too well as the creator of the Eglinton Tournament. The silence about it seems to point to the fact that it was all just a bit of fun and that both players were in on the joke. It was being led by others, so Allan and Tom's kinship was not challenged at all.

After all that noise, not a word. The paper war was over and peace reigned, with Allan still the king.

Tom and Allan played a friendly but competitive repeat of their spring meeting doubles game, with Allan and Sir Thomas Moncrieffe versus Tom and Col. Fairlie in October. This did garner great interest and now we understand why. It was labelled the 'orientals opposed to the occidentals', or, in other words 'east versus west'. Again it was another tight affair, with Allan's side winning the first round 3 and 1, Tom's won the second 4 and 3 and Allan's side won by one over the last holes playing in. Overall, in terms of holes won, they were tied and vowed to play again another day. These were great matches and were repeated every year until 1858.

What is interesting in this whole light-hearted debacle is what Allan considered a challenge for his title. First, it had to be a long match, so not over one round. Second, there needed to be serious backers involved. This was subject to one further and very important sub-clause, which was that if the champion simply did not want to play a young challenger, he wouldn't.

His title. His rules.

Allan and Tom did have matches like the one that started the paper war.

None of them are overly consequential and certainly there was never a title on the line. Remember, Allan and Tom were close friends and had been for years. Even throughout the paper war, when there might have been a perceived grievance, there actually was none. Their kinship saw to that.

In the 1894 *Golfer's Guide to the Game and Greens of Scotland*, author Dalrymple said, 'The first single seems to have been a merry one as was not unusual when the two cronies foregathered on the green. Hamilton, of Cairnhill, Ayrshire, happened to be at St Andrews and gave them a small sum to play for. Allan insisted on a wherewithal for his caddie and this was duly provided off the stake. Tom won at the corner of the dyke [the sixteenth] and Allan proposed double or quits. Tom laughed and Hamilton said, "Take it, Tom. You're never afraid?" "It's not that," said Tom with another smile, "but I never heard him offer that before." They did however go double or quits and the two holes were halved.'

This sounds very much like their first encounter at the end of the St Andrews spring meeting which had sparked the faux war. In his biography of Allan, Adamson mentions a game at Prestwick in June where Tom wins but the scoring is strangely similar to the May match above, so there may be some confusion, where these two encounters are actually one. Tom's scrapbook clearly identifies the match in St Andrews at the spring meeting.

Adamson also mentions a match where they played for a red jacket given by Wolfe Murray of Cringletie. Tom won but Allan is reported to have said that the new wee red coat would fit Tom better. Again, it was merely a fun game.[1]

Allan beat Tom in 1842 at St Andrews and in 1844 at Innerleven. He beat Tom and Dunnie together at Innerleven. Tom won this game in the rain in 1853 and the battle for the new coat, but they were games between friends. Seeing these results in context, you can see why the paper war was, at best, a half-hearted ruse.

There is also an insinuation that when Allan put on his old red coat, in a long match with high financial stakes and proper backers, Allan would have won. He may not have frightened professionals with his long driving like Park, but with a cool head under pressure, he could win.

Not only was a public challenge from backers of Tom a game that Allan did not choose to play, I think Tom also shared that sentiment. There is something about their personal dynamic that leads me to believe that Tom had no burning desire to wrest Allan's title away from him. Throughout all the brouhaha, the two were playing golf together or dining in the evening at social events or co-hosting. When the Open began at Prestwick in 1860, I think Tom was under an incredible amount of pressure. Not only was the event on the links that he designed, but it was also for the title that Allan and, by extension, St Andrews had preciously held for 19 years. It was an altogether easier event for Park. It is not surprising that Tom did not win the first Open, but, to his ultimate credit and his worthy legendary status, he went on to win the next two.

If Allan thought over Christmas in 1853, as news of the Crimean War was reaching St Andrews, that public challenges to his champion title in the paper were over, he was sadly mistaken.

They were only just beginning, and one could perceive a faint but growing rumbling coming from Musselburgh.

Seventeen

GREATEST GOLF MATCH

EIGHTEEN-FIFTY-FOUR passed in a similar way to the previous year, with Allan playing matches with the gentlemen golfers at the spring and autumn meetings. The Union Club, with Playfair at the helm, asked and received permission to remove the large sandy hill in front of Allan's house, so a flat terrace path could be made from Allan's to the new clubhouse, which is still there today.

Allan created the Juvenile Golf Club and gave prizes for the competitions. He donated a silver medal called the Duke of Wellington Medal for the juveniles to play for, with the lowest score over the links winning. It would be played on the anniversary of Waterloo. In 1854 James Kirk and Alexander Strath both came in with a net 97. On the following day, Kirk won. Through the accounts of H. Thomas Peter, and Dr McPherson, we know that Allan was a hero to the boys. In 1855 the winner of the silver medal was future three-times Open champion Jamie Anderson, who was around 13 at the time and went around in 111 shots.

The crack golfer of St Andrews in his day, David Pirie, passed away in March that year. Allan kept a clipping of his death in his scrapbook. Pirie looked after the upkeep of the old Union clubhouse, across the road from Allan's, at the corner where Golf Place meets the Scores. His obituary confirmed his status as one of the senior caddies of St Andrews. 'David Pirie was one of the old guard of St Andrews golfers and upheld the celebrity of the Links some twenty or twenty-five years ago. The family of Pirie has contributed a respectable quota to the ranks and renown of St Andrews professionals, and David was, we believe, the first who made the name famous in a generation now past or passing away. He and his brothers were the "crack" men of our

Links before Allan Robertson and the modern race of notables were known, or at least had required repute. The Piries figured frequently in grand matches during their period, against the heroes of the golfing grounds, singly as well as in "foursomes" with amateurs.'

Tom and Allan did play in professional foursomes against each other with gentlemen. William Tulloch wrote in his book *The Life of Tom Morris* that a foursome match was played in 1854 for a considerable stake of £200, comprising eighteen holes at the St Andrews links. Interestingly Allan was partnered with his adversary Willie Dunn Snr against Old Tom Morris and Bob Anderson. The latter two won the match one up.

The new Musselburgh professional

In October, David, Allan's brother, sent over two small gold nuggets from Australia to The St Andrews Golf Club, saying that he wished them to be played for over the links. George Morris won the heaviest nugget with a 91 and the other was won by the great author Dr James G. McPherson with a 98.

This was also the year Willie Park made his entrance into the golfing scene. With Dunnie at Blackheath, Park was the new crack golfer of Musselburgh. Dr McPherson said Park 'was the most powerful exponent of the game. His style was methodical: not a continued round swing in an upward and downward motion – the former slow, and the later increasingly rapid; but in three distinct movements – one, two, up; and third down. No one ever had a similar style; boys imitated it for a time, but they could not sustain it. Had he been always as careful of his health as Allan and Tom, he might have surpassed even them. But his round shoulders and too marked stoop, as he walked over the course, showed a weakness which in the long-continued efforts told on him.'[1]

Comparing him to Allan, Tom and Dunnie, Dr McPherson said that Park 'had in him the innate power of being the finest and most powerful of all players. But he was more of the "potato-soup" style of feeder, whereas Tom was more of the "ham-and-eggs" type. His weakness was never in style, in pluck, or in golfing resources as to all the niceties – for in all these he was perfect – but in pure physical shortcoming at the crucial point in a great match.'[2]

One example of this funking was during the 1855 autumn meeting, when Allan had one of his best finishes in a match. He was playing with Mr Erskine Wemyss of Wemyss Castle against Mr Archibald Hastie MP and Willie Park in a 36-hole match, with heavy betting on both sides and many followers of the game.

Dr McPherson captures the play as they come down the 17th of the final round:

> Campbell of Saddell was backing the (likely) winners:–
> Hear Saddell say,
>
> 'Now, by the piper who the pibroch played
> Before old Moses, we are one ahead,
> And only two to play – a special coup!
> Three five-pound notes to one!' (announced Campbell)
> 'Done, sir, with you.'
>
> John Blackwood (of Strathtyrum) at once said (accepting the bet), for his faith in Allan was marvellous, almost mesmeric. On went the game, till Park laid his partner on the green, and Wemyss put Allan in the road'.

We do not know how many shots it has taken the players to get to this stage. Allan's side must have arrived in the spot in one less than it took Park and Hastie to find the green. Let us assume it took Park four to reach the green and Allan, over the back in three.

'Yet, though playing two more from such a hazard, the champion would not give in; his pluck never wavered. Think of the odds against him now! A thousand to one would scarcely have been taken.'

So, Allan and Wemyss have already had two goes and failed to make the green. They are now facing their sixth shot, with Park's team looking very assured putting for a five. It is Allan's turn again.

> But we remember Allan cautiously studying the ground; back and forward he went from the hole to the ball – some twenty yards distant. His favourite iron [the frying-pan] he took from Da' [Anderson], who whispered in the champion's ear, 'ye can doo't'. With inimitable balance of golfing genius, he pitched the ball from the hard road up to the top footpath within a hair's-breadth of the spot where he and Da' had calculated the pitch

would require to be, and the ball trickled down the slope and safely landed in the hole. In the hole for a six.

Hastie was paralysed; he funked his putt, and ran it a yard and a half past the hole. Park putted with an unexpected result; the tables were turned:–

'Seized with surprise, th' affrighted hero stands,
And feebly tips the ball with trembling hands;
The creeping ball its want of force complains,
A grassy tuft the loit'ring orb detains.'

In other words, Park was short with his putt, and lost the hole. The match was now square. 'For the last hole Allan played off one of his most brilliant drives – his heart exulting at the marvellous turn, success engendering success in this as in other matters. But Park pressed and "slipped" and "burned" his ball, thus losing the splendid match by one hole. The champion's praises were celebrated in glorious style; the tyro became persuaded that Allan could do anything with the ball and true golfers saw that occasionally the real genius of the game can do wonders just at the critical emergency. This failure of Park's is by no means uncommon … Park funked his putt – but who would not in the circumstances? … The nerves were on him.'[3]

Allan was a hero of Dr McPherson's, who cautioned Tulloch when penning the biography of Tom that it was Allan and Tom, not the other way around. Allan's name always came first. Of the four leading golfers, Dunnie, Park, Tom and Allan, he thought Tom the weakest and Allan, by a long way, the best. Interesting also that the 17th at that time was largely the same as it is today, with the only difference being that it was then the sole main road out of St Andrews behind the green. It would still be a breathtaking shot today.

That was Allan.

Back to 1854 when Park entered the golfing world stage.

On 3 November 1854 the *Montrose Standard* carried a report from the *Dundee Advertiser*: 'As usual at the October meetings, Allan, Dunnil [sic] and Tom Morris, who have been long looked on as the king and princes of the royal game, were to be seen busily engaged on the green. Besides them also appeared on the links a new professional golfer, in the person of Mr William Park of Musselburgh, quite a young beardless boy, who coolly and repeatedly challenged to play any of the three champions above named, which they did not relish well.'

In their defence, it is understandable that golfers who had been playing for years to attain their success and reputation would be reluctant to play someone who had only just arrived on the scene. Having in all likelihood seen Tom and Allan's cordial 1853 'paper war' the year before, Park may have thought that issuing challenges publicly was the right way to do things. It was certainly not unusual for a sporting challenge to be set out in the papers.

Park was born on 30 June 1833. He was 12 years younger than Tom and almost 18 years younger than Allan. When Allan beat Tom Alexander in 1840, Willie was only seven. Now, arriving at St Andrews and publicly challenging the trio of golfing giants, he was a young man of 21. The tone, brashness and audaciousness of his challenge reflected this. He could bang a drum as loud as he wanted, but if the others did not want to recognise the tall drummer boy, they had that right.

On the other hand, from Park's perspective, if you thought you were the best golfer, and you wanted to be recognised as such, you would logically go to the very top and issue a challenge. Why wait?

Allan would have laughed off such a challenge. It was not the way things were done, and certainly not for the trifling amount that Park was offering. Imagine today's multi-million-pound champion boxer's reaction to a £10 challenge fight.

You also get the impression that, in order to play a match for the title against Allan, you had to beat everyone, and you had to do it repeatedly. Winning a match here and there would not have been sufficient.

No one wanted to play Park.

It is often repeated that perhaps they thought Park was just too good, but in reality it may have just been more about earning his stripes before facing the champion. Allan had been at this for 17 years by the time Park arrived. Allan had travelled. Allan had won in front of huge crowds and under immense pressure. It would not have been controversial for the leading players to think that Park needed to put in a hard-fought shift or two before trying to claim the top position.

The Montrose paper continued, 'on Wednesday evening, a council took place in the Golf Inn, to consider how this unexpected Goliath [perhaps referring to his towering physical stature] was to be brought down, and it was agreed that George Morris, brother of far-famed Tom, should play Park on the following morning, which Park agreed to, the bets being £2 by Park, against £1 10*s*. by Morris'.

If you consider Allan's great matches against Dunn for £100 and more, this first challenge is really not a serious proposal.

George worked as a servant in the publisher Robert Chambers' house and was the professional at Carnoustie for around ten years. He was a fine golfer, albeit not in the same league as Allan or Tom. He featured regularly in competitions at the artisan Mechanics Golf Club. Chambers and Morris set out the 12-hole links at Hoylake in 1869. George's son John 'Jack' Morris (1847–1929) was the first professional there, a post he held for over 60 years until he died, extending the links around the summer of 1871. He was and remains a highly prized clubmaker. Jack's wife Margaret Jane Smith (1853–1934) had another golfing connection. Margaret's cousin, the nephew of her mother Esther Ball (1830–1919), was amateur golfing legend John Ball (1861–1940), the eight times winner of the Amateur Championship and 1890 Open champion.

George's match with Park 'was played before a crowd of people, and won by Park by the large number of 10 holes'. It is said that after losing the first seven or eight holes, George exclaimed, 'For the love o' Gode, gi'e me a hauf.' It was a humiliating defeat for the Morris clan.

The report continued: 'A match was then made up by the gentlemen, betwixt Tom Morris and Park, to be played the following morning, the bets amounting to nearly £20. The match was played, and Tom lost it by four holes. Allan and Dunnil [Dunnie] were then expected to come forward and show this youth how he could be beat; but if we are rightly informed, they some way or other declined to play with him. On Friday morning, a number of gentlemen golfers on the links, thinking that the abilities of Park had scarcely been sufficiently tested, asked Tom and him to play a second match for a sum of two or three pounds, which they subscribed for the winner. This time Park lost by three or four holes.'

Other reports at the time had Park losing by five holes. Park wanted an immediate rematch, but Tom had pre-existing match commitments to Col. Fairlie.

What is important to note here is that even Dunnie, Park's fellow Musselburgh man, did not deem the challenge worthy of recognition. It wasn't just Allan.

Far from being about avoiding the game, it seems that Dunnie did not want or feel the need to take on the brusque, colourful challenge of Park, or at least not yet. Nonetheless, this is the start of 20 years or so of Morris v. Park battles.

Given the success of the match and the fact that both golfers were 'on a par', a grand match was quickly arranged for one week later across three courses, namely Musselburgh, St Andrews, and North Berwick. No money was being played for. The papers said this was purely a match the players themselves wanted. Park won at North Berwick but lost at Musselburgh. Overall, he won decisively by nine holes and immediately posted a challenge in the *Edinburgh News*.

It would largely be ignored until the October autumn meeting the next year, 1855. Tom was reported as having thrashed Willie 'on his own green', early in 1855.

That was the defining issue.

Park and Morris were continually winning and losing – they were so well matched. This leaves the question of why Allan or Dunnie would even bother to join the melée.

To think of it in boxing language again, if the undercards beneath him cannot find an undisputed champion challenger among them, then there is no one for the champion to meet.

Willie would beat Tom in 1856 and then, in 1858, a grand match would fall through, due to Willie not having financial backers. After Allan's demise, Tom would win in 1862, defeating Park on all four links of the match at Musselburgh, Prestwick, North Berwick and St Andrews. In 1870 Tom famously walked off the Musselburgh course in the middle of a match, due to unruly partisan crowds.

What cannot be overstated is how all these matches, sometimes over 108 holes, sometimes over 144, created great excitement, with matches gaining more and more column inches. Tom said of Park that he was, 'as good a player that ever lifted a club'. Although never good friends, like Dunnie and Tom, the two of them, Park and Tom, did a service to the game with their gladiatorial matches and feisty challenges in the press.

It could be argued that while Allan was taking it too easy through the latter part of the 1850s, it is Tom and Park whom we should thank for raising the profile of the game. Allan did not respond to a single one of Park's challenges. Many hoped he would and silence the 'braggart' evermore, but alas not. It would be quite wrong to say that Allan had a quiet decade. He certainly did not, as he was playing with professionals and amateurs regularly right up until 1859. Allan did not rise to any singles' challenges that put his title on the line, largely because there was not a single outstanding challenger. However, he did enjoy foursomes.

The greatest played golf match

The year 1855 was good for Allan. He seemed to be playing more golf. Certainly, twice the number of matches were reported than in previous years. Although he was only turning 40 that year, he was like his old self. In their regular game with Sir Thomas Moncrieffe against Tom and Col. Fairlie, Allan's team won, after a few years of tied matches.

Allan even ventured outside of St Andrews. In Crail, on the Balcomie Links, he won their historic Lindesay Medal. Crail Golfing Society varied their play over the original Sauchope course and Balcomie Links at that time. At the prize-giving ceremony Allan said that it was indeed the first medal he had ever won. It is quite hard to comprehend that the best in the world would have no silverware. His winning matches were played for money alone.

Dr McPherson's book showed an 1858 staged photograph by Thomas Rodger, with the four players. McPherson lamented that they had never played an actual match, but they did, which was discovered in old press clippings.

With Allan in good form, The Invincibles reunited for what would be their fourth and final match, in October 1855, as part of the seasonal matches outside of the Royal & Ancient's autumn meeting.

It was the best game ever played, not in terms of match, but in the quality of the players.

Allan and Tom versus Dunnie, who had by then moved to Blackheath, and Willie Park Snr, the new, if somewhat controversial, star of Musselburgh at his second autumn meeting.

Although the game was reported only in passing and sadly lacking in detail, it was actually the most exciting golf match in years. The betting was heavy. Some papers said it was £300, others £400, but the likely sum could have been as much as £500. That was an eye-watering sum and certainly the biggest ever for that time.

The *Fife Herald* dated Thursday 25 October described the match. 'On Thursday a match was played which, as well it might, created very great excitement amongst the golfers, and indeed throughout the whole city. The players consisted of the champion golfers of the day; viz. Allan of St Andrews (the king) and Tom Morris of Prestwick against Dunnie of Blackheath and Park of Musselburgh. It is very difficult to state the total amount of bets made upon this round by numerous parties, but we believe we shall be rather smaller than above the mark when we say from £300 to £400 depended on the issue. A large concourse of people followed the players during the whole round, amongst them were the whole of the gentleman golfers on the Links. Every stroke was keenly watched, and after a well-contested match, the players came in with Allan and Tom having two holes and two strokes ahead of their opponents. Allan and Tom went the round in 94 strokes, while Dunnie and Park took 96.'

The detail of their triumphant hour was not captured fully, but one can imagine the home crowd's jubilation at the moment of victory.

The Invincibles had won yet again and would remain unbeaten evermore. So, in all their grand matches, they truly never lost, apart from when visiting Musselburgh as one leg of a three-course match. Although their winning games were largely at St Andrews, to win and win repeatedly remains a remarkable achievement.

In the article *A Haver with Tom Morris*, Captain Stewart played Tom and Allan with The Invincibles giving him six shots, but this was but a fun challenge, nothing more.

It is curious to note that this 1855 game was the last grand foursomes matches for The Invincibles against the best golfers in the world. Yes, Tom and Allan played more matches with gentleman golfers, and there were certainly some highly competitive professional matches with the two on opposite sides, but The Invincibles never travelled again as a foursome beyond St Andrews. To beat the King or The Invincibles, you had to beat them on their own domain.

One cannot help but look over Allan and Tom's foursomes record and admire what they achieved. The result when money was crossing palms at the end of their four matches was always the same – they won. They were the best and, to the golfing populace of the 1850s, invincible.

Other professional partners

In 1857 Allan Robertson partnered with a young Andrew Strath (1837–68), who would go on to win the Open in 1865. He was the elder brother of Davie Strath, three-times runner-up in the Open (1870, 1872, 1876). Together, Allan and Andrew played against Tom and Park, for the large sum of £100. This was unusual, as Allan could have partnered with Tom but chose a mere boy, the 18-year-old Strath. Additionally, Park and Tom were adversaries throughout most of their lives in these big money matches, so quite why these two fierce rivals would be partners in such a match is not clear. When Andrew won the Open in 1865, he beat Park by two strokes at Prestwick. It is very likely the case that Allan knew what a rich talent young Andrew was. Allan and Andrew won the match by six holes over one round, shooting 84 to 90 strokes by Tom and Park. Like lots of champions throughout the centuries, pairing them up does not necessarily lead to success. Tom and Park were never a great team, and Park often proffered that he would prefer to play against Tom than with him.

This match also shows that Allan was not avoiding professional matches at all.

If the public quietly thought of Tom and Park as the uncrowned princes of the game, he had just beaten them, albeit in foursomes with a young, gifted lad as his playing partner.

Andrew would go on and partner Tom and Sir Thomas Moncreiffe in matches after Allan's demise. He took over at Prestwick around 1865 from Charles Hunter, who had taken over from Tom and lasted eight months before heading to Blackheath. It was this year that Andrew won the Open. Sadly, the Strath family struggled with tuberculosis and Andrew died aged only 31 on 23 February 1868 and was buried in Prestwick. How many more Opens could he have won?

At the Royal & Ancient's autumn meeting later in 1855, Allan and

Andrew paired again, this time against Tom and Park's younger brother David. The outcome was no different. Allan and Andrew won the match convincingly, 7 and 5.

Every time Allan was challenged or when there were rumblings of him avoiding matches, Allan seemed to let his golfing correct the narrative. This 1857 game was the last professional challenge match that Allan was recorded playing in. What an incredible record Allan had. The Invincibles were unbeaten.

In singles matches he rarely lost. If you consider that from 1837 to 1858, out of close to 85 recorded foursomes and singles games, he only lost three times at Musselburgh, a few gentlemen matches, and a couple of times narrowly to Tom.

That is remarkable.

That is why he was called the champion and why Dr McPherson, who witnessed many of his matches, considered him the 'King of Golf', with Park, Dunnie and Tom all beneath him.

Records show that Allan was playing well in the late 1850s, but time was running out. He had one more superlative moment of golfing genius. As final moments go, this was truly special.

Eighteen

LONG LIVE THE KING

As we edge towards the end of the 1850s, Playfair had all but completed his work of transformation in St Andrews. In place of dirt tracks, Allan could now enjoy paved, clean streets and roads clear of dung piles or the horrid stench of fish guts. St Andrews had been re-born as a beautiful, middle-class place to visit and live. From the starveling village of yore, it had blossomed into the town we know today.

In gratitude for his work, the University of St Andrews bestowed an honorary LL.D. on Playfair in 1856 and later that year he also received a knighthood from Queen Victoria. It was only right that someone who had devoted the last 30 years of his life to the town should receive such an honour. It also recognised his service years in India.

The work to protect the links from the West Sands tides was coming along well. With the ongoing and repeated land reclamation, reaching farther into the beach and shoreline, there would be enough land for Tom to create a new separate first hole in 1872.

In July 1857, a portrait of Allan was included in *The Golfers Manual*, the book by Henry B. Farnie (1836–89), which was based on an earlier photograph by Thomas Rodger. This photograph was the first ever of a professional golfer. Yes, there were group-posed golfing shots, but none with a lone professional. Allan was the first.[1] The lithographer was German artist Mr Charles Schacher, who made lithographic prints in the 19th century of many well-known figures, such as Queen Victoria's husband, Prince Albert.

Allan had a keen sense of who he was and his place in the annals of golf. His golf balls and clubs were all signed simply 'ALLAN'. His books and scrapbooks were signed and dated. You get the sense he knew what was coming in terms of the growth of the game and was certain that, as king of the game, items bearing his signature would be of interest and value to future generations. This portrait would have added to that.

The first of the three Grand National golf events in St Andrews took place in 1857, and Playfair was also re-elected once more as provost. Allan partnered up with Mr Erskine Wemyss and won most of their matches against Tom and Mr Cathcart. The match was captured in a posed photograph by Thomas Rodger.

Throughout this year and 1858, Allan played a lot of foursomes with gentlemen golfers, winning the majority of them. There was a spring match with Sir Thomas against Tom and Fairlie, which Allan's side won, and an autumn match when the outcomes were reversed.

To this background, Park and Tom were entangled over a grand match at the autumn meeting that was on and then cancelled when Park failed to raise the finance from backers.

On 7 October 1858 the *Fifeshire Journal* ran a short piece. 'On Monday last Tom had a bout against Allan privately. The play was remarkably close all along. Eventually Allan won by one hole, and that hole by a putt merely – his score being 92 for the round against Tom's 93. In justice to Tom, however, it should be mentioned, that Allan having volunteered on Tuesday [the day previous to the meeting] to take Tom out, in expectation that his [Tom's] match with Park would be played on the Friday following, Tom agreed, and off they started; and after most beautiful play, Tom licked Allan by one hole, so that they are, as far as single-handed play is concerned, a tie.'

It was remarkable that there was but a whisker of difference, if any, between them in 1858. Allan was the older player, but at 43 years of age there are few signs of him declining into twilight years; he was still playing many matches, and indeed his greatest game on the St Andrews links was just about to come.

In a clipping in his scrapbook, the detail of his finest hour in a match against Mr A. Bethune of Blebo at the autumn meeting set out that a week or so later after his matches with Tom, 'A notable event in the annals of golfing, however, occurred on the 15th inst., when Allan – the champion – in a match against Mr Bethune of Blebo, holed the Links at 79, which has never been done before, and will not likely be done again.'

Another clipping said, 'On Wednesday a match of thirty-six holes or two rounds, was played on our Links, between the famed Allan Robertson and Mr Bethune of Blebo, Allan giving three-fourths odds – that is one more for every three holes, and each fourth hole even. Allan holed the first round in eighty-six and the second round in seventy-nine – this being the fewest that a round over our Links has ever been played in. This is a most extraordinary short number to hole a round of St Andrews' Links, and Allan has the honour to be the first and most probably be the only one that will accomplish such a feat. The match was got up by Mr Brown of Balgarvie who backed Allan, and won by Allan beating his opponent by even holes out of the thirty-six. We understand that the £200 match between Mr William Park of Musselburgh and Mr Thomas Morris of Prestwick is to come off shortly.'

It didn't.

No one had ever shot a score as low as 79. Not Dunnie, nor Tom, nor Park, never mind Tom Alexander, nor Davie Robertson (all true legends of the game): Allan surpassed them all. Once again, while Tom and Park are arguing about their match, Allan, as king, let his golf do the talking and simply re-asserted his long reign.

Dr McPherson said, 'He was playing … a single against Bethune of Blebo, giving heavy odds. He forced everything to best his opponent, though so heavily handicapped; he succeeded in all but that [6th] hole, and scored 79 on the round. On the whole, however, Allan combined steadiness and brilliancy; "far and sure" was realised in his play.'

Very far from slowing down, Allan was playing the best golf of his life, birdieing the last hole for the 79.

Knowing the best golfer in the world was playing so well, it made what happened next so very tragic.

The sad decline

The spring meeting came in 1859, but there was no sign of Allan playing his typical list of matches with gentlemen and professionals. In a report for the Grand National Tournament in the *Perthshire Journal* on 4 August, it lamented, 'A few professionals are present on the Links – Tom Morris, Park, Dun [sic], Robert Andrews &c. – but there have been no matches as yet of consequence. Allan, we are sorry to say, has been very ill for some time, and is far from being able to appear on the turf.'

Allan would have been able to hear the comings and goings of the golfers and visitors. His golf parlour may have been open for business, with Lang Willie and Da' holding fort. The *Caledonian Mercury* of 7 September reported, 'Some months ago he was attacked by jaundice, which refused to yield to medical treatment. Many were the inquiries made after his health by visitors of the Links.'

Another reported, 'At the time of the Golf Tournament he was able to appear on the green, and gladly his presence there was hailed by many gentlemen at the gathering. After the tournament he still was able to go out a little, but latterly his disease assumed an alarming aspect. For several weeks back it was observed he was gradually sinking.'

It is beyond reasonable doubt that Tom would have called in to see his lifelong close friend. Allan would have known that the disease had beaten him. Jaundice is noticeable by the yellowing of the skin and in the whites of the eyes. Modern-day medicines target the cause of jaundice rather than the symptoms themselves. In the 21st century, recovery is commonplace, but not so in the mid-19th century. However, the pointed phrasing of 'jaundice attack', according to retired surgeon and golf historian David Hamilton, points us towards viral hepatitis A, which is still dangerous today. Less likely is a pancreatic tumour, which would come on slowly.

Alas, this was one battle where Allan couldn't snoddit them at the burn.

It is tempting to think about Allan and Tom's final moments together with Allan bedridden. In a film script, he might ask Tom to be the new champion and to go out and beat whomever Tom was lined up to play that day, with a few tips about their opponent's Achilles heel. Sadly, this is fanciful. Tom never spoke of their final minutes together and with Allan publicly appearing at the Grand National event, Tom may have even believed or hoped that Allan was on the mend: 'He couldn't be bunkered. Not Allan,' type of thinking.

Allan died in his home, according to the death record, on 1 September 1859 at 1.20 p.m., aged 43.

It is remarkable to think that Tom Morris was only 38 at the time, and would live for another 49 years or so.

Allan's record in the death register noted that his demise was due to a disease of the liver for the previous six months, as certified by Dr John Adamson, who had visited him the day before. Allan's neighbour, John Hastie, was the informant as his brother David was in Australia.

The Union Club, who had not yet amalgamated with The Royal and Ancient Golf Club of St Andrews, issued a fine tribute to him in the following resolution in the meeting for business at 10.30 a.m. at the end of the autumn meeting. The motion was proposed by Allan's partner, Mr Erskine Wemyss, MP and seconded by Sir Hugh Playfair. It said that,

> This meeting have heard with deep regret of the death of Allan Robertson, and they desire to record on their minutes the opinion universally entertained of the almost unrivalled skill with which he played the game of golf, combining a ready and correct judgment with most accurate execution. They desire also to express the sense of the propriety of his whole conduct, and unvarying civility with which he mingled with all classes of golfers, of his cordiality to those of his own, of his integrity, his happy temper, and the anxiety he always manifested to promote the comfort of all who frequented the Links. They desire an extract of this minute to be transmitted to his widow with an expression of their sympathy in her affliction.

Showing that golf was and remains the great leveller, these two gentlemen stood up to speak for Allan. It was a fine honour.

The shock of his passing was also reflected in the national papers. The *Fifeshire Journal* on 8 September said,

> We feel assured Allan's death will be greatly lamented by a very wide circle. To the golfing community his death will prove a blank that cannot easily be filled up. He was admitted to be the champion of the world, and never lost any match he was engaged in … Allan's great forte lay in his nerve. Although a match looked as if it would go dead against him, he never got down-hearted, but continued to play on steadily. The greater the difficulties he had to contend with, the better and more

> brilliantly he played, seeming quite certain that ultimately, he would land himself a winner at the end of the match … In an emergency … it was then his skill showed most – it was then, by some brilliant stroke, often out of a most difficult position, that he astounded those looking on, and staggered his opponents, by the cool, calculating, yet bold aspect of the game. Ah, he was a noble player! We ne'er shall see his like again.

That was indeed Allan's skill. He didn't just impress other professionals. He astounded them. That was the difference between Allan and the professionals of that era. It was Allan who shot 79 when Tom and others were winning matches with a 90. He so bamboozled Park by chipping in on the 17th that Park's next drive sank in the Swilcan Burn.

In *Reminiscences of Arbroath & St Andrews*, the author D.S. Salmond said when discussing St Andrews in 1855:

> I have recollections of seeing Allan Robertson putting. How he calculated every little mound and rough piece of grass in a long and billowy 'putt' is still a subject for admiration. I may be heretical, but I think putting then was a much more 'scientific' as well as more difficult thing than it is now. I have seen the 'champion' to whom I have referred hole putts on very uneven ground with a certainty which makes one speculate as to what he could have done on the present greens … he wore an almost perpetual smile and a red coat when playing.

At each stage of his career, be it in his mid-twenties against Tom Alexander and Dunnie, or in later life, it seemed that, like Tiger Woods in the modern era and with his short red coat on, Allan could switch into another gear even as all seemed lost.

The obituary written by Henry Farnie in the *Dundee Courier* noted, 'Up to the spring of the present year [1859], Allan was a hale, stout little man, with scarcely the memory of an hour's illness. Temperate too, in an uncommon degree, regular in his habits, and enjoying daily exercise on the links; no one could reasonably foretell the rapid change that had taken him from us. In the spring, Allan had an attack of jaundice. After six months weakness he gradually sunk and died on

1st September. God rest him, noble golfer, excellent companion – we will not easily see his like again.'

The *Fife Herald* on 8 September ran the longest of testimonials with Allan's name uppercase throughout. In all likelihood penned by Farnie again, it is certainly worth republishing in full:

ALLAN ROBERTSON, THE CHAMPION GOLFER. ALLAN Robertson, the greatest golf-player that ever lived, of whom alone the annals of the pastime it can be said that never was beaten, was born at St Andrews on the 11th September 1815. He came of a golfing race. His grandfather, Peter Robertson, who died in 1803, was a ball-maker and professional golfer. His father, too, David [Davie] Robertson, who lived till 1836, followed the same trade, and was moreover a good player in his day – nay, few were better on the golfing green. As might be expected from such a generation of golfers, ALLAN took naturally to the Links. It is a fact that his very playthings as a child growing up were golf clubs. This natural tendency joined to a natural desire of his father that his son should continue the business of ball-maker, decided ALLAN's profession, and due course of time he likewise took up the awl and the feathers to learn the manufacture of golf balls.

At that period, golfing was quite another thing from what it is now, or at least its accessories were. Gutta-percha was unknown, and golf balls were composed of stout leather cases stuffed hard with boiled feathers. Their manufacture indeed was both a difficult and an arduous matter; and their expense when finished was such as to restrict the practice of the game, as a rule, to the more wealthy of the community. The Links of St Andrews, in consequence, were less frequented than now; the course was rougher; the sport had an aristocratic and portly mien; and the matches of professionals were as pregnant with interest as any public event. It is not so now; the St Andrews Links are crowded with careless multitudes luxuriating the pastime cheapened to them by the discovery of gutta-percha; and the game is popularised at the expense of its stately traditions.

ALLAN, however, commenced his golfing career what, despite

the clearness of leather, and the paucity of players, Aye must still call (remember) the palmy days of golf. His entire nature was bent on being a golfer. It is yet told on the Links, how ALLAN would rise betimes, and with shirt sleeves rolled up for better muscular play, start alone for practice across the deserted Links still wet with early dew. His success was abundant. ALLAN has improved in his day on the old theories of golf, and to him are owing many of the improved methods and styles of the present game. Some of these we will afterwards more particularly allude to.

In the spring of 1848, Mr Campbell, of Saddell (we believe), brought a few experimental gutta-percha balls from London to St Andrews. They were not very first-rate, to be sure; were not hammered, and flew heavily. Still the material was unquestionably good and adaptable; and consternation stood on every face, ALLAN's included. And no wonder. The leather ball trade was the only one St Andrews could boast, and it was considerable, extending to exports to the colonies as well as home consumption. In ALLAN's shop alone, there were made, for example, 1810: 1,021 balls, 1841: 1,392 balls, in 1844, and so on. The introduction of gutta-percha, which anybody could mould into a sphere, was a dreadful prospect for ALLAN and his brethren, and dire was their alarm. It is even related that ALLAN would gladly buy up all the gutta-percha balls found among the whins, &c, and actually attempted to destroy the obnoxious interlopers with fire!

However, the influx was too great for this system to be pursued any longer, and about 1850 ALLAN entered regularly into golf ball making from gutta-percha and we are glad to know that his labour, whilst it was easier to himself, was not a whit less rewarded than in the old monopoly days of feathers.

The life of a professional golfer like ALLAN, so composed of continuous matches and a certain recurring sameness of incident, that have found it impossible to trace in anything like a consecutive story the incidents of ALLAN's life. All we can do to recall a few memories here and there, and give ... (a select) chronological order of his more important matches and feats.

Who will ever forget ALLAN, having once seen him? What Sir Hugh Lyon Playfair has been to the city proper, has ALLAN been to the Links of St Andrews. They have unwittingly been in close partnership. Sir Hugh renovated a rough, ruined street – ALLAN had eye the while to the improvement of the Links; Sir Hugh attracted citizens, ALLAN, golfers; ah! it was a magnificent partnership, and has done wonders.

The analogy holds good between the two in other respects also. Who could do the honours of the Links like ALLAN? He was as perfectly at home with a descendant of William the Conqueror as with one of the caddies. Without the least tinge of servility, ALLAN could accommodate himself to everybody, and arranged everything on the golfing links with the politeness of BRUMMELL and the policy of a TALLEYRAND …

But it was in a grand match that the figure of ALLAN should live in the memory of all. Who shall describe his elegant and beautifully correct style of play? The champion was remarkable for his easy style, depending on a long cool swing, and never on sheer strength. His clubs were of the toy description, as the slang of the links hath it, possessing no weight or mis-proportion of wood. Indeed, in a word, ALLAN's game throughout was pure unadulterated science. No man, perhaps, so well united in his play in all the bits of the game. Pretty driver as he was, we still stake our belief on ALLAN's short game, especially in quarter shots, and this was an important point in ALLAN's practice.

He it was that introduced the deadly use of the cleek, in playing up to the hole. Previous to about 1848 or 1849, short wooden clubs, the baffing (baffie), or short spoons, were used for this important stroke – both difficult, and frequently inaccurate. But ALLAN employed the cleek to jerk up his ball; however badly it might lie, it was all the same; and this killing game, destructive to a certain extent to the green, is now all but universal.

To return to ALLAN's great matches. His coolness was unique, and almost miraculous. He was never known to funk, or indeed change his off-hand manner the least. He was never beaten – proud epitaph. It is something to be the best in anything, of all the world, ALLAN stood confessed the model player. But it is not only as a golfer that ALLAN is to be deeply deplored. He was possessed of the best heart and kindliest feelings in the world. In the intricate dealings of the Links, in the formation and playing great matches, ALLAN was honourable, just, and gentlemanly, from first to last.

ALLAN did much for golfing both in and out of St Andrews. He has laid out capital Links in various districts, and played thereon himself to the incitement of beginners. Traces of his labour and skill are to be seen at Wemyss Castle, Delvine, Mountquhanie, and many other places, seats of nobles and gentles.

A new era is about to dawn on the golfing links; the old stars are paling, when will others arise? Hugh Philp, who knew how to make a club, is gone; gone too, fine ALLAN, who knew how to handle one.

We have already noticed how impossible it is, especially with imperfect means of information, to give a consecutive or full account of the champion's feats, but we subjoin a few, in hopes that this meagre outline may testify, in some small way, to the merit, as a man and a golfer, of ALLAN ROBERTSON.

i. (1838) ALLAN holed the short hole going out at one stroke, and again in 1846.

ii. (1839) ALLAN drove a teed ball from the corner of dyke hole going out, over all the three ditches – 250 yards. His longest shot.

iii. (1840) ALLAN played grand match with Tom Alexander, ballmaker, Musselburgh, over the St Andrews Links, in October, and beat him by 4 holes, doing the round at 95.

iv. (1842) ALLAN and Sandy Herd, played in a double, against Tom Morris and Jamie Herd, beating them by 2 holes. Strokes 91 and 94.

v. (1842) ALLAN played a match with only a driver and cleek against Robert Chambers, Esq., E Edinburgh, and holed the round at 96.

vi. (1842) ALLAN played a match in December with Tom Morris, beating him 2 holes, and holing the Links at 93.

vii. (1843) ALLAN played during the month of June over the St Andrews Links, a great match of 20 rounds, two each day, against William Dunn of Musselburgh. Allan gained on the tenth, or last day, by two rounds and one to play. As Mr Carnegie sweetly sung on the occasion –

> Ten days they were fighting, ten days, ten days,
> Complete at their weapons, always, always,
> With club, cleek, and putter, my Muse cannot utter,
> A millionth part of their praise, their praise!

viii. (1843) ALLAN played a round at St Andrews in October, with James Calvert, Esq., Montrose, and holed the round at 88.

ix. (1843) ALLAN played a great match of 36 holes with Wm. Dunn of Musselburgh, beating him by 8 holes, and holing the second round at 88 strokes.

x. (1843) In a round with Robert Lindsay, Esq. of Straiton, ALLAN holed the 1st hole, going out in 4, and the second in 3: the whole round was done at 90.

xi. (1844) ALLAN played a match with William Dunn, over three links: 1st, on Musselburgh Links, where Dunn gained; 2nd, at North Berwick Links, where ALLAN was victorious; and 3rd, at St Andrews, where he also won, thus gaining the match also.

xii. ALLAN played a round with Captain David Campbell of Schehallion, and holed the Links at 87.

xiii. In April, ALLAN played another of his matches with W. Dunn: 1st, at Musselburgh, where Dunn beat ALLAN by 7 a-head and 5 to play; 2nd, at St Andrews, where ALLAN won 5 and 3; and 3rd, at Leven, where he also was victor by 6 and 4 to play, thus winning the match.

xiv. (1846) ALLAN played with a single driving club against Captain Broughton, and holed the round of the St Andrews Links at 95.

xv. (1848) ALLAN drove, in two successive rounds, on the same day, a teed ball from the end hole to the foot of the short hole green. This was in September.

xvi. ALLAN played a threesome with Wm. Dunn and Tom Morris, over Dubbieside Links. ALLAN holed 18 holes (two rounds), at 80; Thomas Morris, at 89; and Dunn, at 91 strokes.

xvii. (1849) A great match for £400 was played in the summer between ALLAN and Tom Morris against the two Dunns of Musselburgh, on three links, Musselburgh, St Andrews, and North Berwick. At Musselburgh the Dunns won at a canter, winning 13 holes and 12 to play. St Andrews, however, ALLAN and Tom won their rounds, and retrieved some two or three holes. North Berwick was the deciding place, and at the commencement of the last round of all, the Dunns had four holes a-head, and only eight to play. However, ALLAN and Tom, by a magnificent game, gained the first hole, then the second, halved the third, gained the fourth, halved the fifth, and gained the sixth, thus making the poll all even! and two to play. These two holes ALLAN and Tom also won, thus obtaining the match, one of the most brilliant and extraordinary in the whole annals of golfing.

xviii. (1850) In October ALLAN and Tom Morris played a foursome against the two Dunns for £50 aside. Allan and his partner finished at the burn hole, by two and one to play, holing at 88.

xix. (1852) October, over the St Andrews Links, ALLAN and Tom Morris played a great match of holes with Robert Hay, Esq., and William Dun, Blackheath, for £100 a side. ALLAN and his partner won by six holes a-head, and five to play.

xx. (1853) In October, ALLAN played a round with Captain John Campbell Stewart, 72nd Highlanders, winner at that meeting of the St Andrews Club, of the Royal Medal. This round was halved, though ALLAN was 3 a-head and 4 to play, and dormy at the Burn.

At this time also, Sir Thomas Moncrieffe and Allan played Tom Morris and Captain Fairlie. The first round was won by ALLAN and his partner, at 3 and 1 to play; and the second by their adversaries, at 4 and 3 to play. This foursome was played repeatedly, and on the whole play it may be said to have formed one of the closest matches on record.

XXI. (1857) ALLAN and Andrew Strath, in May, over the St Andrews Links, played a round against Tom Morris and Park ... winning six holes. Strokes, 84 and 90.

XXII. (1858) On the 15th September, ALLAN, in a round with Mr Bethune of Blebo, accomplished the round of the St Andrews Links at 79 strokes, a number altogether unparalleled, and likely to remain so. The following are the particulars of this superb score:–

Going out—1 in 4; 2 in 4; 3 in 4; 4 in 5. 5 in 5; 6 in 6; 7 in 4; 8 in 4; 9 in 4. Total, going out, 40.

Coming in—10 in 4; 11 in 3; 12 in 5; 13 in 6; 14 in 4; in 15 in 5; 16 in 5; 17 in 4; 18 in 3. Total, coming in, 39.

XXIII. At various times ALLAN has holed the St Andrews Links at the following numbers, selecting his best holes: –

Going out—1 in 3 strokes; 2 in 3; 3 in 3; 4 in 3; 5 in 4; 6 in 4; 7 in 3. 8 in 1; 9 in 3; Total, 27.

Coming in—10 in 3; 11 in 2; l2 in 3; 13 in 4; 14 in 4; 15 in 3; 16 in 3; 17 in 4; 18 in 3.

Total, 29. Number of strokes to this selected round, 56.

(In comparing the above scores, it must be recollected that the St Andrews Links are now not nearly so difficult to play as they were 15 and 20 years ago.)

I would add to that. The first hole tee that Allan played was around 50–70 yards farther forward than today, extending down to today's 17th green. The hole came in, looking at Martin's maps, at about 360 yards. Nonetheless, to score a 3 over that hole today would be incredible, never mind with hickory clubs and featherie or guttie ball. With bunker, burn and sandy shoreline, it was an impressive hole. Allan's striking ability and hand–eye co-ordination must have been incredible.

The largest funeral

The funeral of Allan Robertson took place on Monday 5 September 1859. The great and good of golf turned out in huge numbers for their national hero and champion of Scotland. It was said to be the largest funeral that had been seen in St Andrews, attended by over 500 noblemen and gentlemen.

The *Caledonian Mercury* on that Wednesday reported: 'On Monday last, the funeral of Allan Robertson at St Andrews was attended by a number of the inhabitants of that city. Allan was known to everyone on the Links, and he was deservedly and universally respected. He had a kind and genial disposition, an honourable man; and while he took the position as the champion of Scotland's national game, he was never known to be forward presuming ... There seemed to be a general consent of refraining from the game of golf on the day of the funeral. It was … [attended] by Mr E. Wemyss, M.P.; Sir Wm. Dunbar, Bart, M.P.; Mr Whyte-Melville. Mr Grant of Kilgraston, Capt. Maitland Dougall, Mr Sutherland, Captain Lyon and by many from a distance; by Sir Hugh Lyon Playfair, Dr Buist … and many of the townspeople.'

Two hundred people are said to have paid their respects by visiting his resting place in St Andrews cemetery by the cathedral.

Adverts for Farnie's book, in which Allan's lithographic print could be found, now read, 'The only authentic LIKENESS of the late ALLAN ROBERTSON of St Andrews, is a beautiful and correct Lithograph by SCHENCK, in the "Golfer's Manual," after a Calotype by RODGER. Price 2s 6d.'

He was the king of golf and inarguably the game's first star. The champion, when golf started a period of rapid growth, was Allan. Young golfers idolised him and tried to imitate his graceful swing, such as Davie Strath and Captain J.C. Stewart, who, it was said by Dr McPherson, used it to great effect.[2]

Allan was not a tall man, barely 5 feet 5 inches and possibly even smaller, but he left an indelible mark on the links. It wasn't just Allan's demise and the profound loss that was felt, but it was also the end of 250 years of Robertson ballmakers.

The Robertson family had witnessed everything first hand, from the fall of St Andrews following the Reformation, and the era of witches being accused and thrown off the cliffs at the Scores. The Robertsons had seen the open links common land slowly fill up with houses in one triangular piece of ground beside the opening hole. In Allan's time, there were golf shops, but the majority of the houses that face the links came after his passing. To Allan, there were lots of garden gates that opened to the links.

Throughout all this history of St Andrews, the Robertsons were stitching featherie golf balls. It was a remarkable heritage, and few can claim better.

After Allan's death, his wife Jane remained in the area for at least six years. In the census of 1861 she was noted as living at 20 Golf Place, which is where Sandyhill was then, and that she had a lodger. She inherited the not inconsiderable sum of just over £93, but not the property at Sandyhill, which would stay in the Robertson family and transfer to Allan's brother David.

The Royal and Ancient minutes record that, following Allan's death, an annuity was immediately raised for Jane, as proposed by John Whyte-Melville, with £25 being immediately being donated by the Union Club.

David returned from Australia, without his family, and developed plans in 1863 for Sandyhill to become a grand hotel, before his own early demise of a liver complaint on 14 February 1864 (see the Epilogue for more information).

He had plans to expand Sandyhill to at least four bedrooms, which allowed it to be designated a hotel, and was successful in obtaining a licence to sell alcohol. From contemporary photographs we can see that the attic was converted and dormer windows added. David did not build over the garden and bushes that Tom and Allan had planted. That larger extension and the extra layers that created the Allan Villa we know today came soon after.

Jane would stay in Sandyhill until the 1865 sale. It is said that she moved to Edinburgh around this time, but returned to St Andrews some 30 years later, likely to spend her final days.

The Royal & Ancient Golf Club would surpass their earlier tribute to Allan by donating a further £203 annuity to Allan's widow. The 1889 appeal stated,

> The Committee of the Royal and Ancient Golf Club of St Andrews have sanctioned this Appeal being laid on the Tables of the Club House.
>
> APPEAL
>
> The Widow of the famous Golfer, ALLAN ROBERTSON, now in her 77th year, has lately returned to end her days in St Andrews, and is in very straitened, almost destitute, circumstances, through no fault of her own.
>
> A proposal has been made by some who knew Allan, that a sum should be raised by subscription, sufficient to purchase an annuity for her, or otherwise to keep her free from want during the few years of life which may still be left in her. This proposal has been cordially adopted by the few who have as yet heard of the circumstances, and it is believed that there are many who, although they do not remember Allan personally, will be glad to help the widow of a golfer who was never equalled in his life, and has never been surpassed since his death, just thirty years ago. Further information as to Mrs Robertson's circumstances will be gladly furnished by the undersigned, and subscriptions will be received by them or by the Club Steward or may be paid to 'Allan Robertson's Widow's Fund' with the Royal Bank of Scotland, St Andrews.
>
> Alex Kinloch
> W. H. Maitland Dougall
> R. Bethune
> T. T. Oliphant
> The Club House, St Andrews, 2nd September, 1889

With a good few years of salary raised, Jane could live out a comfortable life for the rest of her years.

Allan's last will and testament

On 9 January 1861 Stuart Grace registered an inventory of Allan's estate alongside his last will at the court in Cupar. Made in 1852, the will left 'all my household goods, debts, money, gold & silver coined and uncoined and all moveable effects whatever (except the History of the Bible full of plates and dated 1712, also an old knife dated 1800 it is the shape of a hare, also my late father's old Pinchbeck watch, also the books named the History of the Robertsons, these four things to go to my brother or his family, as heir looms).'

In other words, those select items that belonged to the family in years gone by would stay in the family. As set out on the first page of the first chapter, this book on the Robertsons must have meant a lot to Allan. He truly had a sense of his heritage and where his family came from. The other moveable items were Jane's to do with as she thought best. In the will Allan made sure she was cared for and made her life-rented for the house. In other words, she could stay in the house as long as she lived. At her death, it would transfer to his brother David, or his family if he died young. Jane also had the option of placing debts onto the property if she required money. One addition to the 1852 will, made in 1856, set out that if David died, Jane was given permission to sell the property.

Within a month of the funeral, minds were already turning to consider Allan's successor. On 6 October, the *Fifeshire Journal* said, 'At a meeting of the society … the subject of a successor to the much-lamented Allan Robertson was discussed. The feeling of the meeting lay almost entirely with Tom Morris, Prestwick. Tom is beyond doubt the most likely man to take the place of Allan in the capacity of a professional at St Andrews, Tom is a man of irreproachable character, quiet and unassuming in his deportment, and besides is a native of St Andrews, read and educated to strict proficiency in golf, to which he has attained under the guiding hand of Allan himself. Many a hard-fought match have the two contended in. Now that death has removed the senior partner for the Royal and Ancient Golf club. To attain this end some little difficulties interpose, but it is to be hoped the society will be able to set aside these, and that such an arrangement be proposed to Tom as he may at once see it for his interest to transfer his services back to the golfers of his native town.'

Perhaps some of the members had not forgotten the paper war. Maybe the fact that he was the keeper at Prestwick, with Earl of Eglinton and James Ogilvy Fairlie prominent members there and of the Royal and Ancient, explains the difficulty of the conversation with Tom. There certainly would have been a reticence by the Prestwickians to let him go.

It is striking that Tom did not make plans to return until 1863 and eventually took possession of 6 Pilmour Links, at the end of his garden, his shop, and old Hugh Philp's workshop, at what would become 8 The Links, in 1866. Remarkably, at the time of writing Tom's great-great-granddaughter, Mrs Sheila Walker, who is a wonderful ambassador for Tom and golf heritage, still retains ownership of 8 The Links and the accommodation above it.

Celebrating Allan

Allan was not forgotten.

On 24 July 1869, around the 10th anniversary of his passing, The *St Andrews Gazette* was the first to mention plans for a monument to Allan. 'THE GRAVE OF ALLAN ROBERTSON – Many one asks where this is to be found, for no monument of storied interest yet points out the last resting-place of our national champion of golf. Such diminutive thing was intended now to have been erected, but some friends have recommended delay, as they think it only requires to be known that a monument might be erected to Allan's memory, in order to procure the necessary funds. These would not require to be much – £6 or £7 would do all that is requisite, and we are glad to learn that the matter has been brooked at the Union Club. Allan's resting place is in G Division, No.9, Sec. 1st – being close to the foot-path, south-west of the Square Tower.'

Two months later, on 23 September 1869, the *Edinburgh Evening Courant* ran a piece on the proposals: 'we may notice that the blocks for the obelisk and base for the monument about to be erected over the grave of Allan Robertson have now arrived at the sculptor's yard – Mr James Kirk, Golf Place.'

On 12 February 1870, just over ten years since Allan's passing, *The St Andrews Citizen* talked about the obelisk for Allan:

> MONUMENT TO ALLAN ROBERTSON – In putting up the fine obelisk, which members of the Royal and Ancient Club have just caused to be erected for Allan, they have honoured the national game, of which he was so long the champion; they have honoured themselves, as well as paying a just tribute to golf's greatest proficient. If there is perfection in anything, golf was never nearer played to perfection than by Allan Robertson. Whether in a single, in a foursome, or as an instructor, Allan was always the same. In foursomes, he and Tom Morris beat the golfing world. Although playing a losing game, which of course he did now and again, for the green has its rubs, Allan had always the cheerful, contented, happy smile, so that all who knew him are quite prepared to endorse Lang Willie's favourite expression "We'el never see another Allan again." The monument is executed in freestone by Mr James Kirk, whose forte lies in mural monuments, but it is questionable if he has ever produced one that will be a more lasting memorial of his ability than the present one. Mr Kirk is designer as well … The east face has a bust of the deceased, with the inscription –
>
> In memory of ALLAN ROBERTSON
> Who died, 1st September 1859, Aged 44 years
> He was greatly esteemed for his personal worth,
> and for many years was distinguished as the
> Champion Golfer
> of Scotland.
>
> The north face next to the walk has the game insignia in full relief and full size – cross clubs and balls, with the motto – 'Far and sure.' The south face has a wreath of laurel, with the initials 'A.R.' enclosed … altogether Mr Kirk seems to have entered heartily into his work, and has produced a work of art.

It was a stunning success. Although the lettering may be a little worn, the obelisk is still there today. Please do try and visit on your next voyage to St Andrews.

We have reached the end of Allan's all too short but historic life. He came from hundreds of years of golfing heritage. His ancestors lived through the preaching of Knox, the destruction of the cathedral and the public fear of witches. Some of his ancestors probably played the 22-hole layout. His grandfather Peter was a noted crack golfer. His father Davie was champion golfer, so Park and Tom were certainly not the first; nor were they the first professionals. They were following in a long line of golfing heroes – champions of their era.

Allan lived on the St Andrews links from the age of seven, with his garden overlooking the new gardens on the land that carried the original 22-hole links. The links came right up to the windows at the side of his Sandyhill home.

As a teenager, he saw his father Davie become the champion golfer and the pride of St Andrews. In 1835 he watched his father lose the title to Tom Alexander and then die before he had a chance to win it back. Allan got his revenge in 1840 when he won it back. This can only have been a moment of pride for the Robertson clan, watching Allan become champion golfer like his father. It is a title they held for at least 24 out of 29 years from 1830. Just remarkable. Against the superlative Dunnie he battled and was never beaten by him in a grand match.

When the guttie emerged around 1848, Allan's anger was understandable. Now we know about his heritage – all those centuries of family history were about to go up in flames. Who wouldn't be worried? It was easier for Tom: his heritage was different. To him, the new ball was an exciting innovation. He did not have a ball-making business, nor the wages for staff, namely Allan's cousin Lang Willie, Da' Anderson and Tom. In an era before social security, if you fell on hard times, the pressure on those in Allan's situation would have been intense. To see his own relation, friend and employee Tom play with the new ball, after all the support he had given him for nine years from when Tom was 18 and, by Tom's own admission, drifting, Allan would have thought of it as a betrayal. Tom's position, that he had little choice, is possibly what saved the relationship from turning sour. It is also hard not to get the impression that Tom was evolving himself and ready to set up his own business for his family.

When Tom and Park were battling it out again and again, either on the links or in the papers, with neither taking an upper hand, Allan shot 79. Among all the professionals playing increasingly at St Andrews, it was a record that would remain unmatched for 12 years. When it was beaten by Tommy, when he shot 77, it was on an easier links. Today's bunkers on our opening nine would happen some 20 years after Tommy died.

For Allan and the betting men, there was nothing in Park's challenges for Allan to consider. Park arrived with a bang in 1854, but it quickly fizzled out in matches with Tom.

If during Allan's lifetime Tom or Park had won repeatedly, the betting men would have pushed for a grand match against Allan, but they never did. Just as Park had to beat George to get a game against Tom, it would be reasonable for Allan to think that Park had to beat Tom before he would consider a match for the title. The fact that Tom quickly beat Park if he ever lost, and vice versa, explains why no match was ever organised: it was not the case that Allan was avoiding either of them.

Allan's was a life well lived and devoted wholly to golf. He was, in many respects, golf's first superstar, as golfers, including Tom Morris, were known to have Allan's photograph by Thomas Rodger on their walls.

Allan was kind-hearted. Allan was funny. Allan was simply an exemplary golfer. He actively cared for Tom and that is reflected in his thoughtful silence the night before the Innerleven match. He was proud of Tom, and that is self-evident in the cuttings in his scrapbook.

Allan's sheer popularity was captured by the different classes of people in his funeral cortege. From across Scotland, golfers, including titled gentlemen, all came out to say farewell to their hero.

Hopefully, history will now show that Allan was a genius of the links, fondly admired by his peers, who, when challenged, let his golf do the talking.

Allan Robertson, in his red coat, was simply a St Andrews boy who became 'King of Clubs'.

EPILOGUE

LIFE in St Andrews continued as normal. Of course it would. The 1859 autumn meeting in late September saw Allan's great supporter Sir David Baird win the Silver Medal, Captain Maitland Dougall the Gold Medal, and a Mr M'Whannel the King William IV Medal. At the meeting the R&A poignantly recognised the loss of Allan, which would have been felt so keenly by the members.

The Open

At the end of the Grand National Golf Tournament in 1859, before Allan died, the papers lamented the poor turnout, saying that it resembled the ordinary medal days of the Royal and Ancient. In August a letter suggested that if the event were played at different venues, it might garnish more interest. With Playfair suffering ill-health, the event was never held again.

Allan's passing left an open question – who was the new champion golfer? The title came with a lot of heritage, dating back to Tom Alexander and Davie Robertson in the 1830s, but more likely even before that, albeit unrecorded.

Allan's death led to the creation of the Open. In 1860, and no doubt with Tom's influence, and driven by Earl of Eglinton and James Ogilvy Fairlie, Prestwick invited eleven clubs to send their best and most respectable caddies to play in the tournament. By early autumn, the Champions Belt was ordered and the first Open, though not truly an open event, took place on 17 October 1860.

Tom was widely expected to win the first Open in 1860, but he lost it to Willie Park. He did, however, win the next two events and, in

1862, he also beat Park in a match on all four courses of their match. That was the year of Tom's clear dominance: if Allan had been alive, this would surely have been the time for the money men to have demanded a grand match between the St Andrews friends.

Today, with a doffing of the hat to those early inspiring champions, including Allan and his father, the Secretary of the R&A at The Open prize-giving ceremony announces the 'Champion Golfer of the Year'. It is a remarkable legacy, and the event today is the pinnacle of many players' careers, especially if they win in St Andrews.

Death of the Earl of Eglinton

The year 1861 saw the early demise of two of the most influential people in golf's early history. Playfair, as mentioned, died in January. The Earl of Eglinton was staying for the autumn meeting at John Whyte-Melville's house at Mount Melville.

The press report on 3 October in *The Fife Herald* carried the story: 'a sad and unexpected occurrence threw a damp upon the day's proceedings. The Earl of Eglinton, who has been staying at the baths, was one of the guests at a dinner party at Mount-Melville on Tuesday evening, and on the breaking up of the company was attacked by apoplexy (stroke). His carriage was at the door, and his Lordship was about to take his departure, but the alarming symptoms led to his being carried back to the house. We regret to say that the attack has turned out more serious, the noble earl having, we believe, remained in a state of unconsciousness up until the afternoon of yesterday. The consequence of this deplorable event was that many of the friends of the Earl and Mr Whyte-Melville refrained from appearing on the links yesterday, or at any rate, declined to play.'

The following week, the paper noted that on the Saturday the 'body of the noble Earl was removed Mount-Melville House to the St Andrews Railway Station, whence it was conveyed to Edinburgh by the 3.20 p.m. train. J. Whyte-Melville Esq., was the only gentleman who accompanied the cortege to the Station, the departure having been conducted privately. We understand that the body was to be retained in the vaults of St John's Edinburgh, till yesterday, when it was to be conveyed to Eglinton Castle, where it will remain till the day of the funeral, when it will be entombed in the family vault, in the churchyard of Kilwinning. On Monday last, John Whyte-Melville, Esq., attended upon the registrar for the parish of Cameron, and registered, in due form, the death of the Earl, as having happened at the Mansion-house of Mount-Melville, which though in the vicinity of St Andrews, is within the bounds of Cameron parish.'

The 13th Earl of Eglinton, whose first name was Archibald, and a supporter of Tom Morris, had lived an exemplary life. He not only was a founder of the Prestwick Golf Club and captain in 1851 and of The Royal and Ancient Golf Club of St Andrews in 1853, but he played a huge role in creating the Open. Over 160 years later, it is still thriving. He was Lord Lieutenant of Ireland and is said to have developed the game there at the Curragh.

His competitive streak was recognised by the 1839 extravagant medieval Eglinton Tournament and his 1841 foray into curling, when he became President of the Grand Caledonian Curling Club. He is captured in Charles Lees' *The Golfers – A Grand Match Played in St Andrews Links 1841* and in 1848/9 *Grand Match, North versus South, of the Royal Caledonian Curling Club, at Linlithgow* by the same artist.

The Earl was only 49 when he passed and the suddenness of his demise would have been a shock to many at the autumn meeting. This may explain the behaviour of artist and local teacher Thomas Hodge, who would have been declared winner but on one hole, with his ball resting beside the hole, he simply lifted his ball. The committee did not take long to decide second-placed M'Whannel was the ultimate winner.

His death came much too early, but the Earl left golf in a much better place.

It was also the year that Sandy Pirie died, a man who played a huge part in Allan's life and links education.

Sandyhill

When Allan died, his caddie and assistant in the shop, Da' Anderson, continued to caddie and make a living from golf. He would, in time, move into a house on the links, which is 9 The Links today. His son Jamie, who appeared in photographs with Allan, went on to win the Open three times in a row while living there too.

Da' saw out his days running a de facto golf shop on wheels, at the Ginger Beer hole, where he sold balls, clubs and ginger beer. He was buried alongside Jamie in St Andrews cathedral grounds.

In January 1863 the Star Hotel opened in St Andrews, and a special dinner was held for 30 of the local merchants. One Mr Turner, who was chair for the evening, proposed a toast to Allan Robertson which was 'drank [sic] in silence. A feeling tribute to the memory of one of our warmest hearted men, and most scientific golfer that St Andrews, or Scotland, has produced.'

David, who had come home, but without his family, stood up in reply and talked a little of the family history and said, some thought in jest, that he would soon challenge Tom Morris himself and win the champion golfer title back for the Robertsons.

He never did challenge Tom.

In February that year, there were notices in the paper about his plans to convert Sandyhill into a hotel and updates about his successful plans to get a licence to sell alcohol. David's hotel had a window displaying historic golf artefacts and balls, including a huge featherie.

Tom actually played that year with David against Bob Kirk and Andrew Strath, beating them with an 82 versus 84, and the low scoring was widely lauded.

It is noticeable that Tom did not come back to St Andrews immediately in 1859. It would be four years after Allan's demise, around the autumn of 1863, when he would accept the R&A's invitation to return and be keeper of the green in St Andrews. Tom always referred warmly to Prestwick, and his time there certainly seems to have been happy.

In October 1863 there were newspaper reports that Tom was coming home and that he had bought Allan's house from brother David.

David must have changed his mind regarding the sale as it never came off. He was a larger-than-life character, so it came as a shock when, on 14 February 1864, David died, of liver problems, in his new hotel. He was only 39, but an undeniable pioneer of golf in Australia. The liver issues with both Allan and David seem to point to a genetic issue and not to any alcohol-related problems. We know for sure that Allan was not much of a drinker and, according to Dr McPherson, that both he and Tom looked after their health, unlike Park.

In 1864 Sandyhill was sold by the trustees to Edmund Swan Turner and then auctioned unsuccessfully in 1865 for £500. It was eventually sold in 1866 to Mr Stobbie, who re-named it Allan Villa in Allan's honour.

The *Fife Journal* of 10 May 1866 noted, 'We, along with every citizen and many strangers, especially of the golfing world, are glad to see the house of our late Champion Golfer get a name at length. Everyone knew the kind-hearted Allan Robertson, the man who never was beat, the teacher of Tom Morris, and the introducer of thorough art into the national game. His house stood alone, and he was too unassuming to give it a name. Since his lamented death it has passed through three hands, but in the hands of the enterprising Mr Stobbie, its present proprietor, it has assumed quite a new face and a new form, and it also received the very appropriate title of Allan Villa.'

Allan Villa expanded over the years, building over the garden where Allan and Tom had planted rose bushes. Mr George Honeyman was the next owner, and he created The Golf Hotel in 1867.

From being that tiny Sandyhill house and parlour in the kitchen, it became a popular hotel on the links. Today it has been converted into luxury flats, but, having spoken to a resident recently who is a devotee of golf heritage, it is reassuring to know that Allan Robertson's picture still hangs on the wall there.

David's great-grandchildren still live in Australia and the Royal Sidney Golf Club has one of the finest collections of Robertson artefacts.

Tom Morris

It was said that Tom Morris looked up to Allan as a mentor and superior, and his loss was profound. Tom was only 38 when Allan died. He would live another 49 years, and what a remarkable life he lived.

Tom went on to become the greatest golfer in the world and winner of four Opens. He designed and re-designed over 100 courses. In 1870, some 12 years after Allan, Tom matched Allan's 79, but never bettered it. Although Dr McPherson claimed it happened in 1866, press reports in 1870 said, 'GOLF EXTRAORDINARY – Seeing that the only workable means of conducting competitions for medals, sweepstakes, and other prizes, where there are many players, is by taking the aggregate of the strokes for a round of the links by each player, it has always been a point of rivalry among good golfers to try and carry off, and hold the palm for the lowest score. Seventeen years ago, in a single with Colonel Dougall, Tom Morris holed the round at 82 strokes, which headed the list for ten years, when Allan Robertson, in a single with Mr A. Bethune, Esq. of Blebo, holed the round in 79 strokes. Till Thursday last no one had stripped Allan of his laurels, but on that day, in a single with Colonel Dougall, Tom Morris divided the great honour with his illustrious teacher in the art.'

For many years, Tom has been labelled a ballmaker alone, but, as his registered 1893 and 1894 patents show, he also designed clubs. Although nothing like the scale of Forgan, it would also be wrong not to call Tom a club manufacturer.

As Musselburgh's fame declined, that of St Andrews rose and rose.

Perhaps it was when Young Tom came on the scene that Tom, still just in his 40s, became 'Old Tom'; certainly he was regarded as a golf expert by this time. As Tom evolved from Tom Morris Senior, to Old Tom, with his white beard, he became revered as the Grand Old Man of Golf. He met and golfed with prime ministers, princes and kings. He influenced golf architects such as C.B. MacDonald, who travelled the globe spreading golf. Tom would be feted for his knowledge and professional golfing record.

He died in 1908, after a fall in the New Golf Club of St Andrews after mistaking the door to the cellar for the toilet door. Those steep wooden steps are still there today. Tom fractured his skull and was found unconscious at the foot of the steps. After being taken up to the Gibson Hospital, Tom passed away on 24 May 1908.

It was only six years before World War I. Bing Crosby was five years old. Ella Fitzgerald, who was born nine years later, would live through the music of The Beatles and David Bowie before her death in 1996. Gary Player would meet Willie Auchterlonie at the centenary dinner in 1960. Auchterlonie golfed with Tom Morris, while Player is still golfing today. Time, especially when golf is concerned, is but fleeting, and Allan just a mere few breaths – a couple of lifetimes – from us.

In 2024 a statue was unveiled in St Andrews to commemorate Tom Morris. The committee consisted of Ronald Sandford as chair, and was supported in the endeavour by his brother David, Callum MacLeod, David Strachan, Allan Peden, Athole Reid, Chic Harper and co-author of this volume, Roger McStravick. The sculpture was created by David Annand, whose design was influenced by the picture of Tom standing beside Tommy – the same photograph that was used for Tommy's monument in the cemetery. In November 2025 the statue committee commissioned two Scottish tunes for Old Tom and Young Tommy. They were composed by Pete Clark, one of Scotland's finest fiddle players, who was accompanied on piano by Muriel Johnstone.

Every champion, be it Bobby Jones or Seve, needs and receives help, advice and support, and Tom was no different. It was Allan who gave him a job, keeping him off the handloom weave. It was Allan who chose to partner him as a teenager and taught him much on and off the links. By being with Allan, on his way to becoming king, he would have been a witness to it all. Indeed, in Tom's first year of working in the golf parlour, Allan beat the reigning champion Tom Alexander. There was no finer education in golf.

In 1928 the 82-year-old greenkeeper Alexander Philp of 1 North Street was interviewed about his memories of Allan and Tom. '[Allan] could play, and no mistake,' said Alick. 'I remember him doing a 79 over the Old course, when the fairways were very rough, and there were no tins in the holes. A 79 then was very creditable indeed, considering the state of the course nowadays.'

When I asked how present-day golfers compared with the golfers of the past, he was very emphatic in his reply. 'The present-day golfers ken little aboot it', he said. 'The courses are all cut fine and short, and with the present-day greens, a path is almost made for them to the hole.'

'Would you back him [Tommy] against Bobby Jones?'

'Of course I would, and any more you care to mention. As a matter of fact,' he said, 'I'd back Old Tom Morris and Allan Robertson against any of the leading players today, providing they were playing with the same kind of clubs and under the same conditions.'

Allan and Tom were exceptional. They were never serious rivals. Allan wouldn't have it. They were family and friends. Tom, to his credit, repeatedly called Allan his friend and that is probably the simple reason why they never seriously fell out. Allan would not have begrudged Tom's success. On the contrary, he would have been proud.

What an incredible legacy.

AFTERWORD

In my earliest days working at the USGA Museum and Library, Janet Seagle, the long-time curator at Golf House, provided my first introduction to Allan Robertson. Allan, she explained, was the first golf professional. He was simultaneously player, caddie and ball maker of such renown in his home town of St Andrews that he was able to earn a consistent living wage from golf.

Further, and with greater emphasis, Janet relayed the infamous story of the row between Allan and Old Tom Morris, started the day when Allan discovered that his protégé had been playing with a gutta-percha ball on the links of St Andrews. Oh, the shame. 'We had some words,' Old Tom later recalled, 'and that led to us parting company.' Chastened or perhaps chastised, Tom left for Prestwick, taking new ideas with him and leaving Allan to tend to the traditions of St Andrews golf.

And so it came to pass that my impression of Allan was set, virtually in stone, of a man of many talents, but hopelessly stuck in the past, fearful of change and suspicious of technology. Moreover, it was the image of a self-preservationist, proud and protective only of his own talents and his family's heritage as makers of feather balls, and oblivious to the limitations and high cost of the featherie, which was hindering the game's growth. Those delicate feather balls that Allan crafted so skilfully, so proudly emblazoned with his Christian name 'ALLAN', were time-consuming to make and expensive to purchase. The preciousness of the ball was perhaps the greatest barrier to golf participation in mid-19th-century Scotland.

Traditionalist? Preservationist? Technophobe? The epithets are potentially unflattering. As Roger and Bill have so convincingly demonstrated in this wonderful new portrait of Allan, they are also incomplete. Far more so was Allan generous of spirit, kind of heart, gracious, and honourable to the last. More to the point, he was an innovator, perhaps not of golf balls, but of self.

The St Andrews of Allan's youth and young adulthood was a town undergoing a remarkable transformation. Thanks to the near singular force of will of town provost Sir Hugh Lyon Playfair, the Old Grey Town was transformed from cesspool to sanctuary and its fortunes reversed. In his *Biographical Sketch of the Late Lieutenant-Colonel Sir Hugh Lyon Playfair*, published in 1874, David Louden described the derelict condition of the town in the 1830s: 'St Andrews was fast dwindling into a state of ruinous decay. The streets were overgrown with grass, and it was no uncommon sight to see cows and pigs grazing upon them. Outside stairs, street projections, ruinous walls, dunghills, pigsties, and other abominations everywhere met the eyes, while noxious effluvia everywhere saluted the nasal organs.'

By equal parts force of will and charisma, Playfair washed away neglect, decay and isolation and ushered St Andrews into the age of industry and progress. Grants were obtained from the legislature for the rebuilding of the colleges and the refurbishment of the university's library. Crucially, the railway line was extended to the town, facilitating access to and from Scotland's expanding industrial centres of Edinburgh, Glasgow, Dundee and Aberdeen. The dirty and gloomy West Port gate at the head of South Street was painted, its masonry repointed and a handsome set of stone shields emblazoned with the town's coat of arms installed. These, and so many more projects throughout the public and private spaces of the town, were transformed. In 1856 even the venerable Royal and Ancient Golf Club was elevated with the completion of a new and stately clubhouse.

The author has called it an age of revolution. It was equally a time of re-invention: Re-invention that required vision, confidence, and courage. Indeed, the world was evolving rapidly, driving changes in economic and social structures, patterns of work and leisure, and even the very landscape. Such was the spirit of the age that women and men who comprehended the accelerating rate of change in society could re-imagine and re-position their place and their talents to sit at the leading edge of change and perhaps even become drivers of disruption.

For many Scots of the 1820s, there were few opportunities to advance beyond their station in life. By the 1850s, these could be seized.

The genius of Allan, as now revealed by Roger and Bill, rested in his ability to translate the changes in the physical and social fabric of St Andrews into opportunities for personal enrichment. Within a matter of years, he became the first caddie and golf artisan to integrate into the social life and activities of the R&A. His character and demeanour enabled him to mingle with the 'gentlemen golfers' of the club, albeit not as a peer, but simply as the greatest player of the game. It did not hurt that Allan was blessed with an engaging and colourful personality, when so many of his peers were colourless by comparison.

Without doubt, the members of the club deeply admired (even envied) Allan's talents with club and ball and the honours that followed. To be champion golfer, indeed, had its benefits. Born from such respect, they invited him to participate in the life of the club. In hindsight, the extent to which he was pulled into the activities of the club was extraordinary. He assumed oversight of the spring and autumn meetings. He set handicaps and arranged matches. He modified the hallowed links on which the members played. Indeed, so many of the responsibilities that have traditionally been assigned to Old Tom Morris were in fact first held by Allan. It was Allan who foresaw the need and value of the dedicated golf professional, and it was Allan who first re-invented himself to fill this niche.

As we learn from this volume, Allan's ability to create and invent was not confined to the re-imagination of self. According to H.T. Peter, it was Allan who invented the first wedge, which he dubbed the 'frying pan' and in so doing became the first to master the aerial game. We can now also appreciate that Allan designed far more courses than previously identified, truly making him one of the earliest practising architects in the game. Moreover, he was revetting the faces of bunkers far earlier than any scholar previously understood.

If the impression of Allan many may hold rests largely on his resistance to the gutta-percha ball, we must put his very fears in context. In truth, and quite simply, the new ball was a threat to Allan's life, his business and those he looked after, including his wife, brother, mother and staff. This was the ball he had used from childhood to champion golfer and the ball that sustained his income. The pressures of change must have been extraordinary. Yet he was not stifled, and he did not retreat from the sport. Instead, he found opportunities for change, renewal and re-invention elsewhere within the world where he thrived.

Allan Robertson was playing his best golf in 1858, the year before he died. He was immensely talented. He was kind and funny. And, as a result, he was enormously popular. Young boys would run behind the bushes and pretend to be Allan. What a blessing for the sport to have such a charismatic and creative personality to occupy such a prominent role within the community just as the game was beginning to grow.

For well over a century, historians of golf have largely relied on reports and characterisations of Allan Robertson that appeared in larger texts about Old Tom Morris. At last, with this volume, a full and revealing light has been cast on Allan himself. The portrait that emerges from Roger and Bill's exemplary scholarship allows us at last to appreciate ALLAN, not simply as the name inked on a feather ball, but more fully as Allan Robertson, the game's first superstar.

Rand Jerris
Historian

Appendix

EARLY GOLF LINKS

ALLAN was the go-to expert in setting out links from the 1840s. As mentioned, it was a skill he learned from Sandy Pirie. It would be a little overblown to call him a golf course architect. Allan could set out a course. He did not do incredible earthworks of the scope or scale that we saw in Kyle Philips' inspired design at Kingsbarns. Allan worked with the natural landforms to find hazards and greens. The terms 'golf course designer' or 'golf course architect' were not seen written anywhere until around the 1890s, long after Allan's passing and late into the life of Tom.

The obituary of Allan Robertson in the *Dundee Advertiser* of September 1859 highlighted, 'ALLAN did much for golfing both in and out of St Andrews. He laid out capital Links in various districts, and played thereon himself to the excitement of beginners.' How wonderful it must have been to see Allan play. Inconveniently, the *Dundee Advertiser* does not list those 'capital Links', although the *Fife Herald*, dated 8 September 1859, does mention Wemyss Castle as the work of Allan.

Although the lofty titles of designer or architect were not applied to Allan or even Tom, both, particularly the latter, were responsible for some of the finest links courses, including Carnoustie, Muirfield, Royal County Down, and Prestwick.

Tom mentored or influenced many of the classic golf course designers that followed him, such as Alistair Mackenzie, C.B. MacDonald, A.W. Tillinghast, Donald Ross and Harry Colt. However, it was Allan who taught Tom those basic principles of naturalist and rudimentary design.

These two laid out a golf course by walking the land, visualising holes and placing pegs or stake markers where they perceived a tee box should be, and then the green. Depending on the condition of the land, shots were then played like any golfer would do to gain a feel for the design and the lay of the land. Notwithstanding, everything in between tee and green was simply natural terrain and contours, including natural hazards such as gorse and bunkers, features that had been shaped by wind erosion over centuries.

Allan and Tom derived their technical skills for laying out a course from generations of experience, but also from their personal journeys from boyhood to champions of the game. It was a lived experience. They knew how far an amateur golfer, and those more proficient, could hit a featherie golf ball, so they logically had a good idea where to challenge the player and where there was an interesting approach.

Architectural design plans and Ordnance Survey maps were not a part of their set-up. They set out an entire links with simple, hand-drawn routings and pegs, with their eyesight and imagination as their only work tools. Nonetheless, they still produced remarkable results that were praised by golfers and press alike, be it Carnoustie or Prestwick.

Thomas (Tom) Bendelow, known as The Johnny Appleseed of American golf, was born in Aberdeen in 1868, eventually moving to the USA. During a most prolific 35-year career, he set out more than 600 golf courses in North America. His approach, not surprisingly since he hailed from Scotland, was the 'naturalist' method of course design; much like Allan and Tom, he worked what nature had already provided, such as streams, trees, rock formations and whatever other features nature contributed into his course layouts. Some of his notable courses in the USA include Medinah Country Club, The Apawamis Club, Atlantic Athletic Club at East Lake and numerous others.

Pete Dye, an icon of modern-day American golf course architecture, by contrast, would move tons and tons of earth to mould the very landscape to his vision for the course, rather than letting the natural contours of the property determine the layout. Pete, who passed away in January of 2020, was famous for many golf courses in the USA, not least TPC Sawgrass, the venue of the annual Players Championship with the well-known island green, par-three, 17th hole. The island and surrounding water are completely man-made, but it is still a beautiful hole.

Peter N. Lewis states in *Why Are There Eighteen Holes?* that, in 1832, there were 17 known golf courses, all with a varying number of holes, St Andrews being the only one with 18. Of those 17 courses, 15 were in Scotland and two were in England, namely Blackheath and Manchester. As Allan was only 17 years of age by late 1832, we can safely assume that he was not responsible for laying out any of those courses.

Allan was, however, the first course designer who laid out multiple courses. This was more about necessity, as he was the expert and champion of his era and few knew more about how to set out a links than Allan. His course work is noted below. Hopefully, over time, even more lost or forgotten links by Allan will emerge.

Carnoustie, 1842

Carnoustie, and particularly the Barry Links, have an interesting historical connection to golf; indeed, golf had been played in the Carnoustie area for centuries. We also know from Scottishgolfhistory.org records (accessed March 2024) that it is reputed Sir Robert Maule (1493–1560) played golf on the links there in 1527. 'Robert was said to be tall, fresh complexioned and well-spoken, but prone to anger and pugnaciousness (given to lechery [sic]). Although he never learned to read and write, he became the sheriff of Angus. There is a reference in the Registrum of Panmure in 1560, in the obituary of Robert Maule [which states] that he liked hawking and hunting. "Lykewakes he exercisit the gowf, and ofttimes past to Barry Links, quhan the wadsie was for drink … This was the zeir [year] of God 1527, or thear abouts." It is said that when Sir Robert lost at golf, he would send his servant into the pub and buy everyone a drink, thereby initiating the tradition that the loser buys the drinks.'

Sir Robert died in the Tower of London in 1560, aged 67.

The Maule family, or Clan Maule, arrived in Scotland with the Norman invasion. Maule is a French town, north of Paris, and since 1992 has been twinned with Carnoustie. In 1224, the Panmure Estate, an area covering Monifieth and Carnoustie, passed to the Maule family. With it came the seat Earl of Panmure, which the family lost when the 4th Earl joined the Jacobite rising in 1715. At this point, Panmure went to the Earls of Dalhousie, who would have a significant impact on the Carnoustie links.

One legend, and there are several, said that Carnoustie got its name from a Norse connection. In the 1010 Battle of Barry, King Malcolm II of Scotland defeated the Danes under General Camus and killed him in the battle. The Norse gods were so angry about this that they filled Barry Sands with thousands of crows. The area became known firstly as Craw Nestie and then Carnoustie. This explains the crows in the town's coat of arms. Camus' grave is marked with a cross to this day.

Robert Chambers Snr is said to have set out a links near the land of the Burnside links, called the Balskelly course, around 1834 and 1835, but this was moved due to the arrival of the railway in 1838.

The Carnoustie and Taymouth Golf Club (Carnoustie Golf Club) dates back to around 1842. It consisted of local artisan players and held regular medal competitions, such as the silver medal, which was given by Miss Kinloch of Carnoustie for the best player and won in 1842 by William Anderson.

On 28 June 1848 the *Dundee Courier* noted that the new Caledonian Union Golf Club was founded, with Sir Thomas Moncrieffe as its first captain. The Caledonian Union Golf Club was made up of the best club gentlemen from St Andrews, Perth and Montrose.

Allan, who was also there, said at the time that he preferred his St Andrews links but the Carnoustie course, when properly laid out, would be inferior to no other links in Scotland.

This gives rise to the inference that Allan's work at Carnoustie was closer to summer 1848 rather than the sometimes-quoted 1842. His close connections with Sir Thomas Moncrieffe also supports that conclusion. Given that golf was generally played in the area much earlier, it seems that it was more of a re-modelling and hole-adding input from Allan rather than creating a brand new links.

One month later, an 1848 *Caledonian Mercury* clipping notes of the Carnoustie links, 'the course, which is on a fine links, almost equal to either St Andrew's or Montrose, has been most judiciously laid under the able superintendence of Mr. Allan Robertson. Sir Thomas Moncrieffe, Bart (baronet), has been elected first captain … The course consists of 18 holes, and from their length and general nature, we should say that the course would be well played at 90 strokes; the general average will be about 100 strokes.'

Most historians believe that Allan set out ten holes, based around the course that was already there. Those ten holes could be played as an 18 and certainly were played as 18 by both the Caledonian Union Golf Club and Carnoustie Golf Club.

This and other press references to Allan advising on revisions to the course are, however, evidence of his ongoing role at Carnoustie.

George Morris took over around 1855 and was highly praised for his work. In 1858, George Morris, as keeper of the green, had to resign as he could not make a living from attending to the Carnoustie and Monifieth links. A subscription for him raised £6, but Monifieth soon appointed their own keeper of the green for £2 per annum.

Some reports imply that, in 1867, Tom extended the links at Carnoustie to 18 holes, although this also seems doubtful. Certainly, the course was set out as a ten-hole course in 1867, as evidenced by the fact that a professional tournament was held at Carnoustie in which Tommy Morris, at age 16, won with a final round score of 42 strokes after three previous rounds of the ten-hole course. Three rounds were played, leaving Willie Park Snr, Young Tommy and Bob Andrews tied. Young Tommy won the play-off to gain his first professional victory.

Due to congestion problems over the 10-hole course, The Dalhousie Golf Club of Carnoustie, which formed in 1868, invited Tom to extend and upgrade the links in 1872. *The Field* on 17 May 1873 reported on the opening of the 18-hole course, which measured 4,565 yards in 1873. 'On Saturday afternoon, the new golfing course at Carnoustie was formally opened … Many spectators were present, there being some curiosity as to the score likely to be made by the alteration of the course … The course is about three miles long, and embraces 18 holes instead of 10, as formerly. The outgoing holes are indicated by white flags, and the incoming by red, and on match days large poles will be displayed (as in St Andrews), indicating generally the direction which should be taken. Old Tom Morris laid out the new course, and it is conceded on all hands that he has done his work well. To the Dalhousie Club, at whose expense the improvements have been effected, golfers must feel deeply indebted.'[1]

Interesting to note that Tom was called Old Tom at this stage and he was only in his early 50s. It was more a reflection of his son being young Tommy, rather than any comment on his age.

Allan's modification of the early course lasted for 25 years, before congestion demanded that the course be altered to prevent injury.

Tom's newly extended links lasted until James Braid oversaw many changes to the links in 1926, with new greens and tees, but not the actual layout.

Fundamentally, the course routing has remained the same ever since. On ancient links land, it has produced the most dramatic of championships. The first Open winner at Carnoustie was Tommy Armour in 1931. Allan, Tom, Tommy, Park, Simpson, Park Jnr, Braid, Cotton, Hogan, Player, Watson, Lawrie, Harrington and Molinari all had moments of success and drama at Carnoustie.

Few courses can be said to have such a rich history.

Delvine Golf Club, 1842

Delvine House, Perth, was supposedly laid out by Allan. In 1847 one Dr Fraser Thompson of Perth won the annual silver medal, scoring 100 over 20 holes, so two rounds of ten holes.

Innerleven Links, 1820

Dubbieside Links, better known as Innerleven Links, was situated near the river Leven. It is here where H. Thomas Peter said that Allan saw the new gutta-percha ball in 1848. It has also been suggested that Allan was responsible for extending the early 1820 short course, though historians have a question mark over that claim.

Records and subsequent writings note that in February 1820, 15 gentleman golfers, mostly from Fife, met to form the Innerleven Golfing Society, and their charter called for them to compete on a five-hole course at Dubbieside. The members wore a King Charles tartan jacket.

By the spring meeting of the re-named Innerleven Golf Club in 1844, the golf course had grown to a nine-hole layout, and therefore, quite conceivably, Allan played a part in that.

The *Fife Herald* on Thursday 25 April 1844 noted that, 'The spring meeting of the Innerleven Golf Club took place on the 2nd current, to compete for the silver medal, then held by Mr William Marshall, when Mr David Wallace was reported to have completed the two rounds … at 93 strokes; but before the medal was presented, it turned out that the competition had been contrary to the rules of the Club. It was therefore resolved again to play for the medal on the 19th current. That competition accordingly took place, when Mr John C. Fernie, Balfarg, was reported to have completed the two rounds at 94, and Mr Robert Haig at 96. A respectable number of the members afterwards dined together, when Mr Fernie was, in due form, after dinner, presented with the medal by the Chairman, Mr John Peter, who passed a high eulogium on Mr Fernie for the science he had that day displayed, and the achievement he had accomplished in beating the great champions. The golf medal will be played for in August, when a great turn out is expected, and a more than ordinary battle for the honours of the day. Our poet laureate will no doubt be present, and commemorate the occasion by another of his poetle effusions.'

On 5 September, the *Fife Herald* reported that both Allan and Tom were present at the autumn meeting of 1844, which gives some credence to the notion that Allan could have been involved in extending the golf course to nine holes.

> The autumn meeting took place on Friday and was attended by an unusually great number of members. For several years the enrolment of new members has been considerable, but on this occasion an unprecedentedly large addition has been made to the club. The golfing-green on Friday was crowded with players, and the concourse of spectators was correspondingly great. Never was a more animating spectacle exhibited on the links, and the interest which the spectators showed with respect to the contest evinces the increasing popularity of our peculiarly national game. Mr David Wallace of Belgrummo came in at the very low number of 89 strokes and was declared the successful competitor. Many matches were played after the contest for the medal, but the one which excited most interest was that between the St Andrews caddies, Allan Robertson (Champion of Scotland) and Morris. Their ease, dexterity, and power were admirable, and afforded to golfers a most gratifying and instructive lesson. After the sport of the day, a large party dined at Marshall's Inn – Henry Peter Esq., of Kirkland, the Captain of the Club, in the chair. This was followed by the annual ball,

> at which a large and fashionable party attended. It would be well that the club should turn its attention to the preservation of the most beautiful part of the links, which are fast crumbling down before the invasion of every high tide. Within the last ten years, thirty yards, it is said, have fallen in; and if the present process of destruction should go on (as it must do if not prevented), the sea will in a few years completely wash over the eastern part of the golfing-ground. This should be looked after by some party.
>
> The golfers, as a thriving body, should make some effort to arrest the progress of demolition, and this could be done at no great expense, by the driving in of piles and stones, and by sloping the banks. The proprietors of the village should also take up this matter, as the value and very existence of their property are threatened by it.

The *Caledonian Mercury* of Thursday 23 April 1846 reported on the third leg of Allan and Dunnie's match at Dubbieside. 'The Great Match At Golf – The last game of this match (best of three) was played yesterday on Dubbieside Links near Leven, between Robertson of St Andrews and Dunn of Musselburgh, when the former gained by 6-holes and 4 to play, thus winning two out of three games. A great number of gentlemen interested in the match, and who had taken bets upon it, were present, from both sides of the Firth. As we have before stated, Dunn won the first game at Musselburgh by 7 holes and 5 to play, and Robertson won the second at St Andrews by 5 holes and 3 to play.'

It is said that, due to industrial development, the advent of the railway and the growth of urban building, as well as the ongoing issue of sea erosion, the Innerleven Golf Club moved from Dubbieside to the east of Leven in 1867, where Leven Thistle Golf Club, Leven Golf Club and, later, Lundin Mill Golf Club also played.

The *Fifeshire Journal* on 8 October 1868, reported that since moving from Dubbieside to the east of Leven, the Innerleven Golf Club 'have, by judicious outlay, made the latter green one of the favourite resorts for golfing. Their liberality on the present occasion has been the means of bringing together some of our most celebrated professionals, among whom were Tom Morris, sen., Tom Morris, jun., James Anderson, Tom

Kidd and David Strath … the course consisted of … eighteen holes'. Tom Morris set out the 18-hole course and Tommy, aged 17, won the event, following his first Open victory that year – a proud year from the Morris father and son.'

With the split of Leven Golf Club and Lundin Links to create two courses, James Braid was brought in once more to effect a considerable number of changes. Leven and Innerleven Golf Clubs amalgamated on 1 September 1957 and became Leven Golfing Society.

There are some events at the course that include Allan, and this may point to his involvement, but there is, as of yet, no firm evidence of such.

Monifieth, 1845

According to Panmure Golf Club records, 'On the 6 June 1845, it was reported that Allan Robertson and Alexander Pirie come from St Andrews, examined and laid out the Links in 9 holes, and declared that, in their opinion, the Monifieth Links were well adapted for the game of golf. The fee for these services was 30 shillings. The course was extended to 10 holes, with a total length of 3,131 yards, in 1851, but the layout proved unpopular, and the course put back to nine holes in 1871.'

The Monifieth holes by Allan and Sandy occupied what are today's holes one through to three, and holes 15 through to 18.

The work was carried out at the behest of the Panmure Golf Club, a club formed that year by 17 gentlemen golfers from nearby Dundee. Construction of the railway from Monifieth to Broughty Ferry and Dundee was undoubtedly influential; the club was named after the landowner, namely Lord Panmure (James Maule).

In 1893, due to congestion on the Monifieth links, Panmure Golf Club moved to its present location in Barry.

Old Course, St Andrews

By 1857, the number of known golf courses had risen only to 27, according to the *Golfer's Manual*. Golf as a healthy pastime and the expansion of the railways would change all that. Another boom in the popularity of golf was beckoning, with an explosion in number of golf courses that would last well into the 20th century.

Mythology can sometimes blur into erroneous fact in written golf history. Neil Millar's work on breaking down myths is a credit to him and our new belief that Mary, Queen of Scots was not a golfer is entirely due to his perseverance and research. In the face of decades of misrepresentation about the origins of golf, David Hamilton has changed the narrative so that historians firmly believe golf was a Scottish invention.

There are, in turn, many myths about Allan, such as being golf's first professional, but one of the biggest myths is that during 1848, Allan, who was supervising the St Andrews links, is credited with modifications to the Old Course.

The changes credited to Allan include widening of the fairways and the creation of the famous double greens. It is also said that Allan built a new green on the well-known 17th Road Hole. This is largely unsupported by any official record, such as the Royal and Ancient or Union Club's minutes or, indeed, local newspaper articles of the time.

What we do know is that from 1836, Sandy Pirie and James Herd were reimbursed £5 a year for preparing the course for the club meetings in spring and autumn. It is also known that ad hoc amounts were paid for various additional work, such as tending to the greens ahead of meetings. The work of Pirie and Herd had been causing some displeasure for a number of years, and in 1844 they were officially warned to improve the discharge of their duties or be dismissed.

In 1852 Da' Anderson replaced Herd and Pirie, under the general direction of Allan, on the same annual fee of £5. It was Auld Da' who, in later life, sold ginger beer, and no doubt other stronger substances, from a cart at the Old Course fourth hole, the aptly named 'Ginger Beer'.

In 1836, the fifth hole had two holes on the green, but it was Auld Da' who introduced two holes to the High Hole in 1855, as noted in the club minutes. According to *Challenges and Champions* by John Behrend and Peter N. Lewis, the report of the Royal & Ancient Golf Club, May 1855 meeting stated about the condition of the links: 'They have been in far better condition than at present, the long tack of dry weather having told on them severely. Mostly all the putting greens are innocent of grass, the little there is being wholly covered with sand, thus rendering the short game a matter of more difficulty. Over the course in general, a plentiful supply of sand has strewn during the strong westerly gales which we had for the whole of last month. The Elysian fields especially have received a due share, some portions of that classic locality being nearly an inch deep.'

However, that same year, the overuse of the St Andrews links and the pressure to keep it well maintained was all too much for Auld Da'. He resigned his part-time role when his appeal for a higher salary was rejected.

At the autumn meeting of the Royal & Ancient in October of 1856, it was agreed to make a number of improvements to the links. According to John Behrend and Peter N. Lewis quoting from the *Fifeshire Journal* in December 1856, 'as a result of a decision a few months earlier: "The meeting specially authorise the committee to expend the sum of £25 in placing the putting greens into better order under the superintendence of Allan Robertson." Two payments appeared in the 1856 accounts and a further three the following year, the final payment dated September. One can assume that a major part of this work was the enlarging and returfing of the greens to incorporate second pin positions.'

As noted in *Challenges and Champions*, the *Fifeshire Journal* on 7 May 1857 also detailed the work, 'St Andrews links were never in better condition for golfing purposes than now. Since the meeting in October, the Club has spent some £20 in the repair of the course, in straightening the walls of most of the bunkers, which had become much breached by frequent visitations, and in filling up other little holes and corners. The putting greens have had a thorough over-haul, returfed, and otherwise improved. On each green, with the exception of the first and return, two holes have been placed; the one is played by the parties going outwards, the other in the in-coming. To prevent mistakes, the out-going hole is supplied with a white flag, and its neighbour sports a red one, that being the colour for all the return holes. This is a decided improvement on the old system, preventing confusion and the delays which often had to be put up with, on medal days especially, when a party going out encountered another winding their way homewards, and there being only a hole betwixt them, the one party had to look on until the other party had played out and got under way again.'

On 1 October 1857 the *Fifeshire Journal* expanded on the new work: 'Since last year the Society have expended a goodly sum in their renovations. The greens have been tended with something like parental care, sown out in some instances, and otherwise nursed to beget smoothness. Yawning bunkers, to steer clear of which required a steady hand and a stout heart, have been straightened, their indented sides turfed and patched, thus making these bugbears … more easy to get out of.'

This is quite an important quote as it suggests that Allan was revetting the bunkers. This technique of layering turf to create a bunker wall was used to prevent erosion to the bunker by prevailing winds and, until now, had been claimed to have been a 20th-century invention. Allan's use of revetting to improve the ragged bunker faces would certainly have been one of the earliest recordings of revetting being used.

Therefore, as we see, Allan was contracted to clean up fairways, not widen them, place second holes on the greens, except for the ninth and 18th, and repair the bunkers by revetting. He also incorporated white flags on the greens going out and red flags on the homeward journey. His work during that winter of 1856 and into 1857 was necessary and the Royal & Ancient trusted him. It gave us the eight double greens course that we know today and, once a year, the course is set up to be played in this clockwise way – it was the only links Allan knew. Note that all his famous matches were on the single pin version. It was a narrow course, with unraked bunkers and small greens.

Necessity being the mother of invention, Allan's work was the clearest sign that the game and the links traffic were both growing. St Andrews was evolving, thanks to Playfair's transformative work in the town combined with Allan's superintendency over the links. With more golfing visitors, the links needed not only to reflect that, but also to be better maintained. Articles in the paper lamented over the rise in poor cleek play and heavy divot making.

From 1864 Tom would go even further in expanding greens, creating new greens on holes one and 18, clearing whin away to open the new front nine fairways and eventually creating more bunkers, but it is undeniably true that it was Playfair's work beautifying St Andrews and Allan's early work on the links that went hand in hand to create a new St Andrews.

That is what added to the lure of St Andrews, when Musselburgh was struggling. It was an exciting town on the up and up. Musselburgh was slowly fading.

Fortunes for Tom and Park could have been so very different.

Cupar, 1855

Like many clubs, Cupar Golf Club has a complex history, where the current course is actually the fourth. The first was between Thomastoun and Tailabout Mills (1856); and the second was at Springfield Gardens, which is north of the first course. Then they moved to Ladybank (1876) and shared the course with that club before they finally moved to their current home in the 1890s.

According to Cupar Golf Club, the club, 'is arguably the oldest surviving nine-hole golf club in the country. It was instituted at a meeting in the County Buildings, Cupar, on Monday 7 November 1855. The club's first records indicate that by 1867 there were 37 members playing over a 6-hole course at Tailabout, on part of a farm where "permission to exercise twice a week" was given by the farmer. The course had been laid out by Allan and described as, "The first stroke was over the river Eden, the second hole was over water running out from Tailabout Mill, the third was near the railway bridge, being about the width of a road between the two waters, the fourth returned over the same ground, the fifth was to a corner called the triangle, and the sixth was from the triangle across the Eden to Thomastown. When play was going on, six or more boys were placed on both sides of the water with long-handled nets to retrieve lost balls."'

Allan spoke at the Cupar Golf Club's first medal meeting in 1856, which was reported in a local newspaper, a copy of which found its way into Allan's scrapbook, which illustrates his standing in the community. The report states, 'The first annual competition for the Silver Medal took place on the golfing ground on Thursday last. Allan Robertson, King of Clubs, was present guiding and directing the operations on this first grand day of the infant club. The ground was also graced by the presence of a number of ladies, apparently well pleased spectators of the sport. In the evening, about 30 gentlemen dined. Allan gave the toast [to] "The Game of Golf" and read the members a lecture on the blunder of depriving the ladies of their place and honour in investing the competitors with the ensigns of victory.'

No visible traces of the course remain today, except for the stone footings of a wooden bridge that the golfers would have used to cross the Eden, which probably pre-dated the course.

Wemyss Castle, 1857

Instituted in 1857, just 200 yards west of Wemyss Castle, a nine-hole course was laid out for the estate staff.

Allan was a regular guest and playing partner of the landowner, the Earl of Wemyss, so he played this short course numerous times. Wemyss was also captain of the club. It is pretty much certain that the course, which followed the shoreline to St George's church, was the work of Allan.

Allan's obituary in the *Fife Herald*, dated 8 September 1859, mentioned Wemyss Castle as one of the capital links he laid out. Tom Morris was made an honorary member of the club in 1863, but the club finally closed in 1956.

CONCLUSION

There are other courses that have been set out by Allan, many of which have been found by the *Forgotten Links* historian, Harry Ward. Cambo House Links, Bow of Fife, and Mountquhanie Castle, Fife, are just three with Allan's name attached. Connachan Lodge, near Crieff, is another. This was said to have been set out with James Condie of Perth in 1844, the man who took all Allan's clubs in that fateful match in Perth. Allan is also credited with having set out an early links at Dumbarnie for the Hercules Athletic Club. At the time of writing, research continues to see if Allan's father Davie set out the first links at Scotscraig – he was their official ballmaker in 1818.

It is certain that in the 1840s and 1850s, Allan, as the acclaimed king of golf, set out or re-designed a number of links. Many links, such as Montrose, have a long unrecorded history going back centuries and were constantly evolving to reflect the needs and skills of the golfers. It would not be unexpected if Allan were called upon to advise on this course and others. Allan had connections to earls and lords. He dined with them after play, and there are many tales of Allan regaling them with golf stories of yore.

It was his world, and he was revered for it.

Celebrated golf course architect Pete Dye, who passed away in 2020, paid the utmost tribute, mainly to Tom, but also to Allan, in his book *Bury Me in a Pot Bunker.*

> At St Andrews, we witnessed golf course design in its purest form. Fortunately, Allan Robertson and Old Tom Morris, true pioneers of golf course architecture, respected what God provided and molded it carefully into a golf course. Sometimes

> less is better, and fortunately the designers of the Old Course used great care not to significantly alter the wonderful natural look of the terrain.

Allan's golf was described as the most scientific of professionals. It is not a leap of imagination to think that he used the same skill and approach to set out a capital links.

It was he who taught and passed on those principles to Tom and it is an undeniable skill to be able to look at a piece of earth and create golf holes within that stark landscape. Many of the late 19th-century architects talk of spending time with Tom, but of all those conversations, how many times did Tom echo Allan's words and advice? Those nine years with Allan were among his most prolific years of setting out new links.

When the game was growing in the 1840s and 1850s, albeit not in the same scale as the late 19th century when Tom was setting out courses, Allan was the go-to expert. His was not the era of earthworks and machinery. In many ways, Allan can be seen as the last link to the early golfers of the 1500s, who played with featherie balls and an armful of hickory clubs under the arm of the caddie. Open, wild, sandy links with natural bunkers were their battlefields. The ball was played where it lay and the fun of escaping a hazard added to the joy of the game.

Tom was a little more sophisticated in his greens management, with top dressing, tin cups and introducing the newly invented lawn mower, but seeing a good hole among wild rough terrain was possibly why Allan's services were so frequently requested.

It wasn't a gift he gleaned overnight. Allan was following in the footsteps of centuries of Robertsons tending to the links at St Andrews, which was the best education a budding 19th-century course designer could get.

NOTES

One The Robertsons of Strowan

1 Here the great prelate Wilfrid's body lies,
Who, led by piety, this temple rear'd
To God, and hallow'd it in Peter's name,
To whom the world's Judge gave the keys of heaven.
He deck'd its walls with purple and with gold:
And here a cross, that glorious trophy, placed
Of shining metal; and, by his command,
The Gospels four, in golden letters writ,
Were in a golden casket fitly shrined.
He also the recurring Easter time
Corrected by the true and catholic rule
Fix'd by the fathers: error he expell'd,
And gave his race sure guidance for the rite.
And in these parts he brought together bands
Of monks, and them establish'd in the ways
Taught by the fathers' rule. At home, abroad,
Long time by many grievous dangers toss'd,
Having as bishop spent thrice fifteen years,
He pass'd away, and heaven rejoicing sought.
Grant, Lord, the flock to tread their shepherd's path.

2 I (Roger) was made aware of this book at the Literati meeting on the 20 August 2021, as part of the President's Day celebrations of the British Golf Collectors' Society. I had given a short talk about my ongoing projects, including this book on Allan. Afterwards, founder of the Society, Philip Truett, came up and mentioned the book that was in Allan's will. Furthermore, he had it in his collection and excitingly, there was writing inside by Allan. He kindly offered to let me study it. I am indebted to Mr Truett as the book in itself shows us why Allan had such an augmented opinion of himself. His family name had a noble history and he was

simply proud of this. Knowing the contents of that book opened my eyes to Allan. Modern historians would take issue with the romantic and heroic nature of the book, but in Allan's time, this was regarded as accurate. Allan signed the book in four places:

- i Front stuck down end paper. This also has an address being *Sandy Hill, Links, St Andrews, 1844.*
- ii Title page.
- iii Reverse of title page. This also has an address being *Golf Bank, St Andrews, 1844.*
- iv Page 167, being the final page of text. This has an address being *Links, St Andrews.*

Mr Truett said in correspondence, 'Clearly, he was very proud of this book'.

3 Robertson, Alexander, *The History and Martial Achievements of the Robertsons of Strowan* (Edinburgh *c.*1771).

4 Ibid., p. 6.

5 Ibid., p. i.

6 McAndrew, Bruce A., *Scotland's Historic Heraldry* (2010), p. 181.

7 *www.en.wikipedia.org/wiki/Walter_Stewart, Earl_of_AthollIbid., iii* (accessed 2021)

8 Robertson, Rev. James, *The Barons Reid-Robertson of Straloch* (Blairgowrie 1887), p. iv.

9 Robertson, Alexander, *The History and Martial Achievements of the Robertsons of Strowan* (Edinburgh *c.*1771), p. iii.

Two Medieval Ballmakers of St Andrews

1 *Scottish Shinty and the Origins of Modern Golf, Through the Green,* March 2021, p. 36.

2 *Mary Queen of Scots, Golf and the Seton Necklace, Through the Green*, June 2015, pp. 11–16.

3 *Riches and Reform, Ecclesiastical Wealth in St Andrews, c.1520–1580* (Edinburgh 2020), p. 11.

4 Ibid., p. 14.

5 Ibid., p.16.

6 Ibid., footnote 14, p. 139.

'Following the upheavals of 1559, the leaders of the Protestant Kirk struggled to fulfil this role. Both the superintendent of Fife (John Winram) and the first two Protestant archbishops of St Andrews (John Douglas and Patrick Adamson) faced serious personal animosity from some sections of the St Andrews community. Indeed, relations between

Archbishop Adamson and the burgh's elites deteriorated so much that in 1582 Patrick Learmonth (one of the sons of the Provost of St Andrews) conspired to murder him.'

7 *A True Account of the Horrid Murther Committed Upon His Grace The Late Lord Archbishop of St Andrews* (London 1679), p. 4.

Three The Dark Century

1 Lang, Andrew, *St Andrews* (W.C. Henderson, St Andrews 1951), p. 312.

2 Lyon, Rev. Charles, *The History of St Andrews* (Edinburgh 1843). p. 122.

3 Douglas, William, *Some Remarks on the City of St Andrews in North Britain* (London 1728), p. 7.

4 *Minute book of the cordiner craft, St Andrews, 1570–1796*, University Special Collections, Ref: GB 227 msDA890.S1C7. See also Macadam, J.H., *The Baxter Books of St Andrews 1548–1861* (Edinburgh 1903).

5 www.scottishgolfhistory.org/origin-of-golf-terms/golf-ball-feathery-gutty-haskell (accessed Feb. 2022).

6 Croft Dickinson, William, *Two Students at St Andrews*, 1711–1716 (Oliver & Boyd, Edinburgh 1952), p. xxxix.

7 Ibid., p. xxxix.

8 Ibid., p. xli.

Four Unpardonable Blunder

1 Grierson, Rev. James, *Delineations of St Andrews* (Cupar 1807), p. 92.

2 Hay Fleming, David, *The Links of St Andrews* (St Andrews 1893). p. 15. In the same year of 1797, George Martine, Secretary to Archbishop Sharp published *Reliquiae Divi Andreae*. It was written in 1683, edited by Dr Rotheram, professor of Natural Philsophy in the University of St Andrews, and is a veritable treasure trove of the early history of St Andrews, including the location of one of the earliest Christian churches, St Maria Du Rupe, on the Lady Craig rock formation below the cathedral. According to University of St Andrews archives, 'George Martine of Clermont (1635–1712), was grandson of Dr George Martine, Principal of St Salvator's College, St Andrews. He became secretary to James Sharp, archbishop of St Andrews, as well as being a historian and author of *Reliquiae Divi Andreae or The State of the Venerable and Primatial See of St Andrews*. In 1666 he became commissary clerk of St Andrews, a post he held until dismissed in 1690 for refusing to take an oath of loyalty to William and Mary.'

3 Hay Fleming, David, Notebook 54. University of St Andrews.

4 Hay Fleming, David, *The Links of St Andrews* (St Andrews 1893), p. 15.
5 Whitsunday or white Sunday, was a reference to the white garments worn on the holy day of Pentecost by the newly baptised. It is traditionally the seventh Sunday after Easter and celebrates the Holy Spirit descending upon the apostles. Wit is also said to have been instilled in the apostles at this time. We know it as meaning a humorous intelligence, but it was known for many years as mere wisdom.
6 Hay Fleming, David, *The Links of St Andrews* (St Andrews 1893), p. 24.

Five Rabbit Wars

1 McStravick, Roger, *St Andrews In the Footsteps of Old Tom Morris* (2015), p. 234.

The Real Dempster Family

We all know the very well-documented history of the occasionally violent Rabbit Wars and those pesky Dempster rabbits ruining the St Andrews links. In almost every historical piece of literature, the Dempsters are portrayed as wealthy landowners who would destroy the links in order to make a profit from the rabbits. The damage their farm did to the course and ultimately to their reputation in St Andrews made it practically impossible for anyone to stand up for them.

However, it has recently come to light, thanks to Mr Peter Crabtree, that there is another side to the family, Cathcart in particular, that has not been discussed.

James Howie (1821–70), who lived at 125 South Street, St Andrews, in 1859 and gave guided tours of the town, wrote in glowing terms about Cathcart in *The Intelligible Guide and Manual for St. Andrews: Historical & Descriptive*. Howie says that Cathcart, a former Magistrate, 'lived or was in office 50 years too soon for St Andrews. At the beginning of this [19th] century, the Right Hon. The Earl of Kellie was the nominal or honorary Provost of the City, but he was a "sleeping partner." The entire initiative of everything devolved upon Mr Dempster, either in his capacity as Dean of Guild or Bailie.' An example of this absentee provost was on Friday 5 January 1800 when the boat, *Janet of Macduff*, ran aground on the sands of St Andrews Bay. The waves were too strong for locals to help the stricken vessel and the crew suffered badly. One student, John Honey, swam out and was able to bring the seamen in, one at a time. For his gallantry 'the magistrates invited him to an elegant entertainment, and presented him with the Freedom of the City. Cathcart Dempster, Dean of Guild, spoke that night, 'in the absence of the Right

Honourable, the Earl of Kellie, Lord Provost of this city'.

As a footnote, Honey managed to save the lives of the master of the ship and four seamen who would surely have perished otherwise. It was this incident that prompted St Andrews to have its own lifeboat in 1801.

Howie, who saw Dempster as both philanthropic and a forerunner to Playfair's revolution of St Andrews, lists the many achievements of the Dempster family:

i. They brought the first bank to St Andrews, namely the Bank of Scotland, in 1792. The bank was initially behind 62 South Street but subsequently moved to 43 South Street, then back to 62. In 1871, they went to the corner of South Street and Queen Gardens, where they remain today. It was the Dempsters who actually bought the land on South Street for the new Town Hall and Queens Gardens and built two houses on the corner of that street. In time they sold the corner house to the Bank of Scotland. They would later build another house at 83 Market Street that would ultimately become The Royal Bank of Scotland.

ii. They founded the Butter Market.

iii. They introduced the selling of mussels at the Eden for bait.

iv. They improved the harbour many times and in 1798 bought it for the steelyard.

v. In 1779, they proposed the lighting of the streets.

vi. Cathcart brought in experienced fishermen from Caithness and settled them in St Andrews to show the poor fisher folk how to create a thriving industry. From four boats before this initiative, the fisher folk had 14 by 1859.

vii. They discovered and patented what was known as 'Kyan's Patent Antiseptic'. According to Reverend Grierson, 'The manufacturers of St Andrews are almost entirely confined to two: golf-balls (not clubs) and sail cloths. The manufacture of sail-cloth was first established in 1793, by Mr Dempster of this place, who, about twenty years ago, obtained a patent from the government for an ingenious improvement in the article.' The new sailcloth was no longer 'liable to rot or mill-dew, owing to the twine being properly boiled or bleached before it is woven'. It was also 'more pliable than canvas' and 'for strength, durability and pliability, it far exceeds all other canvases'.

Cathcart's time in office was known as the 'dear years' as he created a fund with which 'the poor working people of St Andrews were supplied with meal at one shilling per peck when the general selling price was three shillings and sixpence. The fund raised 1,000 guineas.'

Before we start to re-write the Dempsters' story completely, the family had many naysayers.

Probably the loudest and most vociferous of all was George Bruce (1825–1904). His book, *Wrecks and Reminiscences of St Andrews Bay* (1884), leaves no doubt in his readers' minds what he thought of the Dempsters. Let's start with the less than subtle, 'Mr Dempster [Cathcart], like his father [Charles], was a pompous, self-interested opinionative official.' Bruce goes on to say that Charles was one-time provost and at around 1760 'farmed the farm of St Nicholas, once (and possibly yet is) the property of the City'.

His son, this Cathcart, erected a factory at the foot of Abbey Street (then the East Burn Wynd), still known as Factory Close, and manufactured what was extensively known as 'Dempster's Duck' or Dempster's canvas, for which he got a patent and was recognised as one of the principal manufacturers of canvas in Scotland, for the British Navy.'

By all reasonable measures this sounds like a very commercially minded family. However, Bruce continues with his ire. 'But he lost both his reputation and his trade by one fatal mistake, viz., allowing the yarn to lie too long exposed on the East Bents [East Sands today], or St Nicholas, before it was converted into 'duck' or canvas; it was, to use a Scotch phrase, 'fusionless', partly rotten.' To highlight how useless the canvas was, Bruce details how two men-of-war were supplied with it, and the first gale of wind 'blew the sails from the spars to ribbons, which also blew away his patent, and closed his factory'.

Of the imported fishermen that Howie talked so glowingly about, Bruce takes an altogether different opinion. Admittedly, Cathcart gave them incentives, including 'ten shillings a week, when they could not get out to sea, and even pay them some money when they went, besides the sale of the fish, when they went, providing they give the citizens the first chance of all the fish they caught, at a fair price – the men to be called the "town's Fishers", and the fish to be exposed for sale at the public Common-House or Butter Market, attached to the old Town Hall, which then stood in the middle of Market Street.' Once again, Bruce's negative comments seemed to be based on complimentary material about the Dempsters. However, he goes on to say that this initiative lasted only two months. You have to wonder exactly how much contact Bruce had with the Dempsters, given that he was born after the Rabbit Wars.

There is clearly a much larger tale to be told, but for now it is simply interesting to note this other side of the Dempsters.

No man or family are as one-dimensional as sometimes portrayed and hopefully in time the full stories and lives of the real Charles and Cathcart Dempster will come out. One thing we know for sure is that they were neither all bad nor all good.

Six House of Lords

1 Baxter, Peter, *Golf in Perth and Perthshire* (Perth 1899), p. 30.
2 Thomas Peter, H., *Reminiscences of Golf and Golfers* (Edinburgh 1890), p. 6.
3 McPherson, Rev., *Golf and Golfers, Past and Present* (Edinburgh 1891), p. 18.
4 Ibid., p. 18.
5 McStravick, Roger, *St Andrews, The Road War Papers* (2019), p. 193.
6 Ibid., p. 126.
7 Lewis, Peter; Behrend, John; *Challenges & Champions: The Royal and Ancient Golf Club, 1754–1883* (1995), p. 55.

Seven The St Andrews of Davie Robertson

1 This poem is from my late uncle Brendan McStravick, who was the Principal of St Paul's in Lurgan, taught English and made writing for me a noble art. It is about my grandfather Cornelius *'Nelly'* McStravick, who worked in Johnson's linen factory in Lurgan, so Brendan, and my dad Joe could have a good education at St Colman's College, known as Violet Hill, in Newry. My late dad talked about granddad's treat of having a bottle of stout on a Friday. My godfather and dad's brother Gerry became the Senior Superintendent of the Royal Hong Kong Police Force. When we achieve any success in life, it is to those people like Granda McStravick that we owe a huge debt of thanks. Giant is on occasion too small a word.

Eight Life at the Golf Parlour, Sandyhill

1 McStravick, Roger, *St Andrews, The Road War Papers* (2019), p. 195.
2 Ibid., p. 88.
3 Clark, Robert, *Golf: A Royal and Ancient Game* (Edinburgh 1875), p. 285.
4 McPherson, Rev., *Golf and Golfers, Past and Present* (Edinburgh 1891), p. 64.
5 For more detail on Alexander's life, please see *Tom Alexander 1802–1841* by Mungo Park, *Through The Green* (June 2018). Also note, Millhill in

Musselburgh is often spelt Mill Hill. Details of Tom's first wife were kindly provided by Mungo Park.

6 Crabtree, Peter; Malcolm, David, *Tom Morris of St Andrews, The Colossus of Golf, 1821–1908* (2008), p. 24.

Nine The Boy Who Would Become King

1 According to *www.jamesboswell.info/biography/george-dempster-mp-dunnichen- and-agricultural-reformer*, accessed on 2 May 2024, 'Dempster was much inspired by the scepticism and liberalism of the Scottish enlightenment (esp. David Hume), and he was probably one of the most progressive Members of Parliament of the time. He eventually gained the nickname "Honest George".

Although originally intended to be a sarcastic sobriquet (as he had to buy his voters, as was the custom at the time), it seemed later on to be a correct description of Dempster who became known as an "independently minded, incorruptible and moderately radical MP".'

He was a lifelong friend of philosopher Adam Ferguson and clergyman Alexander Carlyle.

Following his death in 1818, Sir Walter Scott sent the following epitaph, supposedly written sometime earlier by Dempster himself, to John Wilson Croker (*Boswelliana*, p. 34):

> Pray for the soul of deceased George Dempster,
> In his youth a great fool, in his old age a gamester;
> What you're to know, on this tomb you shall see,
> Life's thread he let go when just ninety-three.
> So sound was his bottom, his acquaintance all wonder'd
> How old Nick had got him till he lived out the hundred.
> To his money concerns he paid little attention,
> First selling his land, then pawning his pension;
> But his precious time he much better did manage,
> To the end of his life from his earliest nonage,
> He divided his hours into two equal parts,
> And spent one half in sleeping, the other at cartes.

2 McPherson, Rev., *Golf and Golfers, Past and Present* (Edinburgh 1891), p. 35.

3 Thomas Peter, H., *Reminiscences of Golf and Golfers* (Edinburgh 1890), p. 54.

Ten Playfair Revolution

1 Playfair, Lieutenant-Colonel Sir Hugh Lyon, *Memoirs of Sir Hugh Lyon Playfair* (St Andrews 1861), p. 3.
2 Louden, David, *Biographical Sketch of the Late Lieutenant-Colonel Sir Hugh Lyon Playfair, Provost of St Andrews* (St Andrews 1874), p. 2.
3 N. Lewis, Peter; Behrend, John; *Challenges & Champions: The Royal and Ancient Golf Club, 1754–1883* (1995), p. 71.
4 *Chambers' Edinburgh Journal*, no. 200 (Saturday, 30 October 1847), pp. 273–5.
5 Playfair, Lieutenant-Colonel Sir Hugh Lyon, *Memoirs of Sir Hugh Lyon Playfair* (St Andrews 1861), p. ix.
6 N. Lewis, Peter; Behrend, John, *Challenges & Champions: The Royal and Ancient Golf Club, 1754–1883* (1995), p. 144.
7 Ibid., p. 144.
8 Playfair, Lieutenant-Colonel Sir Hugh Lyon, *Memoirs of Sir Hugh Lyon Playfair* (St Andrews 1861), p. 4.
9 Ibid., p. 11.
10 Papers of Hugh Cleghorn of Strathivie and the Cleghorn family, University of St Andrews, msdep 53/2/9/240 and msdep53/2/9/8.

Eleven Wonder Years

1 McPherson, Rev., *Golf and Golfers, Past and Present* (Edinburgh 1891), p. 19.
2 Ibid., p. 4.
3 Ibid., p. 19.
4 Ibid., p. 30.
5 Thomas Peter, H., *Reminiscences of Golf and Golfers* (Edinburgh 1890), p. 36.
6 Ibid., p. 54.
7 McPherson, Rev., *Golf and Golfers, Past and Present* (Edinburgh 1891), p. 3.
8 Ibid.
9 Tulloch, Rev. William Weir, *The Life of Tom Morris* (Edinburgh 1907), p. 16.
10 Ibid., p9
11 Ibid., p19
12 N. Lewis, Peter. Behrend, John, *Challenges & Champions: The Royal and Ancient Golf Club, 1754–1883* (1995), p. 97.
13 Ibid., p. 94.

14 Tulloch, Rev. William Weir, *The Life of Tom Morris* (Edinburgh 1907), p. 5.

15 About Willie Robertson. According to Bill's notes, another of Allan Robertson's relatives was William Robertson (1796–1868), better known as 'Lang Willie' due to his towering height. Willie was Allan's cousin, the son of Allan's uncle William who was described in the parish record of deaths of 1868 as a 'golfball maker (deceased)', so it is no surprise that Lang Willie also pursued that trade working for Allan.

Allan's grandfather Patrick, better known as Peter, married Elizabeth Gibson in 1774 and between them they had several offspring, David (Allan's father), William (Allan's uncle) and Elspeth, Allan's aunt. It is through Elspeth that the family connection to Auld Da' Anderson can be found.

Lang Willie was no great shakes as a golfer, but he does go down in caddie folklore with comical tales of mishap. As well as a reputation for being an outstanding caddie, he was also noted for his fiddle play, which made him sought after at various scenes of rejoicing. Besides being a legendary caddie, he also worked with Allan Robertson in his kitchen workshop along with an 18-year-old Tom Morris.

Willie was said to be 6 feet 2 inches, taller than most, and walked with a slouch. With his weathered Lum hat, he towered over everyone. H. Thomas Peter in his book *Reminiscences of Golf and Golfers* describes Willie and something of his character when he caddied for Mr Brown Douglas (Lord Provost of Edinburgh): 'Lang Willie had a tall, gaunt figure and a dry, cynical manner. He wore a long hat, which had seen better days-and that in all weathers. Willie, although generally a sober man, sometimes forgot himself, and would spend all his earnings and remain off the links for a week at a time, if he had the wherewithal to buy whiskey. He had remained sober for a considerable time, when one day when carrying for Mr Brown Douglas' clubs, that gentleman, who, I think, was a strict teetotaler, asked him what he drank now. "Naething but sweet mulk, Sir; naething but sweet mulk;" "Ah!," said the worthy Provost, who was not aware of Willie's weakness and who wished to encourage temperance among the caddies, "There's half-a-crown to buy milk, my man."' Willie was not seen on the links for a week.

James Balfour recounts a similar characterisation on page 41 of his 1887 book *Reminiscences of Golf on St Andrews Links*: 'The greatest character among them (the caddies) was "Lang Willie". He was very tall, about six feet two, with bent knees and a slouching gait, a tall hat, swallow-tailed blue coat, and light trousers. His look was rather stupid but in reality, he was wide awake. He used to insist that he drank nothing but sweet milk, greatly to the amusement of Allan who knew better. He was much taken out as an instructor of beginners, and when one met him and asked him how his pupil was getting on, he had always the same stereotyped answer, "Jist surprising", which might mean either very well or very ill. On one occasion he was teaching one of the professors of the University the noble game. But the Professor was not a very promising pupil. As he hammered away, sometimes "missing the globe", sometimes topping the ball, or cutting up large divots, Willie fairly got out of patience and said to him, "You see, Professor, as long as ye are learning these lads at college Latin and Greek it is easy work – but when ye come to play golf ye must hae a heid! [have a head]".'

Lang Willie was one of the St Andrews characters who claimed to know about most things. The pages of old golf history books are littered with his tales. The Robertson house, Sandyhill, was a hive of golfing activity and Lang Willie was integral to almost everything going on.

There is the story of Mr Campbell of Saddell who would race from the Union Parlour in hot haste and ask Lang Willie, an authority on the weather apparently,

'Is it to be fair?'

'Well sir,' would cautious Willie answer, 'the gless's mair doon the day than she wass yestreen.'

'What does that mean Willie?' ventured Mr Campbell.

'That it'll be aither vera wat or more rain.' Willie retorted.

Willie, like all the caddies at St Andrews, would carry clubs whenever he could. Many of the lesser-known caddies, not a favourite of the club members, would line up outside of Allan's house in the hope of being gainfully employed for a few hours. Lang Willie found himself regular work from the lecturers of the university.

On another occasion a well-known golfer engaged Willie as his caddie. At the last hole coming home the match was undecided, and the notable golfer asked Willie what club he should take for his second shot. "You'd better tak' your short spoon," was Willie's reply. The player took it and missed; and at once threw the club away several yards, with a strongish epithet addressed both to the club and the caddie. Willie spoke no word till the match ended. He then said to his employer, "May I speak a word with you, sir?" "Well, yes," was the reply. "Sir, ye're a great deal worse to carry till than a guid player." "You're right, Willie," the golfer replied, "and here's a shilling for you, to go and drink to my better play."

Willie always dressed not only in his hat but also a tailcoat, which made him a striking figure from some distance.

One near-sighted golfer always requested Willie to caddie for him.

The vision-impaired golfer would knock his ball into the whins and peer forward, squinting, and asking how he lay. 'Ye're in a capital position, sire,' Willie would retort, who had already paid a boy a penny to run ahead, find the man's ball and toss it to a safe spot.

According to H.S.C. Everard's, 'the boy often ran ahead and dropped the ball two hundred or more yards from the tee, further than mortal man had ever driven before.'

The near-sighted golfer swore that he played like a champion when Lang Willie caddied for him.

In Allan's scrapbook, there is a humorous tale of a misfortune that befell Lang Willie. One day Willie was asked to carry the large pieces of luggage of Sir Alexander Kinloch from the Union Parlour to the railway station in a wheelbarrow, a distance more than the length of the eighteenth fairway beyond the 17th green to where the Old Course Hotel is today. The article in Allan's scrapbook dated November 1853 reads,

'Crossing the Swilcan, A Falling in by the Way –

On Tuesday afternoon a gentleman who had been engaged in golfing, was about to leave by railway, and devolved the carrying out of luggage, from the Union parlour to the station, upon that venerable member of caddiedoms – Lang Willie – who, having pressed a wheelbarrow into his service, got under way.

He was advised to take the route by the high road, but being enamoured of a near cut by crossing the Swilcan burn, Willie made for one of the foot bridges, and had just entered upon it, when lo! Shouts of laughter burst from groups of gentlemen, caddies and others about the Parlour – Willie's carriage had got off the rails, and the wheel into the burn, while Willie, saving himself from going the same destination by holding by the barrow shafts, had the pleasure of seeing each and all of the traps – a golf club box, gun case, portmanteau, hat-box, and plaid – launch into the water. Which was considerably swollen, and sail away towards the ocean.

Assistance being at hand, however, the goods and gear were arrested in transit seawards, some of them, not improved by the hydropathic treatment, though, we believe, the contents of the portmanteau were fortunately scatheless. The rueful countenance Willie assumed, and his intimation that he had got a 'gey fricht', increased the merriment that arose among the onlookers at witnessing his exploit, the hero thereof apparently more concerned at his own escape that at any injury the barrow's contents had sustained.'

Willie would forever be reminded of the incident.

From the book *On The Links: Being Golfing Stories by Various Hands* (1889) there are a good number of anecdotes about Lang Willie.

It was generally believed that his origin was higher than his position, as his manners certainly were. 'On the occasion of Louis Kossuth's visit to St Andrews, Willie expressed a strong desire to be present at the public dinner which was to be given to the lion of the day, and applied for a ticket to the Bailie who was in charge of the arrangements. The worthy man, full of the importance of his office, curtly refused the application, saying to Willie that it was "No for the likes of him to be at the dinner." "No' for the likes of me?!" Willie responded. "I've been in the company of gentlemen from eleven to four o'clock maist days for the last thirty year, and that's mair than you can say!"'

Louis Kossuth was a liberal activist who strove for Hungarian independence from neighbouring Austria. He was a brilliant journalist and clever politician, and for a short time he came close to achieving his goal of freedom and self-government. The visit to St Andrews was likely 1849.

Lang Willie had, during his seventy years, several mild heart attacks, which he brushed aside each time as nothing to be concerned about even though a doctor had diagnosed his condition. Later, the strokes impaired his vision and put a tremble in his speech. By 1868, his mouth moved only on one side. On 25 July that year, Willie was carrying clubs for a gentleman when at the 'Corner of the Dyke' hole (16th) he collapsed and never recovered. His place of death is described as Market Street, St Andrews, which was outwith his normal home, which he shared with his sister Margaret, on North Street according to the 1861 census. The signature informant is a George Robertson, likely Lang Willie's son. The undertaker had to make an extra-long coffin. After the funeral Tom Morris, young Tommy and the other caddies drank toasts and shared 'Lang Willie' stories.

16 Thomas Peter, H., *Reminiscences of Golf and Golfers* (Edinburgh 1890), p. 6.

17 Ibid., p. 7.

Twelve The King

1 Due to the quality of records, it was difficult to trace her family but it is possible that her parents were Henry and Jamiel Elliot. This Helen was a twin with her sister named after their mother, Jamiel.

2 Leach, Henry, *The Spirit of the Links* (London 1907), p. 52.

3 Everard, H.S.C., *A Haver with Tom Morris. Badminton Sports and Pastimes*

Magazine, vol I (1895), p. 336.

4 Thomas Peter, H., *Reminiscences of Golf and Golfers* (Edinburgh 1890), p. 28.

5 McPherson, Rev., *Golf and Golfers, Past and Present* (Edinburgh 1891), p. 32.

6 Thomas Peter, H., *Reminiscences of Golf and Golfers* (Edinburgh 1890), p. 38.

7 This image of Allan's scrapbook was kindly provided by Mr John Giannizzi.

Thirteen Golden Reign

1 Here follows two short biographies of Fairlie and Campbell, which are abridged from *St Andrews in the Footsteps of Old Tom Morris* by the author of this book.

Lieutenant Colonel James Ogilvy Fairlie, 1809–70

Tom Morris had much to thank for in his life. One person who helped give Tom an extraordinary life was Lieutenant Colonel James Ogilvy Fairlie. When Fairlie stayed in St Andrews, it is very likely that he resided at Priory House, Saddell's residence, as he was a brother-in-law to Saddell.

Fairlie's family owned Coodham House, near Symington in Ayrshire. His mother Margaret (1781–1845) commissioned the four-storey house in honour of her husband and Fairlie's father, William (1754–1825). On 6 October 1828, the foundation stone was duly laid and by 1831 it was complete, at a cost of £20,000.

William Fairlie was a merchant and banker who worked and lived in Calcutta. William supplied the East India Company's Bengal army with 'elephants, bullocks, camels and victuals before going on to become one of the biggest ship owners in Calcutta transporting rice, indigo, cotton and opium to the China coast'. (*www.historicalportraits.com*)

In 1798, he was described by the then Governor General of India, Richard Wellesley, as 'the best informed in commercial matters in Bengal. I suppose no English house in India has such extensive concerns as Mr Fairlie's, but what I look to is that you may depend upon his giving opinions perfectly unbiased by self-interest. His fortune is very large and his credit seems almost unbounded'. (*www.historicalportraits.com*)

To this day there is a Fairlie Place in Calcutta.

James' parents married in Calcutta in 1798. His mother Margaret was the daughter of John Ogilvy of Murtle, Calcutta. James Ogilvy Fairlie was born in Calcutta on 10 October 1809. When his parents returned to London in 1812, William became a Member of Parliament. They lived at 9 Park Crescent until his death in 1825 and it is at this point that Margaret bought the 90-acre Coodham estate.

The Coodham house was originally called Williamsfield, but, as Malcolm and Crabtree note, 'The original name stuck in local consciousness, however, it was not long before the family estate reverted to it, spelled in Scots phonetic vernacular, Coodham.' (Malcolm, David and Crabtree, Peter E., *Tom Morris of St Andrews: The Colossus of Golf, 1821–1908* (Royal Deeside), p. 62). This is a corruption of the word Cowdam, which the estate was originally called prior to the Fairlie family's arrival.

Tom Morris was James Ogilvy Fairlie's man, so whenever he needed a caddie or a playing partner in the 1840s, he would turn to Tom. They met at the autumn meeting in 1846 and became great friends, so much so that Tom named one of his sons James Ogilvy Fairlie Morris. (Malcolm, David and Crabtree, Peter E., *Tom Morris of St Andrews: The Colossus of Golf, 1821–1908* (Royal Deeside), p. 53). Fairlie was the joint founder of the Prestwick Golf Club in 1851 and it was he who enticed Tom away from his own little shop in St Andrews to the links at Prestwick in July 1851. James had inherited the estate when his mother passed away in 1845.

Tom, of course, created something special in the layout of the 12-hole-layout at Prestwick.

For Tom, the Ayrshire links went from being a daunting foreign piece of ground to a place that he would call home and where he and Tommy would win all eight of their Open Championships.

Fairlie was the Captain of The Royal and Ancient Golf Club of St Andrews in 1850 and is the only person to have ever won gold medals in competitions at the Old Course, Prestwick and North Berwick, which he achieved in 1866.

He had two children, Henry (1841–1922) and Isabella (1834–1935), with his first wife Anne-Eliza MacLeod who died in 1844, and a further seven with his second wife, Elizabeth Constance.

Craufurd, whom he married in 1845, William (1847 -1923), James (1848–1916), Reginald (1850–1932), Esther (1851–1874), Margaret (1853–1932), Francis (1855–1939) and Walter (1860–1943). Three of his sons became Captains of the R&A.

Golfiana says of Fairlie,

> Not an old golfer, but by few surpassed-
> Great Captain Fairlie ! When he drives a ball-
> One of his best, for he don't hit them all-
> It then requires no common stretch of sight
> To watch its progress and to see it light.

When Allan Robertson died in 1859, it was said that Fairlie decided a tournament should be held to settle the question over who was the greatest golfer, since, as Sutherland said, 'Their greatest [Allan] is gone.'

In 1857 Fairlie with Playfair had created the inter-club Grand National Golf Club Tournament, consisting of 13 clubs playing matches in foursomes format at St Andrews. Blackheath won, albeit with two Scottish golfers in George Glennie and Captain John Stewart. So that was deemed acceptable. It was considered a success. In 1858 they changed the format to singles matchplay which, as mentioned, the son of the publisher and writer Robert Chambers duly won. In 1859, with yet another format of scratch golfers and handicap golfers, the attendance had an impact on the attendance of the R&A's autumn meeting, so it was decided that it would never be held again.

When Robertson passed away, Fairlie and the Prestwick members came up with a format that would avoid the frustration in the previous three years. It was a strokeplay event played over three rounds, with simply the lowest score being the winner of a newly created Champions Belt. If the player were to win three years running, he would keep the belt. There was already a precedent of this in boxing. Today, footballers keep the ball if they score a hat trick. Such a tradition thus exists and carries on in other sports.

The members of the Prestwick club paid £25 for the red Moroccan leather belt. This is the foundation and the very beginning of The Open Championship and it is to Fairlie we should turn to thank.

Eight golfers shuffled about like racehorses at noon on the day of the first Open. One of the players that day, in addition to Tom and Willie Park, was one Englishman, G.D. Brown, who would own 8 The Links before Tom. He was a known braggart and the painting of his name on the side of the shop was deemed uncouth, even amongst the lowly artisans. Brown's card, alongside his fellow player Andrew Strath, was marked by Fairlie. After the first round of 12 holes they lunched at the Red Lion Inn, which is still there today, then completed the remaining 24 holes before dark.

When the format for The Open was changed in 1861 to become open to all, Fairlie was the leading amateur. Tom won the Belt that year. How the good friends must have frequently looked back on that day as one of their finest?

Fairlie was a great all-round sportsman, succeeding in equal measure in all sports. He was also the organiser of the 1839 Eglinton Tournament that involved 13 knights who were called the Knights of the Golden Lion. Fairlie, in typically competitive form, won the jousting tournament.

These galas were said to have drawn crowds of over 100,000, including the elite of the elite such as Louis Napoleon.

James Ogilvy Fairlie died on 5 December 1870. This must have been heartbreaking for Tom to lose his mentor, friend, supporter and backer. This was the same year that Tommy won the Open Belt for the third time in a row, making it his own.

For a long time after Fairlie's death, his family kept close relations with Tom. It was Fairlie's own son, James, who was behind the push for a portrait of Old Tom in the R&A clubhouse by Sir George Reid (1841–1913). It was Old Tom who taught the Fairlies to play golf at Prestwick and in the grounds at Coodham House (Malcolm, David and Crabtree, Peter E., *Tom Morris of St Andrews: The Colossus of Golf, 1821–1908* (Royal Deeside). p. 63).

James Ogilvy Fairlie was buried in Symington parish church cemetery in Ayrshire.

We in golf have much to thank the Lieutenant Colonel Fairlie for. Without his support of Old Tom, we may all have lost out on the great man that Tom became. There is something quite fundamental here that gives us a clear insight into Tom the man. Although there was a very clear class difference, they crossed that boundary with ease and to their final days they would have considered each other more than mere acquaintances – they were close friends.

Coodham House was eventually sold in 1871 by Fairlie's eldest son James to Sir

William Houldsworth, who made several improvements to the house and estate.

In winter, the frozen lake was used for curling and skating by visitors.

2 **John Campbell of Saddell 1796–1859**

Mr John Campbell, Laird of Glensaddell (sometimes written Glen Saddell), who was mostly referred to as Mr John Campbell of Saddell or simply Saddell, also owned Priory House.

Tulloch's biography on Old Tom gives a superb insight into the gentlemen in Old Tom's era and their way of life. He describes Saddell as a very tall and handsome man who was one of the Knights at the Eglinton Tournament. 'While a bachelor he lived with Clan Ranald in Pilmuir Place. Clan Ranald was one Eneas Ronaldson Macdonell of Glengarry and Clan Ranald. He was one a bunch of fun loving, high gambling, young 'bucks' of the period.' (Tulloch, William Weir, *The Life of Tom Morris, with Glimpses of St Andrews and its Golfing Celebrities* (London 1907), p. 31).

Saddell and his friends had a considerable reputation for the way they gambled. The playing partner of Clan Ranald and Saddell was George Fullerton Carnegie. He ran through a fortune that provided an annual income of £5,000 a year, which is 'the equivalent of half a million pounds today'. (Malcolm, David and Crabtree, Peter E., *Tom Morris of St Andrews: The Colossus of Golf, 1821–1908* (Royal Deeside) p. 34). After bankruptcy, he turned poet and wrote *Golfiana Miscellanea* in 1833.

Saddell married Miss Henriette Maria M'Leod of M'Leod (1817–1877), one of the Queens of Beauty at the Eglinton Tournament. 'After their marriage they lived for a long time at The Priory.' (Tulloch, William Weir, *The Life of Tom Morris, with Glimpses of St Andrews and its Golfing Celebrities* (London 1907), p. 31.)

Being a buck, Saddell considered himself one of the better golfers in the club and in Carnegie's *First Hole at St Andrews on a Crowded Day*, Saddell, wearing a blue coat (that soon loses its colour as the round goes on), with lots of Gourlays (featherie balls made by Gourlay of Bruntsfield Links), free from spot or stain, 'swears by Ammon he'll engage to drive as long a ball as any man alive' (Stewart, James Lindsay, *Golfiana Miscellanea* (London 1887), p. 86).

In *Another Peep At The Links*, Saddell is not put off playing by his lack of skills on the Links. '[Saddell] Still plays all matches – still is often beat – And still in iced punch drowns each fresh defeat.' (Clark, Robert, *Poems On Golf* (Edinburgh 1867), p. 7.) This poem is by Charles Fullerton Carnegie and is a follow up to his *First Hole At St Andrews On A Crowded Day* (1833).

Like all too many of us golfers, the lack of skill does not deter us from venturing out week after week filled with hope – or delusions of grandeur – on the first tee.

As a frequent backer of the losing side, like Dunn against Allan, Saddell is described in the Carnegie poem as 'a sort of Magnus Apollo with the fashionables of his day. He was a great sporting man and, though a heavyweight, rode remarkably well to hounds. He went in a balloon [ride] from Heriot's Hospital to Fife when such a thing was considered a bold feat. He was a noble-looking man, pompous in his manners, and very irascible. In golf he was well known for his long drive.'

It was when famously playing with Saddell that Old Tom ran out of balls in 1848 and Saddell offered him a new invention, the gutta percha rubber golf ball, to play with. Much is made of the subsequent fallout of Old Tom and Allan but they were playing once again as partners within a very short time. They simply got over it, like good friends do.

The village of Saddell, or Glensaddell, is situated on the coast of the

Kintyre peninsula, Argyllshire, in south-west Scotland. Saddell Castle, the ancestral home of one branch of the Campbell clan, and Saddell House, were built by Saddell's grandfather, Colonel Donald Campbell, who died in 1784, aged 58.

It was there at Saddell House that John Campbell died in 1859, leaving St Andrews and golf much poorer for it.

3 McStravick, Roger, *St Andrews, The Road War Papers* (2019). p. 122.

4 For details on Ferrie, please see Crabtree, Peter; Malcolm, David, *Tom Morris of St Andrews, The Colossus of Golf, 1821–1908* (2008), p. 52. Please also see *St Andrews in the Footsteps of Tom Morris*, p. 5, for details on the tragedy of Ferrie's life where it says, 'Life would take a difficult turn for Ferrie. In 1846 his wife, the daughter of Professor McCormick of St Andrews University, died. In 1847 his military son and daughter-in-law were drowned in the Ganges. By 1850, to add to Ferrie's woes, he and his son William were declared bankrupt.'

5 Baxter, Peter, *Golf in Perth and Perthshire* (Perth 1899), p. 57.

6 Tulloch, William Weir, *The Life of Tom Morris, with Glimpses of St Andrews and its Golfing Celebrities* (London 1907), p. 9.

7 For further details on Innerleven, see *www.golfsmissinglinks.co.uk/index.php/scotland-63/scotland-central-east/fife/1408-sco-innerleven-golf-club-fife* and *www.scottishgolfhistory.org/oldest-golf-clubs-societies/1820-innerleven-golf-club* (accessed 5 Jan 2024.)

From *GolfsMissingLinks*, 'At a meeting on Tuesday 29 February 1820 fifteen gentlemen drew up a constitution for a club, it was to be called the Innerleven Golfing Society. Also at this meeting the members formulated the rules of the game for the club, this was before R&A rules were drawn up. The course of 15-holes would be laid out at Dubbieside (on land later occupied by the Methil Power Station). The gold and silver medals were played for on Tuesday 3rd October 1826 and won by Mr Wallace, Parkhill, and Mr Pattullo, St Andrews. The club continued to prosper and by 1829 there were over 50 members.'

From *Scotishgolfhistory*, 'The Dubbieside course had 18 holes by 1866, which would have qualified it as the third oldest 18-hole course in the world. Unfortunately, by 1866, industrialization and the new railway lines encroached on the ground and the minutes report that at the Autumn Meeting of 1867, the club decided to play on "the popular green" at Leven. The Dubbieside course was abandoned, and later the Methil power station was built on the site, though it too has been demolished some years ago. The entry for the The Golfers Year Book for 1866 is now a fond memory of the course.

Shortly after they moved, in 1870, Innerleven became involved in organising the 'Amateur Champion Medal' competition, believed to be the oldest open amateur stroke-play completion in the world. They also took a prominent part in managing the Links and by 1876, Innerleven was effectively running the Links with contributions towards the upkeep from the other two Leven clubs. At this time, the club sublet rooms above the premises of the golf club-maker Alex Patrick, but in 1894 they built a new clubhouse on ground they purchased beside the eighteenth green.

When Innerleven's membership declined in the mid-1950s, they amalgamated with Leven Golf Club to form the Leven Golfing Society on 1st September 1, 1957, using the Innerleven clubhouse. The Leven Golfing Society and the old Innerleven clubhouse are still there today, playing the Leven Links, radically redesigned in 1909 when the old course was split into two with Lundin taking half the course to form their own.'

Fourteen Dawn of Gutta Percha

1 See Commissioners of Patents, *Patents For Inventions, Abridgements of the Specifications relating to India Rubber (Caoutchouc) and Gutta Percha* (London 1859), for various patents by Charles Hancock. See p. 129 for the use of moulds and machinery.
2 *ScottishGolfHistory.org* (accessed 10 Jan. 2024).
3 Thomas Peter, H., *Reminiscences of Golf and Golfers* (Edinburgh 1890), pp. 12–15.
4 Tulloch, William Weir, *The Life of Tom Morris, with Glimpses of St Andrews and its Golfing Celebrities* (London 1907), p. 9.
5 Stewart, James Lindsay (ed.), *Golfiana Miscellanea* (London 1887), pp. 286–9.
6 McPherson, Rev. J. Gordon, *Golf and Golfers, Past and Present* (Edinburgh 1891), p. 1.
7 Crabtree, Peter; Malcolm, David, *Tom Morris of St Andrews, The Colossus of Golf, 1821–1908* (2008), p. 42.
8 Miller, Rev. T.D., *History of the Royal Perth Golfing Society* (Perth 1935), p. 44.
9 Tulloch, William Weir, *The Life of Tom Morris, with Glimpses of St Andrews and its Golfing Celebrities* (London 1907), p. 30.

Fifteen The Invincibles

1 Thomas Peter, H., *Reminiscences of Golf and Golfers* (Edinburgh 1890), p. 29.

2 Bruce, George, *Wrecks and Reminiscences of St Andrews Bay* (Edinburgh 1884), p. 64.
3 Tulloch, William Weir, *The Life of Tom Morris, with Glimpses of St Andrews and its Golfing Celebrities* (London 1907), p. 72.
4 Ibid., p. 85.
5 Ibid., p. 89.

Sixteen Paper War

1 Adamson, Alistair Beaton, *Allan Robertson, Golfer – His Life and Times* (Grant Books, Worcestershire 1985). p. 26.

Seventeen Greatest Golf Match

1 McPherson, Rev. J. Gordon, *Golf and Golfers, Past and Present* (Edinburgh 1891), p. 7.
2 Ibid., p. 33.
3 Ibid., p. 46.

Eighteen Long Live The King

1 This short biography of Schenck was detailed on www.walterscott.lib.ed.ac.uk/portraits/engravers/schenck.html, accessed 23 Feb. 2024. It said, 'Schenck & MacFarlane - Friedrich Schenck (sometimes spelt Schenk) was born in Offenbach, Germany, in 1811. He trained as an artist and lithographer in Munich and Paris, and was brought to Edinburgh in 1840 by the lithographer and printseller Samuel Leith. In 1842 Schenck married Jane, daughter of the Orcadian poet David Vedder, and established his own lithographic business. He presented several papers on developments in lithography to the Royal Scottish Society for the Arts and was later awarded its Gold Medal for his contribution to Scottish lithography. In 1848 he entered into an informal partnership with the Belgian artist Louis Ghémar, then in 1850 set up the firm of Schenck & MacFarlane with William Husband MacFarlane (b. Dunfermline, 1805). Schenck & MacFarlane established a substantial reputation for the quality and variety of work that they produced, so much so that Schenck was invited to write the article on "Lithography" for the 8th edition of the *Encyclopaedia Britannica*. In 1859 the partnership was dissolved, but MacFarlane continued to operate under the banner of Schenck & MacFarlane until 1871 when failing health forced him into partnership with William Erskine. He died in Italy in 1875. Following the dissolution

of his partnership with MacFarlane, Schenck specialized in artistic work, especially chalk portraiture in collaboration with Otto Leyde. From 1866 to 1868 he worked in partnership with is son Frederick until the latter decided to pursue the study of sculpture. Schenck retired in 1875 and devoted his last years to teaching French and German and to writing historical and descriptive works on Germany. He died in Edinburgh in 1885.'

2 McPherson, Rev. J. Gordon, *Golf and Golfers, Past and Present* (Edinburgh 1891), p. 7.

Appendix Early golf links

1 Overcrowding and overuse of the links would force golf societies to eventually seek their own golf courses. The Honourable Company of Edinburgh Golfers for example were originally at Leith Links before moving to Musselburgh and later to their current home at Muirfield. Monifieth Links was the home for the Panmure Golf Club, the artisan club of Monifieth Golf Club formed in 1858 and several others. Panmure Golf Club would re-locate to its current home at nearby Barry, where it is believed that golf has been played since the 15th century. The clubhouse they left behind is now used by the Ladies Panmure Golf Club and several of the other clubs, excluding Monifieth Golf Club, notably Broughty Golf Club amalgamated to become the Grange Golf Club in 2005.

INDEX